Leadership Basics for Librarians and Information Professionals

G. Edward Evans
Patricia Layzell Ward

THE SCARECROW PRESS, INC.
Lanham, Maryland Toronto Plymouth, UK
2007

SCARECROW PRESS, INC.

Published in the United States of America
by Scarecrow Press, Inc.
A wholly owned subsidiary of
The Rowman & Littlefield Publishing Group, Inc.
4501 Forbes Boulevard, Suite 200, Lanham, Maryland 20706
www.scarecrowpress.com

Estover Road
Plymouth PL6 7PY
United Kingdom

British Library Cataloguing in Publication Information Available.

Library of Congress Cataloging-in-Publication Data

Evans, G. Edward, 1937–
   Leadership basics for librarians and information professionals /
G. Edward Evans, Patricia Layzell Ward.
      p.   cm.
   Includes bibliographical references and index.
   ISBN-13: 978-0-8108-5229-7 (pbk. : alk. paper)
   ISBN-10: 0-8108-5229-2 (pbk. : alk. paper)
   1. Library administration.   2. Information services—Management.
3. Leadership.   I. Layzell Ward, Patricia.   II. Title.
Z678.E895   2007
303.3'4—dc22   2006026885

∞ ™ The paper used in this publication meets the minimum requirements of
American National Standard for Information Sciences—Permanence of
Paper for Printed Library Materials, ANSI/NISO Z39.48-1992.
Manufactured in the United States of America.

For all the future leaders of the information professions
and two young gentlemen (Travis and Trenton)
of the millennium generation.

May their future work life be filled with inspiring leaders.

Contents

Foreword

I have a profound interest in leadership, and on a yearly basis I give presentations and workshops on leadership in our profession. I found this book to be excellent. It was easy reading and full of leadership common sense and realities, backed up by experts through an exhaustive review of the literature, not only in the information profession field but in other disciplines as well. I liked the chapter topics and thought they were positioned appropriately throughout the book. I was very impressed with what seemed an exhaustive review of the literature. I also liked the emphasis on two themes—leading to meet the needs of our users and the concepts of underpromising and overdelivering.

Even though this book is about leadership basics, it should appeal to anyone in our profession interested in leadership. I also hope that folks from other disciplines read it. It is so full of helpful information. As a seasoned leadership presenter, I gleaned something new to think about or use from almost every chapter.

In chapter 1, I appreciated the inclusion of archives and record management. I particularly like the emphasis on leadership and change, which to me distinguishes between leaders and managers. It also provides extra validity for me, having led a massive and much-needed organizational change (much to the chagrin of some folks). Chapter 2 addresses leadership and power and makes some important points, such as needing to recognize the role of power. The review of the literature is also excellent both in terms of covering the types of leadership and of sharing the present and future (especially the concerns for 21st-century leaders). The discussion of developing leadership abilities in chapter 3 is comprehensive and should be very helpful to potential leaders. The leadership assessment overview is particularly useful for beginning leaders. Team building, addressed in chapter 4, is another strong section of the book. I found the effective listening skills section to be especially helpful because this area is not often addressed. Organizational politics, discussed in chapter 5, is a fact of life, and what a fine chapter! I am a strong proponent of strategic planning (chapter 6), and this was one of the best descriptions of strategic planning in one chapter that I have ever read. Again, it is very comprehensive but also succinct. I would refer others dealing with strategic planning to this chapter. The coverage of e-leadership in chapter 7 is excellent and much needed for a leadership book. Chapter 8, "It Isn't Always Easy," covers another crucial topic, especially for beginning leaders. It is all too easy to become disheartened by an early setback or two; knowing others have had ups and downs as well helps you get on with learning and becoming a more effective leader.

Camila Alire, dean of library services
University of New Mexico, Albuquerque

Preface

Leadership Basics is our third collaborative book project. It is our belief that professionals in information services share many of the same challenges and issues regardless of their parent organization (archive, brokerage or consulting firm, library, museum, publisher, records center, and so on) or country of origin. We believe the greatest similarity lies in the managerial area. For that reason, all our books address some aspects of management.

The decision to focus on leadership for this book was relatively easy to make. Information services around the world are facing a host of challenges and changes in the 21st century. One of the most significant changes is a turnover in senior positions as members of the veteran and baby boom generations step down and retire. In many ways, the challenges new leadership faces are more daunting than in the past. Many services, especially libraries, are confronted by growing competition from commercial services such as the Google Book Search website and initiatives such as online book programs by Amazon, Random House, and Microsoft. Long-term viability of the services rests with the leadership making the appropriate choices and decisions in response to and in anticipation of the competition. If and when publishers and database vendors develop reasonable pricing models for individuals rather than for institutions, the competition will be even greater. We explore many of the challenges awaiting new leaders in chapter 1.

All our chapters draw on several sources. Naturally, the current literature on leadership—from both general management and information service fields—serves as our base. We also draw on our own professional experiences in a variety of roles and organizations in different parts of the world. Another important resource is data from our survey and interviews of leaders in archives, libraries, and other information services. A survey mailed in late 2004 and early 2005 provided valuable information, as did our in-person and telephone interviews. The data we collected supports both our ideas and the literature concerning important issues in leadership. The material also created a sense of real-life practicality and utility of the concepts. We would like to thank all those who took the time to share their views and thoughts about leadership in the information services in the 21st century.

We believe this book will assist individuals moving into leadership positions, especially those working in medium-sized and smaller services where it is rare to find institutional staff development programs or outside training opportunities. In today's challenging and competitive environment, all services in the information sector need effective leadership.

A word or two about terminology is in order. Partly in the interest of length and readability, but also because of our strong beliefs about similarities, we chose to use the generic terms *information service* and *information professional*. Certainly we use *librarian* and *archivist* when specific circumstances dictate, but we prefer a generic term rather than a string of labels when referring to the broader group. We fully expect the majority of readers will be librarians (our own principal professional area), but we hope that other information professionals will also find this book useful.

Throughout the book you'll find sections that contain information we want to emphasize. Some are quotations (snappy comments that convey meaning), some contain simple exercises, and others provide resources for more in-depth information. Our goal is that they reinforce the book's key issues.

In addition to thanking all those who took part in our survey and interviews, we want to acknowledge a special debt to three people. The first is Camila Alire, dean of library services for the University Libraries, University of Mexico, who graciously agreed to read and comment on the entire manuscript. Her many valuable insights significantly improved the final product. The second is Margaret Saponaro, manager of staff learning and development, University of Maryland Libraries, who provided equally valuable input on most of the chapters. The third is Martin Dillon of Scarecrow Press, whose experience in working with commercial organizations in the information sector yielded valuable insight. For all their assistance, however, only we are responsible for any errors that exist.

We hope readers will learn to become better leaders and enjoy the role, in part because of this book.

G. Edward Evans, Flagstaff, Arizona
Patricia Layzell Ward, Penrhyndeudraeth, Wales

Part 1

BACKGROUND

CHAPTER 1

Thinking about Leadership

This chapter focuses on the following:

- Leadership and information professions
- Opportunities and challenges for leaders
- The responsibilities of leaders
- The differences between leading and managing
- The routes to leadership
- The organizational culture and climate
- The expectations leaders face
- The development of leadership skills

Defining the term *leadership* presents a challenge. Dictionary definitions include "guiding" and "to show the way." Some writers compare leadership to love, saying it is something you recognize but find hard to describe. This is a good comparison, but we needed to develop a working definition for this text. We feel the following reflects how leadership should be practiced at the present time:

> Leadership for today is a collaborative activity. It generates the opportunity for all members of an organization to engage in visioning and motivating one another to meet the challenges of a continually changing operating environment. The outcome is that the organization moves forward to achieve its goal of fulfilling the information needs of the community it serves. Leaders require specific characteristics and skills to make this happen.

There are many significant words in this definition:

- Collaborative
- Opportunity

- Engage
- Visioning
- Motivating
- Changing
- Operating environment
- Goal
- Community
- Characteristics
- Skills

You can expect to come across these terms frequently in this book.

Leadership is a hot topic today both around the globe and in all sectors of life—in politics, government, education, business, and the information sector. Making the right decision, taking action at the right time, and building trust with the community have always presented challenges, but the way these can be accomplished continues to change dramatically. One example is the impact of new information and communication technology, which enables organizations to reduce back-office tasks and thus cut overhead costs. The result is that the former hierarchies and layers of management have been swept away.

Check This Out

``Inside the Mind of the Leader'' (thematic issue), *Harvard Business Review* 82, no. 1 (January 2004): 1–116.

At the same time, another change is affecting leaders: the way society views their merits. Leaders today find themselves center stage in a bright spotlight. In the past, people moved into a senior role and their constituency was generally accepting of the way they carried out their responsibilities. This leadership style can be described as tending toward the autocratic. The charismatic corporate gurus of the late 1980s were perceived as powerful and strong. Rarely was there any questioning of the approach they took to leading their organizations. But the bubble burst, and today the decisions and actions taken by leaders are subject to much closer public scrutiny and questioning. Leaders can find themselves in a stormy, uncharted sea—buffeted in all directions. They are far less likely to be operating in a comfort zone. This is well illustrated in the political and business sectors. That's the downside. But at the same time, there are greater opportunities and possibilities for leaders in the information profession, as society moves from an information, to a digital, to a conceptual age. This introduces a new architecture for services that will benefit users, since the conceptual age focuses on creativity and is people oriented—think of the Renaissance.

People become leaders in two ways. Some emerge at a time of crisis—something happens that causes a person to come forward to take decisive action and fill a vacuum. When we speak of leaders, it is often the people who have emerged during a crisis that spring to mind.

Check This Out

Encouraged by the emergence of the computer, logical and precise left-brain thinking accompanied the information age. Now comes the conceptual age—ruled by artistry, empathy, and emotion. Read more in Daniel Pink's *A Whole New Mind: Moving from the Information Age to the Conceptual Age* (New York: Riverhead, 2005).

But the majority of leaders in business and the public sector make a conscious decision to move into a leadership position. Taking this step requires careful thought and preparation. Leaders need to accept that they cannot please all of the people, all of the time. Their actions are visible, and this means they become vulnerable to criticism. New leaders very quickly learn that they are exposed. Their habits, idiosyncrasies, and vocabulary are on show for everyone to see and hear. Unpopular choices will likely be made, and it is inherent in human nature to prefer to be liked. This may partly explain why people are reluctant to take up the challenge and why it is becoming difficult to recruit leaders at the top level of many organizations. It can be much more comfortable to accept a senior management role. So the challenge is to identify the people with the right talent, knowledge, and expertise—and let's add the word *ambition*—to step up to fill leadership positions.

Leadership and the Information Professions

Yes, there are challenges, but we firmly believe that there is a pool of people in the information sector who have the potential to move into leadership roles. Drawing together the wisdom of the experts and our personal experience, we want to encourage new leaders to come forward. In this group we also include those who suddenly, and perhaps unexpectedly, find themselves taking a leadership role in the limelight.

In many ways the information sector is no different from any other industry or occupational group. Information professionals are presented with challenges similar to those faced by professionals working in other fields. This is why we have drawn on research and other sources of information about leadership in general (e.g., much has been written about the topic in the business sector).

Some writing is recent, but we have also drawn on writing from the past that retains resonance today.

The text has been prepared for information professionals. The term *information professionals* includes people working in an archive, information, knowledge management, library, or records management service. We refer to these organizations using the generic label of *information services*. The operations and processes used in the different types of services differ, but in essence information professionals carry similar responsibilities. They must know and understand the following:

• The context in which the community served lives or is working
• The range of potential sources and formats of information available to this community

With this knowledge and understanding, information professionals are able to match the users with relevant information that meets their needs as well as to ensure that this information is organized efficiently and effectively.

One of the challenges facing all information professionals is that the service is provided to individuals with varying information needs. In addition, the individual user's expectation of, and response to, the service will differ. Some people visit a public library to find a book to read that helps them relax and takes them away from their daily routine. A student taps into the resources of his college library to find inspiration for an assignment. A historian uses an archive to add to her knowledge about her field of research. A departmental manager consults his records center to check on an event in the past. A physician needs to update her knowledge about a drug. A lawyer needs to check precedents. Information professionals have one fundamental common task: to anticipate and meet these needs.

Check This Out

Winston, M.D., ed., ``Leadership in the Library and Information Science Professions: Theory and Practice'' (thematic issue), *Journal of Library Administration* 32, no. 3/4 (2001): 1–186.

People who use the service play a major role in how it develops. They form one of the groups of stakeholders who contribute to assessing the quality of service received. Users provide feedback that offers essential input to the planning process. Leaders always keep the community served at the forefront of their thinking, knowing that, for users, an information service is but a means to an end. Through the provision of a high standard of service so that information needs are met, the information professional makes an essential contribution to the overall health and well-being of the user and the parent organization. One of the characteristics of an information service that influences the leadership role is that information services are generally not freestanding organizations but are divisions or departments in a larger parent organization. So, many services have another group of stakeholders who contribute to quality control. They are the members of the governing body of the parent organization. They require not only that their information needs be met but also that the service achieves its goals effectively and efficiently.

Check This Out

Although the following text is targeted at librarians, other information professionals will find it useful:

Cihak, Herbert E., and Joan S. Howland, eds., *Leadership Roles for Librarians*. AALL Publications Series, no. 66 (Buffalo, NY: Hein, 2002).

Information services, in common with all organizations, are experiencing a relentless increase in the rate of technological change that affects service delivery. New approaches to service provision are evolving, new competition is emerging and growing, and outsourcing and collaboration are playing a greater role in delivering services. Social change influences the information-seeking behavior of users at the same time that educational achievements continually rise. Users are increasingly "information savvy."

Check This Out

Riggio, Ronald E., and Sarah Smith Orr, *Improving Leadership in Nonprofit Organizations* (San Francisco: Jossey-Bass, 2003).

It is all too easy to become preoccupied—particularly in times of rapid change and close financial scrutiny—and temporarily overlook the outcomes and impact of the service, as well as the needs and the power of the user and the governing body. Leaders must continually monitor what is happening in the operating environment—both externally and within the organization. Both use and nonuse need to be monitored, together with what is being used and the frequency of use. What is no longer being used? What information needs can be better satisfied by delivering the service in a different way? The leader has the responsibility of ensuring that supervisors and managers collect quantitative and qualitative information to use when the team makes decisions together. This informs the strategic direction of the service.

The information professions need to encourage new leaders to come forward. These leaders must be drawn from a pool of people with the proper skills to work collaboratively with a team. Working together, the leader and the team drive the change process to create the information services that will meet the needs of today's and tomorrow's users and satisfy the parent organizations.

Opportunity and Challenge

Opportunity is what everyone is looking for, particularly in a new position. Change is the greatest challenge that everyone faces. It is a constant factor in our lives, and the information sector is no exception. Further, the ever-increasing rate of change is both fundamental and wide-ranging. In the information sector, information technology has moved information retrieval from punched cards to digitization in half a century. Where will it be in 2050? We won't offer a prize for the correct answer, but just think about it and make some predictions.

Try This

What developments in information and communications technology would you expect to see in

- five years' time?
- ten years' time?
- fifteen years' time?
- twenty years' time?

Research predictions that are emerging from general, trade, technical, and professional sources.

Technology makes the most obvious impact in the information sector. At its simplest level, it enables people to select how they access information services. They work from their offices, homes, or dorms and so need to make fewer, if any, visits in person to a service point than they did a decade ago. People expect to have 24/7 access to a fast, accurate, cost-efficient service, delivered to them through their personal computers, personal digital assistants, landline telephones, or cell phones. The Internet revolutionized the way we think about information and knowledge. One example is that the introduction of knowledge management lets people work together in teams to share information and create new products or services, often across the globe. Knowledge is transformed more quickly as advantage is taken of time differences around the world. New languages emerge that reflect the changing technologies—consider the ways that we communicate by cell phone. Language itself becomes transformed. Some critics say that the information gained in this way may not always be accurate or up to date, but the response is immediate and can be drawn from a range of sources.

One outcome of these changes is that people in the community at large now need more support when seeking or using information than they did in the past, and information literacy becomes a more important part of the school and college curriculum. Having gained the basic skills, people also need to keep up to date with changes in technology and its uses so that it can benefit their work and lives in general. Users need to learn how to use new technology and services efficiently and effectively, so more user coaching is vital. We use the term *learn* because today's information professional takes on the responsibility of coaching users. People know *how* to use the Internet but may not have *learned* how to use it efficiently and effectively.

The information service provided to the members of the community served must be, in the opinion of that community, excellent, cost effective, and user-friendly, because they have other options to turn to. That is why use and nonuse must be closely monitored. Increasing competition in the information sector opens up a range of options to people seeking information. Think of higher disposable incomes and the pressures of work and life. People may not need to visit a public or academic library because books can be easily purchased at discounted prices from Amazon and other online booksellers. Individuals can download articles from many journals and newspapers without charge, or perhaps for the price of a cup of coffee. Some professional associations offer access to online journals and abstracting services as a benefit of membership and provide a specialist information service via their website. As archive services make more information available online, personal visits may be less necessary. Using the online catalog of the archive and records service, a user can spend more time preparing for a visit instead of going to the archives to check the catalog before requesting documents.

So the options for how books, documents, and information can be delivered and used are subject to continual change, requiring enhanced skills in communicating with users. The downside and challenge for providers of information services lie in the capital and recurrent costs of providing access and of training staff. Training and development costs in terms of purchasing courses and down time for staff are budget elements that continue to increase.

A significant benefit of technology is that it enables staff to work at a distance. Some staff members may be able to work from their homes or, at a different level, link with colleagues based in offices across the globe. International legal firms and mining companies use networking to run their operations located on different continents.

Competition has emerged in a variety of ways. The information sector has long had cooperative arrangements between services within a country and international partners. Such arrangements operate at little or no cost. However, new providers have emerged through outsourcing in the same way that occurred, for example, in banking. Developments in call center technology result in a sophisticated 24/7 information service being available to the United States through collaboration with similar services operating in different time zones. Commercial vendors can also supply virtual reference services.

Legal, regulation, and deregulation issues have become increasingly important. Copyright has long been an issue, and the question of rights has extended into the field of digitization. Access to the Internet is an issue in some U.S. states and countries overseas, as is the question of privacy.

Government policies exert an increasing influence on the community. Within the information sector, some challenging questions have arisen about access to information through censorship, privacy, or technology. Policies have been implemented that hold down spending in the public sector, and at the same time, businesses trim costs to give a better return to stockholders. Both the capital and recurrent budgets of information services can be affected. One action taken by governments has encouraged greater collaboration between services within and across the information sector. Cross-sectoral agencies, such as the Institute of Museum and Library Services, link together archives, information, and library and museum services to create new alliances, providing the synergy for change. In return, government agencies offer grants to oil the wheels of this collaboration and provide central services.

At the same time, the workplace is also changing. Conger and Benjamin (1999) write of the need for "workplace savvy leaders," stressing the importance of fully understanding the complexities of diversity and changes in demographics. These include working with staff, volunteers, and users from different generations—from veterans to "gen next"—and different lifestyles, beliefs, and cultures. The different groups within the community may approach their work in different ways. Family-friendly policies form an essential element in human resource management. An interesting statistic to consider is that two-thirds of those entering the civilian workforce in the United States are women or are from racial minorities. Winston (2001) draws attention to the relationship between diversity and organizational success.

The recruitment of volunteers is one aspect of diversity that is growing. Volunteers can be a valuable resource, particularly if they have special expertise or knowledge. But to become effective members of the team, they need to receive training and be provided with a contract that sets down their expectations and responsibilities, along with those of the host organization. Again, different generations approach work in different ways and have different expectations of what can be achieved.

One of the new responsibilities of leaders in the information sector is serious revenue raising. In the past, this was often needed for add-ons or "like to haves." Now it is likely essential for obtaining additional income streams to provide what were once regarded as core services. In the private sector, there is generally an internal accounting process that imposes a charge for the use of central services, including information services. In turn, the information service buys into central services. Marketing and good public relations become increasingly important, both external and internal to the information service and organization.

Organizations are often not stable at the macro level. In the private sector, mergers and takeovers take place, both inside and outside the organization, as businesses come together to increase market share. Universities and colleges merge internal departments such as IT with library services and bring related academic disciplines together. Governments restructure departments or create new ones to provide services to meet perceived changes in society.

But we emphasize that for every challenge there is an opportunity, and leaders should be, by their very nature, optimistic. Every threat should be turned 180 degrees to assess what benefits can be gained. In some areas of the information sector, the level of charges should be reexamined. One school of thought says that when people pay for something, they value it more highly, and that can be very true in the for-profit sector. Changes in generational attitudes mean that younger, affluent members of the community are more likely to expect to pay for services that were available without charge a decade ago. Now, we are not suggesting that every service should or can levy charges, but rather that sometimes creative thoughts might produce an opportunity.

Try This

Some opportunities and challenges have been noted already, but clearly not all that are likely to emerge across the information sector have been identified. Think about the type of service you are working in, and draw up a list of opportunities and challenges. If you are about to move into the information sector, list the aspects you feel you need to know better.

People who become leaders want to bring about change. Leadership offers the challenge of working with a team in order to develop a service that anticipates and identifies opportunities and takes action to develop plans and policies to meet changing conditions. Change will be constant and will happen at an ever-increasing rate, but the nature of the change will be different over time. Spotting a development that will likely affect a service, gathering and assessing information and data, judging the likely impact, factoring it into strategic planning, and ensuring change is successfully implemented are the challenges to be met—all while watching the horizon to see what is likely to happen next. . . . This sharpens the mind of the leader.

The Responsibilities of Leaders

The role of leader carries a number of responsibilities. First and foremost, leaders must take a proactive role and anticipate the future. Although they can't foresee everything that might happen, they can take a helicopter view, looking to the horizon to see what influences are emerging. Leaders look for trends that are likely to affect the direction of the parent organization and therefore the information service and how that service should be delivered. An environmental scan covers inputs such as the international scene, national political decisions, new technology, economic conditions, and social change. It includes "hard" information such as data and statistics. For example, in the case of services for the public, demographic data are examined, and in the corporate field, profit and loss data for the parent organization and those of competitors are studied. "Soft" information is also gathered, using such tools as opinion surveys and focus groups. Both hard data and soft information are valuable inputs. Taken together, they inform the vision that guides strategic planning and identify the changes needed to keep the service moving forward. This is a major responsibility of leaders.

Leaders must also be accountable to the stakeholders for the delivery of the service. The stakeholders comprise the community served (the users, nonusers, and ex-users), the leader's immediate team, and the governing body of the parent organization.

Another responsibility relates to forward planning, which is carried out in collaboration with the stakeholders. Unless the stakeholders have trust in the leader and his actions, and understand what is happening, the leader is likely to fail. If a leader fails, it carries major implications for the organization, the service, and the team. In addition, the leader must create momentum and move forward by working with a high-performing team to implement and monitor the strategic plan.

The responsibilities are therefore considerable, and there can be a fine line between success and failure. Carrying out these responsibilities requires skills such as gathering information, analyzing situations, interpreting data, solving problems, thinking strategically, communicating, consulting, negotiating, motivating, delegating, facilitating, and coaching. Leaders must demonstrate personal motivation, ambition for the organization rather than themselves, self-knowledge and self-confidence, an understanding of values and ethics, and people and political skills.

We subscribe to the view that, generally, leaders are made, not born. Some people are natural leaders, having the advantage of being born with the essential traits that, particularly in a time of crisis, elevate them into a leadership role.

An Example

Ernest Shackleton was a British polar explorer who saved the lives of twenty-seven men who were stranded with him for nearly two years on an ice floe in the Antarctic. His experiences have been written up as a series of readable case studies, a graphic account of how Shackleton emerged as a leader:

Morrell, Margot, and Stephanie Capparell, *Shackleton's Way: Leadership Lessons from the Great Antarctic Explorer* (London: Brealey, 2001).

But for most people, leadership skills develop as a result of awareness, experience, and training. Our experience indicates that the learning process never stops.

And let's make the point once again—the key to success in the information sector lies in meeting the needs of the community served. Without achieving this goal, the service has no reason to exist. The danger is that the people served can slip out of sight when leadership is discussed. We stress that leaders who forget that they lead for a purpose do so at their own peril.

Leading and Managing: The Differences

Moving into a leadership position generally means that a formal shift has been made from a managerial or supervisory designation, but this isn't necessarily so. People can find themselves in a leadership role even though their designated position is that of a manager or supervisor. However, there is an important distinction to make. Leadership isn't simply managing or supervising at a higher level. There are significant differences between the roles of a manager or supervisor and those of a leader. But, drawing on our experience, we can safely say that having been a manager or supervisor makes it easier for a new leader to understand the responsibilities and viewpoints of members of their work team. This increases leader effectiveness.

At the outset we mentioned that it is not easy to find words to describe a leader. However, it is much easier to analyze the role of a manager. The responsibilities and tasks of a manager can be readily identified, described, and quantified. Researchers (e.g., Mintzberg, 1973) have found a number of tasks common to the work of most managers, in any sector. There is a strong generic content in their work.

The Expert

``Management is mechanical—it's about resource allocation, efficiency, optimization . . . and there are processes you can follow to help you manage effectively. Leadership is different; it's about vision and fire and winning people's hearts as well as their minds.'' (Alan Thompson, managing director of Toshiba Computer Systems, quoted in Lucas, 2000, p. 11)

Bennis and Goldsmith (2003) make a clear distinction between the two roles in their list of differences between the manager and the leader:

- The manager *administers*; the leader *innovates*.
- The manager is a *copy*; the leader is an *original*.
- The manager *maintains*; the leader *develops*.
- The manager accepts *reality*; the leader *investigates* it.
- The manager focuses on *systems and structure*; the leader focuses on *people*.
- The manager relies on *control*; the leader inspires *trust*.
- The manager has a *short-range* view; the leader has a *long-range perspective*.
- The manager asks *how and when*; the leader asks *what and why*.
- The manager has his eye on *the bottom line*; the leader has his eye on the *horizon*.
- The manager *imitates*; the leader *originates*.
- The manager *accepts the status quo*; the leader *challenges* it.
- The manager is the *classic good soldier*; the leader is *her own person*.
- The manager *does things right*; the leader *does the right thing*.

Moving into a leadership role from a supervisory or managerial post will test any individual. If you consider the description of the two roles, you find that, in many ways, they are diametrically opposed. Yet it is from the managers and supervisors that the leaders generally emerge. So it calls for a major shift of perspective. From being responsible for ensuring the smooth running of part of an organization and focusing on the bottom line, the new leader takes a wider, forward-looking perspective. Leaders ask what should be done and why, working closely with their teams. Leaders must gain trust, innovate, and develop the service. Remember, the shift calls for new leaders to move up a notch, anticipate the future, and take action to move the service forward. This means they must develop the skills and understanding to inspire the team to anticipate change, and they must readily adapt to meet the emerging needs of users and the challenges of delivering the service that lie ahead. By contrast, the manager's responsibility is to implement plans and ensure the smooth day-to-day operation of the service.

The Expert

"Great managers know and value the unique abilities and even the eccentricities of their employees, and they learn how best to integrate them into a coordinated plan of attack. This is the exact opposite of what great leaders do. Great leaders discover what is universal and capitalize on it. Their job is to rally people to a better future. . . . This doesn't mean a leader can't be a manager or vice versa. But to excel at one or both, you must be aware of the very different skills each role requires." (Buckingham, 2005, p. 20)

A common comparison is made between a leader in the business sector and the conductor of an orchestra. The conductor works with a group of highly skilled musicians, each playing a different instrument. The musicians will be demanding colleagues since they possess different personalities and talents and make varying contributions to the pieces played. They must work as a team in harmony, each playing the right notes, to the right rhythm at the right time, as defined in the score. It is the role of the conductor to bring it all together to produce the performance. Without a key figure, a cacophony will emerge. The conductor inspires the orchestra to create a memorable performance. Mintzberg (1998) observed the conductor of the Winnipeg Symphony Orchestra at work in order to explore the metaphor. As a result, he suggests there are differences between leading musicians and leading professionals. He describes "covert leadership," where the role of the leader is to act quietly and unobtrusively in order to produce an inspired performance. The emphasis in the professional setting should be placed on inspiring rather than on empowering. We think Mintzberg's view should be remembered.

Point of Reflection

Think about leaders you have worked with—perhaps in the information sector, another job, or a voluntary organization. Would you describe their approach as being either empowering or inspiring? How would you describe the differences?

Working at this level requires that the leader accept responsibility for making the right decision at the right time and communicating it effectively to the stakeholders. It is easier to arrive at judgments about the longer term than to ensure that the appropriate action is taken at the right time and, most important, that the outcomes are evaluated and action taken. Evaluating outcomes with the work team, users, and the board or boss—and taking appropriate action—is essential for a learning organization. So often an emphasis is placed on what has been a success, but the "not so successful" also needs careful analysis and action.

A Tip: Communication and Feedback

Writing about leadership, Rudolph Giuliani offers sound advice. Working in a crisis situation during 9/11, he held a short meeting with his team at the start of each working day. The purpose was to brief each other to ensure that essential information flowed between the leader and the team. It helped strategic planning and to fine tune decisions. Under normal conditions a daily meeting may not be feasible, it may have to be weekly, but it shouldn't be less frequent. And today's technology brings the benefit that everyone doesn't necessarily have to be sitting around the table. (See Giuliani with Kurson, 2002, pp. 29–34)

The literature of leadership is extensive, and many experts have written on the subject. From our readings we have drawn out the most common leadership traits, skills, experience, and knowledge that they identify as being central to the leadership role. And from our experience we would add three aspects of knowledge that are particularly important to new leaders in the information sector:

- A deepening awareness of the culture, values, and mission of the parent organization; what it exists to do and how it does it; and the broad community it serves and works with. No two organizations are alike—and no leader should assume that they are.
- An awareness of how the last occupant of the post operated, his plans, and his leadership style. Change should evolve—there shouldn't be a revolution.
- An awareness of the community served and an understanding of individual needs and the ways to deliver high-quality service that will add value to work, study, or daily life.

Leaders have a responsibility to develop the next generation of leaders.

Try This

The following lists experts' views of leadership traits, skills, experience, and knowledge. Number the items in each column in your order of importance for a leader, then use them as a checklist to see how you rate your traits, skills, experience, and knowledge. What are your strengths and weaknesses at this time? Prepare an action plan to overcome the weaknesses.

Traits

☐ Intelligence
☐ Empathy
☐ Initiative
☐ Integrity
☐ High achievement
☐ Self-confidence
☐ Optimism
☐ Loyalty
☐ Curiosity

☐ Reliability
☐ Adaptability
☐ Strong values
☐ Courage
☐ Sense of humor
☐ Thick skin
☐ Patience
☐ Inspiration
☐ Decisiveness

Skills

☐ Diplomacy
☐ Self-knowledge
☐ People skills
☐ Communication
☐ Building trust
☐ Congruity
☐ Motivation
☐ Persuasion
☐ Delegation

☐ Politics
☐ Analysis
☐ Time management
☐ Planning
☐ Mentoring
☐ Organization
☐ Coaching
☐ Public relations
☐ Professional skills

Experience

☐ Staying the course
☐ Networking
☐ Anticipating change
☐ Setting goals
☐ Seeing the big picture
☐ Knowing how to make a difference
☐ Being a good judge of people
☐ Admitting errors

☐ Flexibility
☐ Successful planning
☐ Organizing major events
☐ Working in committees
☐ Being receptive to new ideas
☐ Working in teams
☐ Leading teams
☐ Working with top management

Knowledge

☐ Operating context of the parent organization
☐ Structure of the information sector
☐ Style of the preceding leader
☐ Management and leadership
☐ Corporate culture and climate
☐ Reading a balance sheet
☐ Emerging trends at international, national, and local levels

☐ ICT benefits and challenges
☐ Professional theory
☐ Networking
☐ Ethics
☐ Data analysis and interpretation
☐ Pedagogy
☐ Psychology
☐ Marketing
☐ Research methods
☐ The community served

Routes to Leadership

Earlier we noted that people move into leadership roles through a number of different routes, and so we need to briefly review the various ways. It isn't always a question of seeing a vacancy and applying for it, for leadership generally calls for preparation.

Some large organizations manage succession planning by recognizing the problem of identifying and developing leaders. Each department works closely with human resources and is involved in the process of succession planning. Employees who demonstrate a potential for leadership are recruited into a program designed to test their capabilities. As part of a personal growth program, the potential leaders move around the different departments to deepen their understanding of the total organization and the way it operates. This develops both their individual skills and their experience. During the training period, an understanding is gained of the specialist roles and knowledge needed to ensure the efficient and effective functioning of the organization. The outcome is that potential leaders can be tested on the job. This benefits both the organization and the potential leaders. Individuals can discover how well they are likely to perform and how comfortable they would feel in a leadership role. The employer gains added benefit from internal recruitment at this level, as the newly promoted leaders will have an understanding of the organizational culture and climate.

Within the information sector, few organizations are large enough to be able to offer an in-house program for leadership development. Leaders emerge in other ways, perhaps as natural leaders or as a result of their own career planning; some find themselves becoming accidental leaders, while others are hidden leaders.

Some people possess the personality traits that make them natural leaders. They move into a leadership role without apparent effort, and often their style is described as being charismatic. Their skills are likely to have been identified and developed within a community group or youth movement or through voluntary work.

Others choose to take a leadership path, making strategic career moves along the way. They deepen and widen their technical expertise and knowledge of their work sector, follow a program of study or reading, build a network (probably in their professional field and management), and choose an appropriate mentor or role model. Linking this with a self-awareness of their strengths and weaknesses, they gain the confidence required to step up the career ladder.

In the case of natural leaders and career planners, a number of avenues are available for professional development. Professional bodies in the information sector organize short courses and workshops. Universities offer formal courses on campus or through distance learning. A starting point is to read—the literature is extensive and comes in a range of styles.

Check This Out

Very sound and practical advice for the accidental leader is provided in Harvey Robbins and Michael Finley's *The Accidental Leader: What to Do When You're Suddenly in Charge* (San Francisco: Jossey-Bass, 2004).

One of the most challenging routes emerges at a time of rapid change or crisis, when accidental leaders come forward. Accidental leaders find themselves thrust into an unexpected situation. They may be given the responsibility of leading a team within the information service, receive promotion, or need to take action when a disaster occurs. All too often the pages of professional journals report the effects of fires, floods, hurricanes, earthquakes, and other disasters. Accidental leaders find themselves in a tricky situation. They will probably have had limited training, or perhaps none at all, and are unlikely to have experience in the information sector to draw on. They may have no one to turn to for advice. But they find themselves in a role or given a job title that designates them as a leader. To operate successfully in this situation, accidental leaders need to possess a natural ability for leadership, be quick thinkers, learn on the job with limited time to reflect, plan ahead, think themselves into the role, and inspire those around them. That inspiration will probably need to extend up the hierarchy as well as to immediate colleagues.

Check This Out

Ciampa, Dan, ``Almost Ready: How Leaders Move Up,'' *Harvard Business Review* 83, no. 1 (January 2005): 46–53.

The final category consists of the hidden leaders. Hidden leaders from an interesting group. They are not usually the most senior people in the company, they do not have a job title that suggests organization. Hidden leaders possess a natural talent for leadership, see beyond their daily job, and use their interpersonal skills to encourage others to perform at a high level. With a team approach to management in place, most information services staff are empowered, so some will naturally take a leadership role. This becomes the training ground for their personal development since some will be in supervisory rather than management posts.

Sometimes people recruited for leadership roles in the information sector come from a different field and therefore lack work experience in information services. Possessing an understanding of the different roles and what is needed to create an effective service within a given sector helps a leader settle in at this level. We believe this is helpful in the information sector. Leaders who are appointed from outside the information sector *may* be less effective and *perhaps* not stay for any length of time. The thinking behind recruitment from another sector is that it brings new insights to the organization. However, if leaders lack training and practical experience in a sector that is new to them, they are likely to face a greater challenge. They will lack a professional vocabulary, an appreciation of how different parts of the service operate, and a professional network. They will have to work harder and faster to gain this understanding and make the vital contacts. Many have been successful, but a person moving from one sector within the profession to another is likely to be on a very steep learning curve.

Try This

Which route have you taken, or are you likely to take, to move into a leadership role? Is this a result of career planning or of an internal development program? Could you be an accidental or hidden leader? What are the pluses and minuses of this route? Do you feel you possess the natural traits? What do you still need to learn?

Organizational Culture and Climate

Another factor to think about when considering a move into a leadership role, particularly if it is a shift to a different organization, is the question of culture. To what extent is the culture of the organization likely to be familiar and resemble earlier experience?

The culture of an organization is generally related to its age. As an extreme example, an older traditional university is likely to have a very different culture from that of a new business enterprise. Taking a leadership role in an organization that has a different culture may require a different skill set.

A newly established organization needs leaders with entrepreneurial skills. The organization then moves into a steady state of consolidation that requires the skills of checking systems and processes. There is then a further shift through a change process, where the entrepreneurial skills are once again vital. Reflecting on our experience and conversations with those working in a range of information services, particularly in the private sector, we suggest that not everyone has the appropriate skill set for each of the different stages of development. Some people are better working at the entrepreneurial stage; some are better leaders when the service is in a temporary steady state. Further, certain sectors are more volatile than others (e.g., the mining industry and, increasingly, services in the public sector).

The Experts

Mayo and Nohria (2005, p. 48) describe Zeitgeist leadership in a paper that charts the context of U.S. business in the 20th century, identifying three archetypes of leadership: "*Entrepreneurs* are often ahead of their time, not necessarily bound by the context in which they live. They frequently overcome seemingly insurmountable obstacles and persevere in finding or launching something new. *Managers* are skilled at reading and exploiting the context of their times. Through a deep understanding of the landscape in which they operate, they shape and grow businesses. *Leaders* confront change and identify latent potential in businesses that others consider stagnant, mature, declining, or moribund. Where some see failure and demise, this breed of executive sees kernels of possibility and hope."

Expectations

Everyone taking up a new post has expectations. But new leaders are not the only people with expectations. The management team, the staff of the service, the board or boss, and, of course, the users will also have expectations. Examining the different expectations of each group underlines the skill sets needed by leaders and identifies the attributes that contribute to success.

No matter how good the previous incumbent was in the position, a newcomer carries hopes for the future—and often for a new start to the service. So everyone eagerly anticipates the new arrival. The management team and staff will probably have been involved in some way in the recruitment process and are likely to have a favorable impression of their new colleague. The board or boss has high hopes: A large investment of visible and invisible costs have been made, and a return is expected. The users think about the improvements they would like to see made to the service. They do not necessarily think that the previous incumbent wasn't good at the job—but this person is new! He is expected to bring a new perspective—and the leader is visible, oh so visible.

We have already noted that these high expectations come at a time when the task of a leader has become more demanding. There is also a closer scrutiny of output and quality, with targets that must be met or even surpassed. Technology has replaced the secretarial staff who, in the past, were able to provide a barrier when required (and produce coffee as necessary). Even if the leader has a good personal assistant (PA), she will still likely be swamped with e-mail messages, cell phone calls, and text messages that come directly to her desk.

Against this background, let's take the expectations of the community served. Many members of that community will have the experience of using similar services and will know what they would like to see introduced. (The National Archives in London sets high standards. It provides a fast, high-tech, high-quality service coupled with comfortable surroundings and excellent coffee that the users would like to find in their local record office. However, it is not immediately obvious to the users that there are differences in the levels of funding allocated at the national and local levels.)

It is important to hear not only the views of users but also the tone in which they are offered. Do users expect some fine-tuning, or are some fundamental questions being posed? The new leader needs to go out and about and gather their different views. Some users visit the service in person. Contact with other users or potential users may be more easily made at the watercooler, in the coffee bar, or at the canteen. The leader must be visible and must listen. If the users and potential users are based at different locations or access the service remotely, then they need to receive a friendly message asking for their opinions. The leader should get worried if no one responds, yet remember that if an overwhelming number of replies comes in, it will not be possible to meet everyone's expectations.

Interacting with colleagues to prepare a strategy for handling the comments puts the leader on a different learning curve. It presents an opportunity to see how the work team reacts to user feedback and how the group works together. The leader and work team should discuss the outcomes and then deliver the findings to both the users and the senior staff in the organization, together with an action plan. This demonstrates to everyone that the leader, working with different levels and groups in the organization, means business.

Determining user expectations also helps the service staff better understand the leader. They learn how the leader prefers to work, how the leader communicates, what the leader does and doesn't know about the service, and what they need to teach him. It is a way they can demonstrate pride in their work. The immediate colleagues also have expectations: Their leader should be a good communicator who can listen as well as talk. They want to be inspired, to share the vision, and to know in what direction the service is likely to be heading. We feel it is a myth that people don't like change to occur in their daily work. Often the staff of an information service know what needs to be done but haven't always been encouraged to make their views and ideas known. The channels of communication may have been blocked, or perhaps they felt they had made suggestions that were not considered, and so they stopped making them. They expect their leader to possess good interpersonal skills and be visible and accessible to them. Chatting around the watercooler provides opportunities to gather informal feedback. But for them, it is also important that the leader is visible within the organization, presents an appropriate image, and quickly gains the trust and respect of staff, both inside and outside the department.

The staff will also expect that their boss be human and understand the complexities of life that affect the workplace from time to time. Informal contact will likely uncover family matters (e.g., illness, changes in circumstances) that may temporarily affect performance. An inquiry about the progress of a sick relative demonstrates a personal interest in colleagues in the work team.

Trust is an important factor in working with everyone in the organization, but it is a key issue in working within the service. High ethical standards are essential. Handling a clash between professional and organizational ethics is a test for the leader. Communication is vital, and sharing information is paramount unless it is confidential. It works both ways because staff at all levels will have their own networks. Empowering the staff of the service builds trust and good communication, contributes to forward planning, and promotes sharing the vision for service development, and that is halfway to introducing change.

Boards and bosses have their own expectations when making a senior appointment. Recruitment can be an expensive process, and they need reassurance that they have selected the right person who possesses the right skills and experience to lead the service forward. They may have needed to make a difficult decision to select the appropriate person in relation to the stage of service development. Remember that young services need someone with an entrepreneurial flair. At times someone needs to move behind an entrepreneur to ensure the service is working efficiently and effectively. A long-standing service may be in need of radical change. This is a factor that appointment boards take into account. In addition, they expect to be kept informed of the good—and sometimes perhaps the not so good—news. Basking in reflected glory is something we all enjoy, but if bad news is likely to emerge, then they need ample warning before it happens. Think of the IT contracts that do not always go according to plan. This is not always the fault of the person in charge. Bosses know that even with good planning and organization, a hitch can be encountered. Demonstrating that plans have been subject to risk assessment builds confidence. Bosses take a keen interest in the bottom line but welcome positive feedback from users and the community at large.

Meeting deadlines a little ahead of schedule brings brownie points. Underpromising and overdelivering instills trust in the leader. The board requires loyalty from their leaders and anticipates that leaders will be able to accept, and act on, any critical feedback they may offer.

The Expert

''Too much distance makes leadership—like pornography—just a mechanical act.'' (Bennis, 1998, p. 53)

A major investigation by Hernon, Powell, and Young (2003) gathered the views of directors, assistant directors, and associate directors about the qualities that will be required by the next generation of U.S. library directors. The highly valued attributes sought in the next generation of leaders are summarized here as the "traits wanted." There were, however, some surprises in the lowest-rated personal characteristics, which were labeled as "we'll keep your résumé on file." Following are the "traits wanted" attributes:

• Trustworthy
• Evenhanded
• Self-confident
• Fine-tuned moral compass
• Stress-proof suit
• Good at juggling
• Excellent vision
• Astute
• Inspiring

Following are the "we'll keep your résumé on file" attributes:

• Sense of humor
• Plays well with others
• Asks the right questions
• Time-management maven
• Team-builder
• Accountable

Perhaps it is not surprising that we have found that meeting expectations is more readily achieved in smaller organizations. People work more closely together, and feedback comes more readily in a situation where the staff and users are in frequent informal contact. So conversely, the larger the department or organization, the more difficult it is for leaders to meet people and receive feedback. They need to work that much harder to meet expectations.

Here is our list of expectations:

1. The board expects that its leaders will do the following:
   - Be effective in anticipating, meeting, and surpassing the needs of the user community
   - Be efficient in terms of the use of resources—financial, human, physical; the lower the request and the higher the output the better
   - Develop and monitor a strategic plan that has the support of users and the commitment of staff to its delivery
   - Meet performance targets
   - Be visible within the community served, the profession at large, and the wider community
   - Be at the forefront of understanding about change as it relates to both the parent organization and the professional practice
   - Not rock the boat
   - Keep the board informed of developments, both good and bad
   - Show loyalty to the board
   - Enable the board to bask in pride and reflected glory
2. These expectations will be shared by the staff of the information service, who also
   - Want to be part of a high-performing service that is visible in the places where it matters
   - Like reflected glory
   - Realize that change is essential—but not too fundamental or often
   - Would prefer that change be matched to their comfort levels
   - Like their leader to be nice and meet their needs
3. The community served expects the following:
   - That the service will anticipate their information needs
   - That these needs will be met in a timely manner in a preferred format
   - That the financial or time cost will be at an acceptable level

Clearly, meeting the needs of the immediate work team will be a challenge, especially when they are in closer contact with the leader than is the board. This is where the skills to inspire, negotiate, build trust, and persuade are needed.

And there will probably be some downsides when the expectations of users, the team, or the board are not met. This may happen for a number of reasons. Perhaps it may be a time of rapid environmental change. Misjudgments can occur, mistakes creep in, and plans are upset. If this occurs, then people become less happy. At the same time, the leader's expectation of the level of what might have been achieved will fall. It is so easy for everyone to become frustrated. It is particularly important for the leader to demonstrate that she has a well-developed sense of humor and a thick skin. Time has to be taken to pause and reflect carefully on exactly what has happened. The situation needs to be analyzed to work out what has not gone according to plan—and why. If an error has been made, then it must be acknowledged by the leader and those affected, making everyone more likely to accept the situation and find a way to overcome the problem. The team will learn that errors can be brought into the open rather than covered up. Leaders are human too. But leaders must remember that they shouldn't make mistakes too often!

Developing Leadership Skills

Successful professionals make a long-term investment in their continuing education and development. We suggest a mix of professional development in the information sector and in leadership. This provides an insurance policy if the leader decides to return to an information role. Not everyone wants to stay in a leadership role until the end of his working life. And with later ages of retirement, not everyone should, because people slow down as they get older. Some hold that workers reach their career peak in their mid-forties. When a leader tries to hang on, it also frustrates the team, because it may delay the possibility of promotion. And as we noted earlier, for any service a change of leader is also essential at different stages of its development.

Learning about leadership is a developmental process. The basics can be acquired from short courses and reading. But a leader needs experience to find out what works best for her—there is no one magic path. Learning happens away from the job, and it happens on the job. It comes from feedback. It comes from successes as well as the "it didn't work out quite as I expected" situations. Self-analysis is part of the process.

Try This

Consider people you have observed in a leadership role. Take one person you consider to be a good leader and one person you feel is less successful. List the reasons and compare the outcomes in these two categories: the good leader's appeal and the less successful leader's problems.

It is essential that leaders keep in touch with developments in their own area of the profession so they can make informed decisions and are able to talk with some confidence with the specialists within the team. Just think about the rate of change in technology. . . .

A basic way to start learning is to think about leaders you have known and consider their leadership style. They might have been colleagues, thereby providing an opportunity to observe them at work firsthand on a daily basis, or it could be someone on a professional committee or a person in the public eye. The point to consider is, who are the good leaders? What is attractive about their style and approach? And it's also instructive to think about those who may not have been so successful. What made them less successful as leaders? Why was this so? The following exercise can help identify these factors. Remember we all can learn from the good and the less good.

Generally, the leaders we warm to are those who recognize us as individuals, even if we are in a lowly position. These leaders take a personal interest in others and ask about their work. For leaders, it is a useful way to keep in touch with what is happening at the grass roots. And it is good for people at the grass roots level to be able to recognize the boss. Recognition makes everyone feel good, too. Followers may have a less warm feeling for leaders who are rarely visible, hide in their offices, walk around looking straight ahead, and don't have a public profile. Much can be gained by pondering on the good and the less good as examples of how, or how not, to behave.

Managers learn the basic skills they need by taking a formal course such as an MBA. Many moving into a leadership role are likely to have an MBA, which provides a foundation on which to build the skill set now required. But we believe that you can't learn to be a leader in just one course.

The Expert

Leaders grow over time, and we agree with Frances Cairncross (2004): ''I think that leadership can be learnt, but I'm not sure it can be taught. You can teach leaders the skills that they need. You can teach them to read numbers. You can teach them something about corporate history. You can teach them the rudiments of accountancy. . . . But I'm not sure that the knack of leading a large number of people is something you can learn in a business school.''

Granted, Cairncross is writing about the business sector, but information services operate in the same way as business enterprises. The bottom line matters.

So leadership skills are gained over time using a variety of learning processes. Bennis (2004) endorses this idea in his description of "the seven ages of the leader." In this article, he looks back on his personal development and identifies different stages in his career.

Bennis starts by writing about his first experience of leadership as a lieutenant in World War II at age nineteen. He arrived on the front lines in Belgium in the middle of the night and made a low-key entry into the platoon, joining them in a bombed-out house. He was offered a place to sleep with the rest of the men, and being scared, he pretended to be asleep. He lay there and listened to what the men had to say, learning about the soldiers he would be leading. Their conversation revealed that they needed the person they would later teach him to be. They taught him how to lead, often by example. He learned the value of a good first move: making a low-key entry.

Taking Shakespeare's seven ages of man, Bennis identifies the first age of the leader as being an Infant Executive, entering a frightening place, who needs a mentor. The second age is that of the Schoolboy with a Shining Face, when "everything about you is fair game for comment, criticism and interpretation and misinterpretation" (p. 49). At this stage the new leader learns what it is like to be in the spotlight. This is followed by the third age in which the Lover, with a Woeful Ballad, is "sighing like a furnace . . . as they struggle with the tsunami of problems every organization presents" (p. 49). The leader who is promoted internally discovers it is not easy to relate to former peers who now report to her.

In the fourth age, leaders become more comfortable with their role as the Bearded Soldier, but some communication problems can emerge as "they might assume that what they are hearing from followers is what needs to be heard" (p. 51). It is the point when the leader needs to recruit people who are better than himself so the leader can shine in reflected glory. The next step up is to the General at the height of a career, when the leader learns to listen; many younger leaders just don't want to receive bad tidings. The penultimate stage is that of the Statesman, with Spectacles on Nose. This is the time when the leader starts to think about stepping down and gets ready to pass on what has been learned. The Statesman then becomes the Sage, who becomes the mentor—ambition has passed and life can be enjoyed, "waking up each morning ready to devour the world, full of hope and promise" (p. 53). Out of this research comes the most important quality a leader needs—the capability to adapt to the different stages of leadership.

The seven stages underline our experience that the skills and attributes should be gained over time. Instead of being a one-shot process, it needs a variety of inputs at different points in a leader's career development. So the experience of growing into a leadership role identifies the skills that need strengthening.

Although many large organizations provide a development program, some information professionals will be working in situations where this is not available in-house. However, some basic understanding will have been gained from their first professional course in management and communication skills, together with a sound foundation in professional skills and understanding. Working in a team situation develops communication skills on the job, helped by the feedback gained from appraisal programs.

Information professionals have opportunities for informal learning through membership in their professional associations. Benefits include current awareness magazines, academic journals reporting research, association websites, meetings and conferences, and opportunities for committee work and conference presentations. Association membership can be the first step on the ladder to leadership. Being active in a professional body means you are in touch with the latest developments. You can hone your communication and committee skills and start to be noticed, and for the right reasons. Upwardly mobile career planners get involved with professional associations both within their field and within the field of management. They get nominated to committees and progress through local, regional, and national levels, and may choose to move on to the international scene. Yes, it means an investment of time and personal finance, but the opportunity to learn from a peer group is invaluable. The benefits gained reward the investment of time and money. A network involving a peer group provides feedback regarding how well a person is performing, and perhaps if things are not going well, someone will whisper in the leader's ear. Feedback from peers is to be welcomed. So much can be gained so quickly, and it can be enjoyable, too. It develops the knack of looking beyond the daily role to the horizon. Informal learning is very important.

Mentors provide another mode of informal learning. A mentor may be identified from within an employing organization or from the profession. One example of how mentoring is organized within a profession comes from Australia, where a number of local groups of the Australian Library and Information Association have set up and evaluated mentoring programs (Ritchie and Genoni, 2002). Basically, the purpose of mentoring is to provide a support system that helps people grow in their careers, and it is generally organized on a one-on-one basis. Sometimes a mentoring relationship develops during a qualifying course of professional studies and continues over the long term. Over time both parties get to know each other well, both strengths and weaknesses, and the mentor, on request, can offer advice and comment. However, moving upward into a leadership position may require a different kind of mentor, one who has experienced the highs and lows of being a leader. Through dialogue trust develops, and challenges and experiences are exchanged. If mentors can talk, in confidence, of things they feel they could have done better, that is welcomed by a new leader. A mentor must be a good listener, shouldn't offer comment or advice unless it is requested, and is always honest. Through a relationship built on trust, a mentor can help steer a mentee through difficult situations. Isolation is one of the greatest challenges a leader encounters, and a good mentor can help overcome this danger.

In the business world it is becoming common practice for new executives to feel the need to work with a leadership coach, particularly if the organization is undergoing fundamental change. In this situation, executives may need to examine their competencies and orientation to the employing body. Coaching can be delivered in a one-on-one program or in small groups. The participants are in a learning mode that supports their role in a specific situation. Good coaches are expensive to hire but can be a sound investment if the new leader learns self-awareness and develops new skills rather than uses the coach as a crutch.

After some experience in a new job, we know what we don't know. There are gaps in everyone's understanding of their role and what is expected of them. Reading is a good start to fill the gaps, and bookstore shelves offer many titles about leadership. Because leadership is a hot topic, publishers have been busy, and there is a varied and wide range of information available. Some books that distill the essence of leadership are designed for quick scanning; others are popular quick-to-read titles or biographical stories, and still others are academic in their approach. Browse and remember that most have merit—just check out the publisher—and make a choice.

Try This

What's the last book you read about leadership? What are the three points that stick in your memory? List the newspapers and journals you read *regularly*. List the e-groups you regularly visit. Put them in order of their value to you in terms of information content that contributes to your daily work. Are there any gaps that need to be filled? Is there any duplication so that titles can be dropped to make better use of your time? There are many interesting e-groups—but a choice needs to be made. Which are the most important for your current work?

Keeping up to date with new developments with the intention of bringing best practice to the service is easily done through the journals provided for the various sectors in the information professions. Perhaps it is a pity that there is not yet one that covers the whole of the information sector. For keeping up to date with the field of leadership, we turn every month to *Harvard Business Review*, which offers authoritative, current information presented in a readable style. Alongside that, a weekly covering of current political and economic issues (e.g., *The Economist*) broadens awareness. Finally, a quality national newspaper completes the core reading. All can be read online, but reading the print editions at leisure makes it easier to think through the implications of current trends.

One common frustration is that having to absorb the content of so many reports and internal documents often results in speed-reading. It isn't always easy to read more slowly, but sometimes it is essential as well as being enjoyable.

The Most Important Factor

We finish with yet another reminder that the most important factor a leader must take into account in the information sector is the community served—the users, ex-users, and nonusers. The leader must understand the community's current and future information needs and develop ways to meet these needs that will increase user effectiveness, whether it is for work or relaxation. The users need the team, and the team needs its leader.

Summary

Leadership is not an easy topic to define. It is easier recognized than written down, but writers such as Bennis (2004) have described the role of the leader. Leadership is an issue in many occupations, and it assumes an even greater challenge in the 21st century. Leaders are very visible and are vulnerable to criticism that can come from any direction. As a result, leaders need a good sense of humor and a thick skin to survive.

People become leaders through a variety of routes—through an internal selection and development program, by pursuing a career plan, or even by accident. There are also hidden leaders within every organization. One point that is paramount is that being a leader isn't being a glorified manager. There are some distinct differences.

A range of challenges and opportunities have resulted from the ever-increasing rates of change. People have great expectations of a newly appointed leader, even if the predecessor was successful in the post. Because a person is new, the expectations of users, the team, and the governing board are raised. Each group has an investment in the appointment, and it is vital for the new leader to make contact with them.

Leadership skills can be developed in a number of ways—through courses, reading, and professional associations. Involvement in professional committees provides a peer-based network.

We know from writing about management that it is easy to focus on the means and make it seem that the ends are not important. So we stress from the outset that the most important factor resides in the community served—in other words, the user.

References

Bennis, Warren G., *Managing People Is like Herding Cats* (London: Kogan Page, 1998), 53.

Bennis, Warren G., "The Seven Ages of the Leader," *Harvard Business Review* 82, no. 1 (January 2004): 46–53.

Bennis, Warren G., and Joan Goldsmith, *Learning to Lead: A Workbook on Becoming a Leader* (New York: Basic, 2003).

Buckingham, Marcus, "What Great Managers Do," *Harvard Business Review* 83, no. 3 (March 2005): 72–79.

Cairncross, Frances, "A Discussion with Frances Cairncross, Managing Editor of *The Economist*," *The Economist*, October 23, 2003, at www.economist.com (accessed May 1, 2006).

Conger, Jay A., and Beth Benjamin, *Building Leaders: How Successful Companies Develop the Next Generation* (San Francisco: Jossey-Bass, 1999).

Giuliani, Rudolph W., with Ken Kurson, *Leadership* (New York: Hyperion, 2002).

Hernon, Peter, Ronald R. Powell, and Arthur P. Young, *The Next Library Leadership: Attributes of Academic and Public Library Directors* (Westport, CT: Libraries Unlimited, 2003).

Lucas, Erika, "Tooling Up for Leadership," *Professional Manager* 9, no. 5 (September 2000): 11.

Mayo, Anthony J., and Nitin Nohria, "Zeitgeist Leadership," *Harvard Business Review* 83, no. 10 (October 2005): 48.

Mintzberg, Henry, *The Nature of Managerial Work* (New York: Harper & Row, 1973).

Mintzberg, Henry, "Covert Leadership: Notes on Managing Professionals," *Harvard Business Review* 76, no. 6 (1998): 140–148.

Ritchie, Ann, and Paul Genoni, "Group Mentoring and Professionalism," *Library Management* 23, no. 1/2 (2002): 68–78.

Winston, M.D., "The Importance of Leadership Diversity and Organizational Success in the Academic Environment," *College and Research Libraries* 62, no. 6 (November 2001): 517–526.

CHAPTER 2

Leadership: Past, Present, and Future

This chapter focuses on the following:

- The basics of several traditional approaches to leadership
- Post-9/11 approaches to leadership
- Five areas of concern for 21st-century leaders
- Effective behaviors for 21st-century leaders

For a long time, scholars have attempted to define leadership and to understand how to identify and develop leaders. Some studies of leadership traits go back more than eighty years, while a relatively recent book on library leadership (Hernon, Powell, and Young, 2003) devotes a substantial amount of text to the "qualities" of library directors. Some scholars have chosen to focus their research on behavioral aspects, while still others use a contingency/situational approach. Additional approaches include transformational, charismatic, transactional, normative, attribution, and leader-member exchange. Scholars from several fields have contributed to the study of leadership, in particular psychology, management, sociology, and political science. In this chapter, we briefly discuss these different approaches and attempt to draw some lessons from them as well as from interviews and from our own experiences.

Trait Approach

Studies of leadership traits started appearing in the early 20th century and were the focus of researchers' attention until the late 1940s and early 1950s. Early trait studies involved efforts to determine what differentiated leaders from non-leaders. Although often labeled trait theories in the literature, they are less theories than an approach to understanding what a leader *is* rather than how a leader *leads*. Many of the leadership self-tests found in popular literature are trait based, the outgrowth of "personality tests" researchers used in their original studies. The trait approach usually covers physical, social, task-related, and personal characteristics. Researchers would select a type of institution or organization to study and administer tests to both "leaders" and "followers." Their scores were compared for significant differences.

One such researcher was Ralph Stogdill (1948), who published an article reviewing 120 such trait studies. His purpose was to determine if there was a core set of traits that most studies agreed were distinctive of a leader. He concluded that traits alone could not differentiate between leaders and followers. Follow-up studies reached much the same conclusion (Gibb, 1954; Mann, 1959). By the 1950s, new approaches shifted attention away from traits; however, some work did continue in the area, linking traits to aspects of the newer approaches. This essentially acknowledges that traits are but one factor in what leadership is and how it manifests itself in the working world.

That said, there are some lessons to be learned from trait studies. A few traits do arise more often than not in terms of managerial success and career development—high energy level, ability to handle pressure situations, communication skills, self-confidence, and emotional maturity (Kirkpatrick and Locke, 1991). In our survey, respondents cited these traits in their self-assessments, although energy level was not frequently listed. As Kirkpatrick and Locke state, "Traits *alone*, however, are not sufficient for successful business leadership—they are only preconditions. Leaders who possess the requisite traits must take certain *actions* to be successful" (p. 49). Clearly, having a high energy level and the ability to tolerate stress helps individuals in leadership positions cope with constantly changing circumstances. Communication skills of a high order are crucial for working effectively with the various stakeholders in an information service environment. Being consistent in one's views and expressed values is a hallmark of an effective leader. Demonstrating confidence in plans and goals is another important characteristic of true leadership. (Note: there is a significant difference between showing an appropriate level of confidence and being considered arrogant or brash.) Both consistency and self-confidence were frequently mentioned by our respondents. Effective leaders must have a high level of emotional maturity and accept negative comments and views without overreacting.

As Gary Yukl and David Van Fleet (1992) point out, skill and motivation also play a role in leadership effectiveness. Having a trait is one thing; having the motivation and skill to employ the trait is another matter. Yukl and Van Fleet divide skills into three broad groupings: *technical skills, conceptual skills,* and *interpersonal skills*. Most organizations are complex, with a variety of technical and functional activities, and it would take a highly exceptional person to have in-depth technical skills in all areas; however, having some successful experience in more than one functional area is usually important for a leader. One of the authors of this book had experience at the reference desk, as a cataloger, as head of a serials department, and as a subject bibliographer before becoming a director. Those experiences made it easier for the staff to accept that there was "frontline" experience backing up suggestions and ideas.

Technical and professional skills are necessary for leaders and managers; however, in leadership positions there is also a need for a vision of where the organization should be going (see chapter 6 for a discussion of visioning). Again, a number of our respondents mentioned vision sharing as one of their strengths. Effective visions are grounded in a careful analysis of complex events and issues, in seeing the issues in creative ways while at the same time factoring in practical concerns (conceptual skills). Strong interpersonal skills are necessary to "sell" the vision to the various stakeholders and to secure the best efforts of staff to achieve the vision.

Trait research that examines skills usually does so in the hope of identifying "universals" that differentiate between leaders and followers or managers. To date, the results suggest that the differences vary by situation (see the discussion of the contingency/situational approach later in this chapter). This in turn has led trait researchers to take a holistic approach to their studies. An example of this type of study is Zaccaro, Foti, and Kenny's (1991) research on leadership flexibility. In their conclusion, they suggest that several styles of leadership become necessary as tasks change. As might be expected, the holistic approach does suggest that balance is necessary in traits and skills. That is, while self-confidence is important, too much confidence can result in failing to listen to contrary views or information, which in turn can lead to disastrous outcomes. Balancing also involves trade-offs such as those illustrated in the familiar "managerial grid" of Blake and Mouton (1964), in which differences in concerns for people and production have an impact on leadership style. Some balances include personal concerns versus organizational concerns, subordinate concerns versus supervisor concerns, and the desire for change or innovation versus need for predictability.

A leader cannot lead anything without followers. As Gary Wills (1994, p. 13) writes, "The leader most needs followers. When those are lacking, the best ideas, the strongest will, the most wonderful smile have no effect." In today's team environment, a better descriptor might be *collaborators*, in the positive sense of the term, rather than *followers*. Mutual dependence has become increasingly clear, and the leader's behavior has an impact on the followers (or collaborators).

Behavioral Approach

The behavioral approach emphasizes what leaders do and how that behavior influences their effectiveness. In 1939, Lewin, Lippitt, and White published a classic study of the results of an experiment examining three leadership styles—autocratic, democratic, and laissez-faire. The article's importance was in defining leadership in terms of behavioral style.

After World War II, leadership research turned more and more toward looking at how leaders act when operating as a "leader." Researchers at Ohio State University developed a questionnaire in the late 1950s (called the Leader Behavior Description Questionnaire), which is still widely used in leadership surveys.

Check This Out

View the user documentation and try the Leader Behavior Description Questionnaire (LBDQ) for yourself at the Ohio State University website: www.fisher.osu.edu/offices/fiscal/lbdq.

Originally the questionnaire was a two-factor instrument, measuring task-oriented and people-oriented behavior. Efforts to develop a more complex format have met with limited success. The two factors probably bring to mind some of the basics of motivation and research in that field (McGregor, 1960; Blake and Mouton, 1964; Herzberg, 1959; Fielder, 1978). This is not surprising; a leader's behavior will clearly have an impact on the motivation of the people working with him.

Check This Out

A good review of basic motivational theory and its relationship to leadership appears in Gisela von Dran's article "Human Resources and Leadership Strategies for Libraries in Transition," *Library Administration and Management* 19, no. 4 (2005): 177–184.

Regardless of the questions asked, behavioral researchers are searching for the outcomes of each type of behavior in the hope of identifying a core of successful behaviors. To date there has been limited success, especially in terms of the task- and people-oriented factors. One reason is that research treats the two as mutually exclusive behaviors, which, of course, is not a true reflection of the real world. Leaders can, and often do, engage in behaviors intended to be both task and people oriented. Another factor is the situation; some situations (such as dealing with a flood or a sudden budgetary crisis) call for one type of behavior more than another. (The situational approach to leadership is covered shortly.)

One type of leadership behavior that has had a great deal of attention and writing devoted to it is "participative management." While the general sense is that such behavior is a good thing, years of research indicate the results are mixed (Yukl and Van Fleet, 1992). Sometimes there are good outcomes, and sometimes the results are less than positive. In today's team-oriented environment, some form of shared decision making is essential. However, that process is, by its nature, different from participative management in that effective teams require shared rather than just consultative decision making.

Although behavioral studies have not produced the "magic leadership bullet" (the behaviors that will lead to success), they have produced aids for assessing situations. Perhaps what is clearest is that both task- *and* people-oriented behaviors are necessary, and their relative importance varies from situation to situation.

One aspect of behavior that has received special attention is how a leader uses power. Every leader has some power; how that power is or is not used as well as the type of power often determines if a leader is successful or not. *Power* is the ability to make people do something they would not otherwise do. *Influence*, on the other hand, is the ability to change people's minds to get them to do something they had not thought about doing. Influence tactics are the behaviors a person employs to change people's minds.

French and Raven's (1959) classic paper outlines five types of social power, something that all leaders need—expert, referent, legitimate, reward, and coercive. *Expert power* arises from a leader's knowledge or skill level. The greater the knowledge or skill, the more people recognize and accept the leader's expert power position. *Referent power* is derived from the relationship between the leader and other people and its influence on others' behavior. *Legitimate power* is the power that resides in the position the leader holds. People accept or reject directions to do or not do something in part based on their view of the leader's legitimate right to issue those directions. *Reward power*, as the label suggests, is a result of the leader's ability to give or withhold desired benefits or resources. *Coercive power* is the ability to impose sanctions on people who do or do not do something.

Leaders make use of all five powers from time to time. When and how often they employ a particular type of power appears to have some impact on the leader's success or failure. As one might expect, an emphasis on expert and referent power is more likely to lead to success than is employing frequent use of reward and coercive power. However, leaders do need to be aware of the five types, as they will all likely be used at one time or another.

Sharing power or influence is another way leaders lead. One label for this process is the *leader-member exchange theory*. This concept and process usually involves selected members rather than all the group members. However, effective leaders involve every member of the group at some point in time, making certain there are no "second class" individuals.

Influence tactics are part of the sharing process. There are at least nine such tactics—rational persuasion, inspirational appeals, consultation, ingratiation, personal appeals, exchanges, coalitions, pressure, and legitimizing. Using logical arguments, facts, and data is an example of *rational persuasion* behavior. Emotional or enthusiastic appeals to followers are examples of the *inspirational tactic*. *Consultation tactics* occur when the leader involves people in planning activities or when modifying ideas based on input from followers. *Ingratiation* takes place when the leader engages in behavior that is intended to make people feel positive before putting forward ideas, plans, and so on. *Personal appeals* make use of friendship and feelings of loyalty in moving an activity forward. *Exchange tactics*, as the name indicates, is a trading of favors or an offer of future benefits to gain support for a plan. *Coalition tactics* differ from consultation in that the leader enlists a few supporters to help change the minds of others in order to gain acceptance of a concept. *Pressure tactics* make use of threats or constant emphasis to gain the requisite influence over others to carry out an activity. *Legitimizing tactics* employ the positional power of the leader to accomplish her goals. Few, if any, leaders employ just one tactic for a given goal; using multiple tactics appears to be the most effective approach

Limited research into tactics suggests the most common tactic used with other tactics is rational persuasion. Power and influence research has provided some useful insights into effective leadership. Effective leaders make use of multiple factors rather than one or another alone. They use noncoercive power to direct efforts while employing sharing power (the consultation tactic) to empower and generally motivate others to greater effort. How and when one applies a particular type of power, influence, or tactic is in large measure a function of the situation.

Advertisements for library directors often contain lists of desired characteristics such as high energy level, outgoing, innovative, excellent public speaker, or proven track record in a team setting. Such lists are a reflection of the major purpose of the trait approach—identifying prospective leaders. When applying for such a position, one should expect the interviewers to test the traits identified in the ad in a variety of ways. Further, the list should be considered reflective of what the organization members see as qualities the new director or leader should possess.

Situational Approach

Studies of how *situations* affect leadership arose from the recognition that just looking at traits and behaviors did not provide fully satisfactory explanations about leadership. It is clear that different behavioral styles of leadership are more or less effective as circumstances vary. Thus a key factor in leaders' success is the ability to read and understand the situation they and their followers are in.

Research shows that three major aspects of a situation influence the appropriate leadership behavior or style—the nature of the work, the nature of the staff, and the nature of the environment. Hersey and Blanchard (1969) explored staff skills and abilities in what they labeled "subordinate independence" in a relatively simple context. They suggest there are two styles of leadership (directive and supportive) to consider, depending on the degree of confidence or independence of the subordinate(s). For example, when the subordinates have low confidence or independence, using a highly directive style is more effective than using the supportive approach. Just the opposite is true for individuals who have somewhat high confidence or independence. Hersey and Blanchard's work, in many ways pioneering, was based on a noncomplex model.

A more complex model that relates to the nature of the work is Vroom and Yelton's (1973) decision-making theory. Their model examines five decision procedures—autocratic decision, autocratic decision after seeking additional information, consultative with select individuals, consultative with the group, and group decision. Seven situational variations were also part of the model—the importance of the decision's quality; the structure of the decision; the amount of information already available to the leader; the importance of group acceptance for effective implementation; the degree to which an autocratic decision will be accepted by the group; how much the group shares the leader's organizational goals; and what, if any, conflict exists among group members. Vroom and Yelton formulated a series of guidelines for various combinations. For example, group decisions are not likely to produce quality outcomes when the group and leader do not share common goals. An example of where a group decision would be effective is when goals are shared and group acceptance is important. A leader must, of course, recognize that at some point decisiveness on his part will be required. Maintaining a balance between being decisive when necessary and a tendency to "take over" to move things along can be a challenge.

Perhaps one of the best situational models is Frederick Fielder's contingency theory (1978). Like many others, he believes there is no single best way to lead. His model contains three main variables—leader-member relationship, task structure, and leader's power position. Each variable has two subcomponents—good or bad relationships, structured or unstructured tasks, and strong or weak power position. Another factor is whether the leader is relationship or task oriented. Fielder's research suggests that task-oriented leaders generally do better in situations that have good relationships, structured tasks, and either a weak or strong power position. When relationships are good, the task is unstructured, and the power position is strong, they do equally well. The other situation task-oriented leaders do well in is poor to moderate relationships, unstructured tasks, and a strong power position. Relationship-oriented managers tend to do better in all other situations.

A theory called "leadership substitutes" (Howell et al., 1990) indicates that in some situations the supportive or instrumental behavior of a leader is unnecessary or at least irrelevant. Exactly how this relatively recent research will play out in the workplace is unclear; however, results make it clear that the leader is affected by situational factors.

Charismatic Leadership

In many ways, Max Weber can be viewed as the individual who started the serious study of "great man" or "great woman" leadership. *Charismatic leaders* can be thought of as individuals who apparently have exceptional abilities to carry out difficult activities and inspire their followers to extraordinary levels of effort and commitment. Generally when people think of charismatic leaders, thoughts turn to people such as Alexander the Great, Hitler (not all charismatic persons are "good"), Gandhi, or Martin Luther King. Three examples from business organizations are Steve Jobs (Apple Macintosh computers), Lee Iacocca (Chrysler), and Mary Kay Ash (Mary Kay cosmetics).

Often studies of charismatic leaders take the form of biographies, from which different readers take away different ideas about what constitute the key elements of charisma. One factor that comes out of both biographies and research is that situations do matter, and a charismatic leader might succeed in one setting while failing in another. Charismatic leaders frequently arise in crisis situations or when followers are unhappy with the status quo. Research suggests that charismatic leaders share four traits—need for power, very high self-confidence, willingness to take risks, and commitment to the "correctness" of their views.

Robert House (1977) identified three behaviors of a charismatic leader. One is a clear and compelling *vision*, put forward with behavior that reinforces the leader's belief in that vision so that followers keep their confidence in both themselves and the leader. The leader also communicates *high expectations* for the followers' performances in achieving the vision. Further, the leader expresses great *confidence* in the followers' ability to carry out the necessary activities. Alternatively, as Nadler and Tushman (1995) put it, charismatic leaders are envisioning, energizing, and enabling.

Conger and Kanungo (1998) propose that charisma is something individuals gain as the result of others (followers) attributing characteristics to a "leader." Followers observing a leader's behavior attribute characteristics (charismatic or noncharismatic) based on their observations and the outcomes of the behavior.

Conger and Kanungo assume the characteristics vary in level depending on the situation. They identify three important behaviors of charismatic leaders—proposing visions that are very different from the existing situation and yet within the capabilities of the group, taking risks or making sacrifices to achieve each vision, and taking unconventional steps to assist in successful accomplishment of the goal(s). Further, they identify several traits that enhance charisma—very high self-confidence, the ability to create strong positive self-images, exceptional ability to assess a situation and possible actions, and outstanding "people" skills (e.g., empathy, understanding) when it comes to assessing followers' needs and values. Like other researchers, Conger and Kanungo see charismatic behavior arising in highly fluid situations or when the status quo is unsatisfactory. Their research draws on survey data from both charismatic and noncharismatic organizational leaders.

Research suggests that charismatic leaders are not in themselves sufficient to "institutionalize" the changes. When the charismatic person is gone, more often than not, many aspects of his vision fall away. This happens for a number of reasons. Perhaps the most significant of these is the development of unrealistic expectations among the followers. Sometimes a vision requires broad-based changes (e.g., social, economic, organizational) that take years to occur, if at all. Very often there is reluctance, or in some instances fear, to disagree with the charismatic leader. (High self-confidence can be a double-edged sword for a person unable or unwilling to listen to contrary points of view.) There is also the danger that lower management may become disenfranchised—that is, the meaningful messages (directions, views, motivations, and so on) appear to come *only* from the charismatic leader.

Two potentially interrelated issues that may arise in a charismatic-led organization are dependency and the limitations of a leader's skills or interests. Charismatic leaders by their nature often spur strong psychological responses in their followers. Occasionally this reaches a point where followers become so dependent on the leader that they do not act on their own. When that occurs, the danger of personal skill or interest limitations comes into play. No one is equally interested and skilled in all aspects of management (collection development, fund-raising, technology, fiscal management). In all likelihood, there will be some aspects that a leader does not or cannot handle effectively; if the followers have become dependent on the leader, serious problems can arise. When that happens, some of the leader's "magic" begins to fade. If too many problems crop up, dependent followers become confused and even less able to act to address the problem.

With these factors in mind, it becomes clear that while charisma may be an important factor, it is not enough in itself to guarantee long-term organizational success. Warren Bennis (2003, p. 145) makes the following observation:

In the course of my study, I met many leaders who couldn't be described as charismatic by any sort of rhetorical stretch, but they nevertheless managed to inspire an enviable trust and loyalty in their co-workers. And through their abilities to get people on their side, they were able to effect necessary changes in the culture of their organizations and make real their guiding visions.

Such leaders fall into the next type of leader that we will describe—transformational.

Transformational Leadership

James MacGregor Burns (1978) formulated the concept of *transformational leadership* in the 1970s. It is a blend of the aforementioned behavioral and trait concepts. A key element in transformational leadership is influence—the leader and followers influence one another. Burns further identified two interrelated types of leadership depending on the nature of the influence: transformational and transactional.

The works of Burns (1978) and Bass (1994) are key studies in the area of transactional and transformational leadership. Because of the similarities between transformational and charismatic leadership, it is important to note their differences as well as to differentiate between them and transactional leadership.

While charismatic and transformational leaders are characterized as possessing such attributes as vision, self-confidence, and the ability to arouse strong follower support, transformational leaders have at least two other key components—intellectual stimulation and individual consideration. These leaders have greater concern for their followers and their development. *Intellectual stimulation* describes the leader's sharing of information to increase the followers' awareness of issues so they will think about how to handle them. *Individualized consideration*, as the phrase suggests, is focused on individual needs for support, development, encouragement, and so on. Essentially, transformational leaders attempt to empower and develop their followers, while charismatic leaders have little or no focus on those aspects. Burns viewed transformational leadership as a two-way process—leaders influencing followers and followers influencing leaders. He saw it as appealing to higher rather than baser values or motives.

In contrast, both Burns and Bass view *transactional leadership* as taking place when there is an exchange of valued "things" between a leader and followers, such as economic rewards and support. Also, both recognize that a leader may at one time or another switch between transactional and transformational as circumstances change.

As noted by Humphreys and Einstein (2003, p. 85), the key to transactional leadership is the "exchange between the superior and the subordinate. They influence each other in a way that both parties receive something of value. . . . In this transaction, leader influence is based on the premise that it is in the best interest of the subordinates to follow."

A transformational leader instills feelings of confidence, admiration, and commitment in the followers. He is charismatic, creating a special bond with followers and articulating a vision the followers identify with and are willing to work for. Each follower is coached, advised, and delegated some authority. The transformational leader stimulates followers intellectually, arousing them to develop new ways of thinking about problems. The leader uses contingent rewards to positively reinforce performances that are consistent with the leader's wishes. Management is by exception. The leader takes initiative only when problems arise and is not actively involved when things are going well. The transformational leader commits people to action and converts followers into leaders.

Transformational leaders are relevant to today's workplace because they are flexible as well as innovative, and they form effective teams. While it is important to have leaders with the appropriate orientation defining tasks and managing interrelationships, it is even more important to have leaders who can bring organizations into futures they have not yet imagined. Transformational leadership is the essence of creating and sustaining a competitive advantage.

We end our brief review of transformational leadership with a discussion of a relatively recent study of that approach and two other aspects of successful not-for-profit organizations. Jaskyte (2004) explored the relationships between the following:

- Transformational leadership and organizational culture
- Transformational leadership and organizational innovativeness
- Organizational innovativeness and organizational culture

The results were mixed, and there was no significant statistical correlation between transformational leadership and innovativeness, but there were such correlations for the others. This suggests transformational leaders should be aware that situations requiring innovation will probably require their extra attention.

Servant Leadership

At about the same time as Burns and Bass were publishing their research on transformational leadership, Robert Greenleaf (1977) introduced the concept of *servant leadership*. His idea was that people who are viewed as great leaders are first servants. Further, Greenleaf proposed that such leaders moved into the leadership role by first feeling the need to serve, followed by the conscious choice or desire to lead. In his view, those served would grow and develop—and might become servant leaders themselves. Servant leaders are much more likely to be trusted, according to Greenleaf. Some of the other attributes of the servant leader include initiative, thoughtful listening, an active imagination, empathy, persuasiveness, foresight, and community building.

Greenleaf suggests that leadership is "bestowed" on individuals who are trusted because of their status as servants. The trust arises when a person is empathic and accepts followers as they are, is always dependable, and leads by example. A servant leader, by being a servant, also generates the trust of the organization. Essentially, for Greenleaf, servant leadership is both a product of and an antecedent to leader and organizational trust. He views trust as being created through the following:

- Genuinely empowering workers
- Involving employees early
- Honoring commitments and being consistent
- Developing and coaching skills and taking risks
- Applying an appropriate management style
- Building trustworthiness through integrity and competence
- Engaging in thoughtful and full communication

The concept has much to offer potential and existing leaders if the idea indeed translates well to the workplace. Joseph and Winston (2005) tested four hypotheses, one of which was that servant-led organizations have higher levels of trust than do nonservant-led organizations. They found statistical support for that hypothesis and suggest that trust plays an important role in organizational effectiveness in areas such as the following:

- Job satisfaction
- Organizational commitment
- Turnover intentions
- Belief in information provided by the leader
- Commitment to decisions

Check This Out

A key website for servant leadership is that of the Greenleaf Center for Servant-Leadership: www.greenleaf.org.

A vast majority of writers on leadership today (e.g., Joseph Badaracco, Warren Bennis, John Kotter, James Kouzes, John Maxwell, Henry Mintzberg, and Barry

Posner) employ elements of the various research approaches covered so far in this chapter. Each writer tends to focus on one or two aspects of leadership, but a careful reading shows they all believe that leadership is a complex concept, and one single aspect cannot explain what leadership is or how one goes about becoming and staying a leader.

The Present

The postmillennium years have been filled with stress and uncertainty. In the United States in particular, the events in New York and Washington, D.C., on September 11, 2001, and elsewhere in the recent past have changed our personal sense of security and increased our desire for effective leaders, at least for most of us. That desire was probably a contributing factor in the increased publication of books and articles addressing leadership concerns. Some publications describe how individuals handled crisis situations (Morrell and Capparell, 2001; Giuliani, 2002). Some provided more complete discussions of some aspect of leadership (Goleman, Boyatzis, and McKee, 2002). Some were updated versions of earlier works (Bennis, 2003). Still others drew on general leadership lessons from a particular organization (Snair, 2004). One study even examined attributes of library directors (Hernon, Powell, and Young, 2003). What follows is a sampling of those works, which is but a small proportion of the publications that have appeared in the recent past. The items selected do demonstrate the broad interest in the topic in today's society.

Shackleton's Way by Morrell and Capparell (2001) is an interesting mix of the "great man" biography and a general discussion of leadership. Sir Ernest Shackleton, a British explorer with a special interest in the Antarctic, led an expedition to that area in 1914. Between January 1915 and May 1916, the group faced an ever-increasing series of crises that probably should have killed everyone. Instead, Shackleton's leadership brought everyone to safety. The story is enjoyable and exciting in itself; however, the authors break the story down into chapters that reflect elements of leadership. At the end of each chapter, after describing the story's pertinent events, they relate the experience to lessons for leadership in today's climate. For example, chapter 1, "The Path to Leadership," concludes with a list titled "Shackleton's Way to Develop Leadership Skills." A sample of that list (p. 45) follows:

- Cultivate a sense of compassion and responsibility for others.
- Do your part to help create an upbeat environment at work.
- In a rapidly changing world, be willing to venture in new directions, to seize new opportunities and learn new skills.

• Learn from past mistakes—yours and those made by others. Sometimes the best teachers are bad bosses and the negative experiences.

This book provides insights into leadership in general, as well as how to handle life-threatening situations.

Another account of a "great man" handling a life crisis that takes a dual approach is Rudolph Giuliani's *Leadership* (2002). He states in the preface that he had started work on the book some time before the New York events of September 11, 2001; the book was "a self-imposed program on how to run an organization" (p. ix). The dual approach arises because the work turned out to be in part a discussion of how he led/ran the city of New York as mayor as well as a discussion of his experience in handling the crisis of 9/11 and its aftermath. Unlike the Shackleton title, which drew lessons from the events, Giuliani shows how his existing leadership style assisted him during and after the crisis. The core of the work, and what probably would have made up the book in its entirety except for the events of 9/11, is part II of the book, fourteen chapters describing his personal management philosophy. The chapters also make reference to how the topic covered played out during the crisis. His chapter titles provide a summary of his views about leadership—"First Things First," "Prepare Relentlessly," "Everyone's Accountable, All of the Time," "Surround Yourself with Great People," "Reflect, Then Decide," "Underpromise and Overdeliver," "Develop and Communicate Strong Beliefs," "Be Your Own Man," "Loyalty: The Vital Virtue," "Weddings Discretionary, Funerals Mandatory," "Stand Up to Bullies," "Study. Read. Learn Independently," "Organize Around a Purpose," and "Bribe Only Those Who Will Stay Bribed." Given this is a book by a politician, the last chapter title probably deserves an explanation—it is about the importance of trust. The first and last chapters specifically address the events of 9/11 and their aftermath. Prospective and existing leaders can benefit from spending some time reading Giuliani's book.

Shifting away from the "great man" approach to leadership, we turn to *Primal Leadership* by Goleman, Boyatzis, and McKee (2002). Although, as we noted earlier, most of the writers on leadership during the past ten to fifteen years have drawn on the elements of earlier research described in this chapter, some writers have promoted an added element or two to the list of leadership skills and attributes. Daniel Goleman has been a leading proponent of the importance of emotional intelligence (EI) for effective leadership (see chapter 3 for a more detailed description of EI). In the preface to *Primal Leadership*, the authors state that "the primal job of leadership is emotional" (p. ix). They expand on this statement by suggesting that EI underlies how well things will work for a leader. (EI, very simply, is understanding one's own emotions, understanding others' emotions, and making use of that information in a positive manner.) Dividing the text into three sections, the authors make the case for why EI is a powerful tool for leadership, then move on to the topics of creating emotionally intelligent leaders and organizations. This book gives readers a full understanding of what EI is and how it can be useful to leaders.

In addition to new titles added to the leadership literature, Warren Bennis's classic *On Becoming a Leader* was updated and expanded during this period. Bennis is one of our favorite writers when it comes to leadership. (This is one of the reasons we followed his approach when conducting our own survey of library leaders as part of our preparation for this book.) He has produced more than fifteen books on management and leadership. *On Becoming a Leader* first appeared in 1989 and was based on interviews of people in leadership positions. Bennis notes:

> My paradigm, then, is leaders, not theories about leaders, and leaders functioning in the real world rather than some artificial setting. . . . They [are] all people whose lives have made a difference—thoughtful, articulate, and reflective. (p. xxviii)

Drawing on real-world experiences and formulating leadership lessons is a hallmark of his research and writing. If you have only limited time to devote to reading about leadership, spend some of it on this book. You will be well rewarded.

A prospective or existing leader of an information service should not be put off by the title of Scott Snair's 2004 work, *West Point Leadership Lessons*. As Snair himself notes, "The purpose of this book is to offer West Point leadership philosophies—personified by leaders of yesterday and today—that can be applied to any management scenario. The Academy's enduring messages are meant for supervisors facing uncertain times, morality dilemmas, and team challenges" (p. viv). Snair uses both Academy and non-Academy graduates to illustrate his points. The book suggests that a West Point leader, and by extension any leader, does the following (pp. ix–x):

- Displays absolute integrity
- Maintains technical competence
- Takes care of subordinates
- Respects others
- Is goal oriented
- Sets high standards for self
- Possesses supreme confidence
- Shows superb people skills
- Chooses leadership over "managership"

- Has high physical and mental drive
- Holds the ability to choose the "harder right" over the "easier wrong"

This list could be a summary of research that focuses on leadership skills and abilities.

The Next Library Leadership by Hernon, Powell, and Young (2003) explores which attributes are appropriate for directors of academic and public libraries. As the authors note in their introductory remarks, "This book identifies those traits needed by the next generation of academic and public library directors, and suggests strategies that individuals can use to prepare themselves for leadership positions and challenges ahead" (p. ix). The authors employed the Delphi survey method, content analysis, and in-person and telephone interviews to collect their data. The major portion of the text addresses the attributes of leadership and how the authors developed the impressively long list of traits needed. It does have a brief section on how to prepare oneself for a leadership role, but that is not the primary focus of the book. One may at first be intimidated by the long list of attributes (which appears on pages 115–119 of the work), but for the most part, the traits they suggest are manageable to acquire, and most people already possess many of them. The list makes it very clear just how complex the concept of leadership is and what it takes to become a leader.

Gazing into a crystal ball carries risks—but we will stick our necks out and envision the future for up-and-coming information service leaders. Unfortunately, we believe that life is not likely to get more comfortable for leaders. Aside from the growing geopolitical challenges, the marketing of services will increasingly be required; technological change will not slow down, nor will licensing become less expensive; and staff will be more mobile and require a greater investment in their training, and their personal needs will have to be taken more closely into account. Funding bodies will seek even greater accountability. These factors point to a tremendous challenge for tomorrow's leaders—they will believe they are making a major impact as they develop and change the nature of tomorrow's information services. Attributes such as those described in this chapter will help them meet those challenges in an effective manner.

What We Can Learn from the Writings on Leadership

The preceding brief discussion highlights some of the major leadership theories and research. We emphasize the fact that the coverage is brief and far from comprehensive. Indeed, there are full books addressing the theories and their variations, such as the *Encyclopedia of Leadership* (Goethals, Sorenson, and Burns, 2004). One lesson to take away from the review is that no single approach will work all the time in any situation. Another lesson is that each concept has something of value to consider when putting together a personal approach to leadership. Since most of the leadership theories and approaches were formulated in the last half of the 20th century, they now must take into account the changes and issues of the early 21st century.

We will touch on five areas of concern for 21st-century leaders—globalization, increasing stress on the environment, the speed of change within the field of information technology, the speed of scientific and social change, and increased uncertainty about the future. In terms of *globalization*, the world is becoming increasingly interconnected, and events in one region of the world can and do have an impact in other parts of the world. Economic changes are the most obvious, and leaders who fail to monitor such changes risk having unpleasant surprises popping up at inopportune times. People are moving from one country to another in growing numbers. Workforces are becoming more diverse as a result; effective leaders recognize and respond to this trend. (Much of the research on leadership was conducted on what was a rather homogenous workforce, which could mean results do not apply to today's situation.) Globalization also means that a leader's environmental scanning (monitoring) must be broader in character than it was in the past. Information professionals must keep up to date with what is happening in the field worldwide, not just what is occurring nationally.

Environmental stress—pollution, deforestation, global warming, the search for renewable energy sources, and so on—may seem far removed from the concerns of the information professional. At one level that is true, but from a long-term perspective it seems clear that society must address these issues, and resolving them will be costly and perhaps even disruptive, because they appear to be best resolved on a global rather than a country-by-country basis. A leader's vision that does not factor in potential economic consequences will likely fail to materialize as planned.

Everyone in the information professions recognizes that the *speed of change in technology* is not slowing down. It is not just the equipment and software changes that are a challenge; the way people are using the technology is also important. Effective information leaders pay close attention to the "how used" factors, perhaps even more attention than to the technology side. The end user is the key point to successful information service. Asking how, when, where, and why users are doing what they are doing with information resources should be a major consideration as visions for information services are developed and modified.

Scientific and social changes are also areas a leader should monitor. The social side seems obvious for information service programs. The challenge is to maintain a broad perspective. Although it is frequently the local end users that are the focus of any successful service, regional, national and even international social shifts may be forerunners to local shifts. In some countries, such as the United States, there is an increasing link between social and scientific change and research. Some areas (e.g., evolution and creationism) are often interrelated in ways that can affect services and collections.

Uncertainly about the future has become a greater concern, especially in light of the terrorist attacks around the world. Although incidents may be local in character, their impact is worldwide. People know they are now less secure. To some degree, personal values (i.e., what is most important to individuals) have shifted. Family and other nonwork activities have taken on greater significance, and work-related issues are frequently of lesser importance. Leaders who are unaware of such shifts and who do not respond to these changes may find it increasingly difficult to develop effective teams.

What are some leadership implications that arise from these and other 21st-century changes? One implication is that leaders must be effective in working with their followers in the process of handling change. Often in the past, a work team would face the need to change, make the change, and then have a fairly long period in which there was no change. Today, change is ongoing, and there is little time to settle into one way of doing something before the pressure is on to change yet again. Take the ever-changing nature of database interfaces or the frequent improvements in OPAC services, for example. Also, changes are coming in multiples, rather than singly, making the process ever more complex. The issue of managing change is also discussed in chapter 6.

Check This Out

A good book for leaders who wish to help staff through the change process is the revised edition of Susan Curzon's *Managing Change* (New York: Neal-Schuman, 2005). The work includes tips for preparing the organization for change and offers several ``change scenarios'' worth reviewing. Although it was written for the library sector, it will be helpful to those in other sectors of the information professions.

Complexity has always been with us; however, today it is making the leader's task more difficult. Thinking in terms of systems has always been the hallmark of a good manager or leader. Because of the interrelated aspects of so many of today's challenges, a leader must be willing to share leadership responsibilities in order to draw on diverse points of view.

Rapid change, complexity, and interrelatedness tend to increase tensions and sometimes create differences in values. Such tensions and differences can develop within the leader's group itself; that in turn places even greater emphasis on the leader's ethical behavior, especially when it comes to balancing differences between individuals. For the information profession, there is a need to address the growing gap between the "information rich and poor." Social justice, economic, and organizational issues create a mix of factors that are often difficult, if not impossible, to balance in a completely satisfactory manner. There are several constituencies to consider (e.g., staff, community served, governing boards, funding authorities), not all of whom will share the same values (see chapter 5 for a discussion of the political aspects of leadership).

Finally, although it may have been thought of as a nice benefit in the past, in today's organizations, continuing education is a must in order for staff to remain effective. Although leaders can only do so much (limited funding for training is often outside their effective control), they can still coach staff and otherwise encourage self-learning by team members. Making use of various staff members' expertise can also promote ongoing learning among the staff. The requirement of ongoing learning may originate from the leader, but the teaching and coaching can come from anyone. Mentoring, teaching, and coaching are explored in more depth in chapter 3.

Check This Out

The American Library Association's Continuing Library Education and Networking Exchange (CLENE) Round Table provides a network for individuals with an interest in education for library personnel. Among its activities, the round table sponsors an annual training showcase at the ALA conference. More information is available at www.ala.org/ala/clenert/aboutclene/aboutclene .htm (accessed May 1, 2006).

21st-Century Leadership

We believe that 21st-century leadership should be nonhierarchical, shared, cooperative, collaborative, inclusive, or some other word that implies leadership is a joint activity. (A leader without followers is leading nothing.) Today's information professionals are highly educated, self-managing, lifelong learners who approach projects in a people-focused manner. Such individuals require a 21st-century approach to leadership. An idea put forward in an *Economist* special supplement on leadership is particularly valuable for today's leaders to keep in mind: "People oriented, knowledge-based businesses need to be led from the centre, rather than from the front" (2003, p. 18).

All the foregoing led us to add yet another definition of leadership to the hundreds that already exist. Certainly we drew on the thoughts of others, especially Burns's and Bass's concepts of transformational leadership, but we wanted to formulate a definition that matched our views of where professional leadership should be going. Our definition is as follows: Leadership for today is a collaborative activity. It generates the opportunity for all members of an organization to engage in visioning and motivating one another to meet the challenges of a continually changing operating environment. The outcome is that the organization moves forward to achieve its goal of fulfilling the information needs of the community it serves. Leaders require specific characteristics and skills to make this happen.

Some readers may think this a somewhat speculative definition, and perhaps it is; however, it draws on a large body of literature that looks at 21st-century leadership issues. We also believe it reflects what will be necessary as those in generation X and the millennium generation move into leadership roles.

Check This Out

An article that explores how real-life experiences can be used to make you a better leader is Susan Metros's "A Heart to Heart on Leadership," *College and Research Libraries News* 66, no. 6 (June 2005): 447–450.

We see such leadership resulting in an organization that is team oriented, with team accountability and rewards. In this environment, everyone can be (and sometimes will be) a leader, and people are focused on doing the "right things" rather than simply "doing things right" (without forward thinking). It is also an environment in which context and processes play a greater role in work activities. In today's environment, information professionals often need to engage in more risk taking or be more entrepreneurial. With more competitors around, staying with "tried and true" methods and approaches to service is not likely to lead to long-term success. Drawing in all the staff is one way to address the need to be more innovative and foster a change orientation. Effective leaders will also commit some resources to coaching, teaching, and lifelong learning for all staff members.

We think the following quotation from James Neal reflects the 21st-century leadership approach: "A leader is an individual who can attract innovative people and provide the working environment for those individuals to thrive and grow individually and collaboratively to get things done" (Sapp, 2005, p. 64).

What are some of the behaviors that may be most beneficial for today's leaders? As one might expect, articulating a clear and appealing vision is a key element in building group commitment. It is the vision that helps guide activities and decisions of organizational members; this is especially true where members are to have a high degree of autonomy or discretion in their activities.

Effective leaders also explain how the organizational vision is attainable. In addition, leaders must not assume they have all the answers—group feedback and thoughts are keys to success. Nevertheless, leaders should present their thoughts about steps needed for the successful accomplishment of the vision. Without such input, staff may have serious doubts about the vision's feasibility. Concrete examples of actions required can also help demonstrate how each team member's contributions further the vision and increase commitment.

Acting confidently is another important behavior for today's leaders, especially when there is uncertainty in the environment. Nothing kills commitment more quickly than a leader who shows a lack of confidence in the goals and achievements of the organization. A leader needs to be especially aware of this danger when there are setbacks and unexpected problems—they can and do crop up all the time in any vision or plan. Obviously, visions and plans will need to be adjusted at times in order to address any crisis that may arise. One need only look at the widespread impact of the 2005 hurricane season on the south central United States to see the numerous challenges faced by the leaders of archives and records services and the many libraries in the region.

Demonstrating optimism is equally important for success. This becomes a significant issue when facing prolonged delays or setbacks, such as budgetary constraints or ongoing issues with facilities or technology. Even when the leader may not be feeling particularly optimistic, she should make every effort to be positive about the ultimate outcome. Another behavior that builds commitment is expressing confidence in the ability of the group and its members to achieve the desired outcome(s). It is the rare vision that does not call for changes in services and activities. Often this means people will need to stop doing something they are comfortable with and take on new duties or use new skills. Understandably, some people will have difficulty with such changes, either because of discomfort or because they are not sure they have the necessary skill set(s). Building individual and team confidence is essential for long-term success and the ultimate achievement of the vision.

Coaching and teaching are additional behaviors that build confidence and commitment. Coaching, teaching, and training can take many forms, from one-on-one sessions to outside workshops and conferences. We emphasize once again that such opportunities should be available to all staff, not just professional personnel.

Taking symbolic or dramatic action in reference to key values or aspects of the vision can focus the group's attention on those issues and can help reinforce their importance. For example, if a key element of the vision is providing state-of-the-art technology for users, the leader could take responsibility for seeking external grants or funding to enable the purchase of the needed items. Care should be taken so that the group does not misinterpret such an action as meaning only the leader need take steps to ensure the successful realization of the vision.

Leading by example has always been a hallmark of effective leaders. Today, setting an example is even more important. Individual contribution is one area where it is crucial to set an example and maintain credibility with followers. Leaders must not just talk about collaborative efforts, saying that "everyone can be a leader" (at least some of the time), but also act on those concepts by welcoming input. Failing to do so will quickly kill trust and faith in a leader.

Setting examples becomes more effective when the leader empowers people. Empowerment leads to greater commitment to the vision and the efforts to achieve that vision. We see empowerment as one of the most important elements in the toolkits of today's leaders. What empowerment means is that individuals and teams get to help set goals and objectives within the broad framework of the vision, as well as help determine strategies. When a leader empowers people, it means trusting them as well as giving up some power and control. For some individuals, such a step is difficult to take, but it is one a true leader must take.

Keep in Mind

To be effective, today's library leaders should be prepared to do the following:

- Articulate a clear and appealing vision
- Explain how the vision is attainable
- Act confidently and optimistically
- Express confidence in the group's ability to achieve desired outcomes
- Provide coaching, teaching, and training opportunities for staff
- Take action as needed to reinforce the vision or mission
- Set an example and welcome input
- Empower their staff

Since 2002, *Library Journal* has published a supplement titled "Movers & Shakers." Each issue profiles fifty or so individuals, from all types of information services, who are, in fact, demonstrating that one can lead from any level in an organization. Most of the people are at either the front line or middle level of their organizations. The supplements suggest that the featured individuals are actually behaving along the lines we outline in this section. An example is Mary

Graham of the Brooklyn Public Library ("Movers & Shakers 2004"). In talking about her project to rethink branch libraries, she said the goal was "to transform neighborhood libraries and the way they function, both internally and in their local communities, by building and nurturing autonomy at the local level" (p. 9). The profile further notes her interaction with the staffs of the branches, where there was natural concern about the vision of "transforming" internal operations. Graham's role was to provide encouragement and to remain open to concerns. "She soothed fears about their changing roles, welcomed their feedback, . . . invited them to generate solutions, . . . modeled respectful and inclusive communication with all levels of staff, and provided an environment that encouraged respect, risk-taking and creativity" (p. 9). Almost every one of the profiles reflects similar behavior by these "leaders," which they are, even if *Library Journal* does not use that term. Reading "Movers & Shakers" gives us a very strong sense that the future of the information profession will be in good hands as these individuals move up to senior-level positions.

Almost all of our own survey respondents indicated in one way or another that they too were engaged in these important behaviors. This suggests to us that perhaps, at least in some settings, there may not be as big a generational difference in the field as one might expect from reading the literature, at least as far as leadership is concerned.

Summary

It appears clear from the foregoing discussion of leadership concepts that leadership is behavioral—there are certain things one must "do" to be a leader. Some traits are important, such as self-confidence, ability to envision and articulate a plan, and high energy. Certainly it is clear that how leaders behave will dictate the situations they find themselves in. The 21st century brings with it additional issues, especially in the area of staff involvement.

The trait, behavioral, and situational approaches to group leadership all have significant implications for leaders. Traits describe how a person's personality may determine whether other group members see that person as a leader. Behavior concepts explain the effect that the leader's behavior has on group members. Situational approaches help leaders select appropriate behaviors as situations change and also reveal how successful a leader will be in differing group situations.

Three issues come into play when looking at effective leadership—the leader, the collaborators or followers, and the situation. There are no simple or single answers to the question of what results in successful leadership. A leader must assess his skills and values, assess his staff's skills and values, and assess the given situation. Knowing how to respond as a leader calls for experience, knowledge of both leadership theory and practice, and an accurate assessment of one's own abilities. Even then, a leader must understand that what worked well in what appears to have been a similar situation may not work this time. We discuss some of the tools that can assist in self-assessment in the next chapter.

References

"A Survey of Corporate Leadership," *The Economist*, October 25, 2003, at www.economist.com (accessed May 1, 2006).

Bass, Bernard M., *Improving Organizational Effectiveness through Transformational Leadership* (Thousand Oaks, CA: Sage, 1994).

Bennis, Warren, *On Becoming a Leader*, rev. ed. (New York: Basic, 2003).

Blake, Robert, and Jan Mouton, *Managerial Grid* (Houston: Gulf, 1964).

Burns, James M., *Leadership* (New York: HarperCollins, 1978).

Conger, J.A., and R.N. Kanungo, *Charismatic Leadership in Organizations* (Thousand Oaks, CA: Sage, 1998).

Fielder, F.E., "The Contingency Model and the Dynamics of the Leadership Process," in *Advances in Experimental Social Psychology*, edited by L. Berkowitz (New York: Academic, 1978), 60–112.

French, J., and B.H. Raven, "The Bases of Social Power," in *Studies of Social Power*, edited by D. Cartwright (Ann Arbor, MI: Institute of Social Research, 1959), 150–167.

Gibb, Cecil A., "Leadership," in *Handbook of Social Psychology*, edited by Gardner Lindzey (Cambridge, MA: Addison Wesley, 1954), 877–920.

Giuliani, Rudolph, with Ken Kurson, *Leadership* (New York: Miramax, 2002).

Goleman, Daniel, Richard Boyatzis, and Annie McKee, *Primal Leadership: Learning to Lead with Emotional Intelligence* (Boston: Harvard Business School Press, 2002).

Goethals, George R., Georgia J. Sorenson, and James MacGregor Burns, eds., *Encyclopedia of Leadership* (Thousand Oaks, CA: Sage, 2004).

Greenleaf, Robert, *Servant Leadership: A Journey into the Nature of Legitimate Power and Greatness* (New York: Paulist, 1997).

Hernon, Peter, Ronald Powell, and Arthur Young, *The Next Library Leadership: Attributes of Academic and Public Library Directors* (Westport, CT: Libraries Unlimited, 2003).

Hersey, P., and K.H. Blanchard, "Life Cycle Theory of Leadership," *Training and Development Journal* 23, no. 2 (1969): 24–26.

Herzberg, Frederick, *The Motivation to Work*, 2nd ed. (New York: Wiley, 1959).

House, Robert J., "A 1976 Theory of Charismatic Leadership," in *Leadership: The Cutting Edge*, edited by James Hunt and Lars Larson (Carbondale, IL: Southern Illinois University Press, 1977).

Howell, Jon P., et al., "Substitutes for Leadership: Effective Alternatives to Ineffective Leadership," *Organizational Dynamics* 19, no. 1 (1990): 21–38.

Humphreys, John H., and Walter O. Einstein, "Nothing New Under the Sun: Transformational Leadership from a Historical Perspective." *Journal of Management History* 41, no. 1 (2003): 85–95.

Jaskyte, Kristina, "Transformational Leadership, Organizational Culture, and Innovativeness in Nonprofit Organizations," *Nonprofit Management & Leadership* 15, no. 2 (2004): 153–168.

Joseph, Errol, and Bruce Winston, "A Correlation of Servant Leadership, Leader Trust, and Organizational Trust," *Leadership & Organizational Development Journal* 26, no. 1 (2005): 2–22.

Kirkpatrick, Shelly A., and Edwin A. Locke, "Leadership: Do Traits Matter?" *The Academy of Management Executives* 5, no. 2 (1991): 48–60.

Lewin, Kurt, Ronald Lippitt, and Ralph White, "Patterns of Aggressive Behavior in Experimentally Created Social Climates," *Journal of Social Psychology* 10 (1939): 271–299.

Mann, Richard D., "A Review of the Relationship between Personality and Performance in Small Groups," *Psychology Bulletin* 56 (1959): 241–270.

McGregor, Douglas, *The Human Side of Enterprise* (New York: McGraw-Hill, 1960).

Morrell, Margot, and Stephanie Capparell, *Shackleton's Way: Leadership Lessons from the Great Antarctic Explorer* (London: Viking, 2001).

"Movers & Shakers 2004," *Library Journal* supplement to March 15 issue (2004): 1–52.

Nadler, David, and Michael Tushman, "Beyond the Charismatic Leader," in *The Leader's Companion,* edited by J. Thomas Wren (New York: Free Press, 1995), 108–113.

Sapp, Gregg, "James Neal on the Challenge of Leadership: An LA&M Exclusive Interview," *Library Administration and Management* 19 (Spring 2005): 64–67.

Snair, Scott, *West Point Leadership Lessons* (Naperville, IL: Sourcebooks, 2004).

Stogdill, Ralph, "Personal Factors Associated with Leadership: A Survey of the Literature," *Journal of Psychology* 25 (1948): 35–71.

Vroom, V.H., and P.W. Yelton, *Leadership and Decision Making* (Pittsburgh, PA: University of Pittsburgh Press, 1973).

Wills, Gary, *Certain Trumpets* (New York: Simon & Schuster, 1994).

Yukl, Gary, and David Van Fleet, "Theory and Research on Leadership in Organizations," in *Handbook of Industrial and Organizational Psychology,* edited by Marvin D. Dunnette and Leaetta M. Hough (Palo Alto, CA: Consulting Psychologist Press, 1992), 147–197.

Zaccaro, Stephen J., Roseanne J. Foti, and David A. Kenny, "Self-Monitoring and Trait-Based Variance in Leadership: An Investigation of Leader Flexibility Across Multiple Group Situations," *Journal of Applied Psychology* 76, no. 2 (1991): 308–315.

CHAPTER 3

Developing Your Leadership Abilities

This chapter focuses on the following:

- How various generational groups view the workplace and respond to leadership
- What to consider when answering the question "Do you want to be a leader?"
- How to assess your leadership potential
- How to develop or maintain leadership skills and abilities

In the last chapter, we explored the major concepts and theories related to leadership as put forward by leading researchers and scholars. We also addressed what we view as the needs of leaders in the 21st century—collaborative style and empowering behavior. In thinking about the research, what the many contemporary writers on the topic have to say, and the changing environment we face in the 21st century, one might well think, "I cannot be a leader; I don't have all the skills and abilities required." In this chapter, we hope to demonstrate that such thinking is off the mark. In fact, *everyone* has leadership potential, and by undertaking a thoughtful self-assessment, combined with a willingness to learn and study, a person can "grow" into an effective leader.

It is the exceptional person who is born with all the requisite skills for being a great leader. Most of us need to develop such abilities and knowledge over time. Looking at the professional literature, one gets the impression there is a leadership crisis, at least in terms of potential leaders. However, if everyone has the potential, and we believe that is true, then John Berry's editorial seems most accurate when it states that "the best of us achieve leadership or have it thrust upon us" (Berry, 2002, p. 8).

As we have suggested, leadership roles exist at various levels in an organization. Having the role "thrust upon us" can happen at any point in one's career, from soon after accepting a first job to many years later when beginning to think about retirement. Developing leadership skills is something everyone should consider, even those who do not aspire to become leaders. In today's world, with its growing emphasis on teamwork, the likelihood of becoming a team leader is rather high. We explore the issues of team leadership in general and at the senior level in chapter 4.

One of the issues that everyone agrees on is that effective leaders keep their organizations viable by recognizing the need to have a sense of the future and a plan for how to change the organization as the environment changes (i.e., a strong, accurate vision). For many people, both in the general public and recent professional school graduates, today's information services are too unchanging and bureaucratic in character to survive long in the 21st century. (However, some recent graduates believe that with the proper changes, today's information services will not only survive but also thrive.) Such views would suggest there is a leadership problem in the field. Perhaps there is, or perhaps the field is just not making the most effective use of the leadership potential that already exists in most information services.

Staff Composition and Leadership

Today's information services very likely have a paid and volunteer staff made up of several generations—veterans, baby boomers, generation X, and generation Y. The "generations" have rather different general approaches to the work situation, and often such differences create some tension. (It seems clear that every new generation has some issues with the generation "in control" of the workplace. How those differences are handled is what leads to success or failure.) Let's briefly explore the generational differences and see what if any implications there are for leadership. Keep in mind that these differences are no more than generalizations, and many exceptions exist.

Check This Out

One very good resource is Michael Coomes's *Serving the Millennial Generation* (San Francisco: Jossey-Bass, 2004).

Veterans, or those born before 1946, are becoming fewer and fewer in number in the paid workplace. Those who have not yet retired are likely to be in senior positions, but there are some rank-and-file staff members that fit this category.

Generally, these individuals are disciplined in their approach to work, with a strong respect for orderly processes and a stable organization. Most are inclined toward maintaining stability and are probably less likely to see the environment as posing serious threats to the organization. Those veterans who are still in the workforce, or those who recently decided to retire, are probably the exceptions rather than the rule for their generation. Going against "type," they see the need for change and take steps to implement changes that do in fact keep information centers viable. However, the younger generations still view the veterans as past oriented and overly concerned with history or status quo. For the younger generation, veterans, while perhaps willing to consider change, are too inclined to want to move slowly. There are few implications for leadership from this group because they will soon be completely out of the workforce. When they depart, so will a significant part of the organization's corporate memory. Such memories were and are important for effective operations, a fact frequently undervalued by the younger generations.

Baby boomers, born between 1946 and 1964, are the largest of the generations and represent many of the senior managers today. In their youth, they were considered "rebellious," experimenting with many things as well as questioning operations and authority. However, by middle age they had become rather conservative in their approach to work. They are optimistic, ambitious, and highly loyal, and view job status and symbols as important. They are more likely to focus on workplace process and output rather than on implications and outcomes. They do monitor the environment and see change as a necessary part of organizational life; however, again the younger generations do not see changes implemented by this group as taking place fast enough. In terms of leadership, there is a tendency to talk about inclusive and collaborative leadership, but often there is more talk than action, at least in the eyes of the junior staff members. This group is sometimes referred to as the "sandwich generation" because they are often called on to support elderly relatives as well as care for younger family members. Such situations, although outside the workplace, sometimes carry over and impact work performance.

Generation Xers ("latchkey children") were born between 1965 and 1979. Very often, they grew up in a home where both parents worked and thus were on their own sooner than the earlier generations. They tend to be very self-confident, individualistic, self-reliant, and often irreverent, especially about the older generations. In terms of work, they tend to focus on relationships and outcomes rather than on processes and organizational structure. As a result, they need a leadership style that is inclusive, collaborative, and empowering. They can be very loyal to and work hard for a vision to which they are committed. They embrace change and are reasonably comfortable with uncertainty. As they move into higher and higher leadership roles, they will face many challenges and must be able to address the issues of upcoming generations.

What are some of the motivators for generation X? For most, it is enough to tell them what needs to be accomplished—don't tell them how to do it. When there are multiple tasks at hand, gen-Xers prefer to set the priorities. They expect to be asked for feedback and to be listened to when giving feedback. They relate to coaching and mentoring more than to training. They expect leaders to live up to talk about values.

An informative profile of a gen-X librarian appears in an OCLC environmental scan (2003). The young lady is an energetic, altruistic, self-motivated person with a strong drive for collaborative activities. The profile concludes with the following, "Gen-X and Millennial librarians may be more comfortable with change and technological gadgets than their Traditional and Boomer compatriots but at the bottom, they seem to be very much like we were at their age."

Check This Out

Pixey Anne Mosley published a good article on mentoring gen-Xers in a 2005 issue of *Library Administration and Management*, titled "Mentoring Gen-X Managers: Tomorrow's Library Leadership Is Already Here," (19, no. 4: 185–192).

Generation Y (the "millennium generation," born after 1980) is just coming into the workforce; however, they are doing so in relatively small numbers; as with generation X, the birth rate was substantially lower for generation Y than for the baby boomers. Generation Y is considered *the* technology generation; these individuals grew up with the World Wide Web and all the other information technology we take for granted today. They are more than adept at multitasking—talking on their cell phones while doing something else or listening to music off the Internet while working on the computer is second nature to them. They are a *now* generation, and they are not used to waiting long for anything (even responses from supervisors). Patience is not seen as a virtue. (A colleague of one of the authors of this book frequently finds herself purposefully refraining from immediately responding to e-mail queries and "demands" from a gen-Y employee she supervises, in an effort to demonstrate that not every request for information can be responded to at the drop of a hat. She's not sure how effective this is and continues to struggle for ways to explain that what may appear to be "crucial" to a gen-Y may not be all that important in the greater scheme of things.) Change, and rapid change at that, is a part of their lifestyle; if nothing else it is part of their technology-based approach to life. They are highly tolerant of diversity—just visit an educational campus and look at the variations in hair color or body piercings. They have a great tolerance for variation, and they expect to receive the same type of tolerance toward themselves.

What motivates generation Y? First and foremost, these people want to know how they fit into the "big picture" and how they can make a difference. Coaching is a preferred method for gaining new skills, and continuous learning is something they are very comfortable with. Respecting their creativity and diversity is very important. They respond better to informal and electronic communication than they do to formal written material. Above all, they expect state-of-the-art technology to be available in the workplace and that staff will make effective use of the technology's capabilities.

Two recent articles describe some of the generational differences just outlined. Newhouse and Spisak (2004), two newly graduated librarians, reported on a survey they conducted of 124 recent graduates (recent was defined as being on the job one year or less). In their opening paragraph, they state, "In our first year, after coming up against bureaucratic brick walls and resistance to new ideas for libraries, we were almost convinced the field of librarianship was virtually unchangeable" (p. 44). Their survey results suggest that while that view might be too strong, there is strong agreement that change needs to be quicker in coming. More than 40 percent of survey respondents disagreed with the statement that for new librarians, libraries are open and affirming. The authors state that new librarians "are unhappy with how libraries are run and operated; . . . they did not anticipate rigid upper administration" (p. 45). Most distressing was the news that many of the respondents were not sure they would stay in the field. Another fact they noted, but did not support with statistics, is that many of the new librarians did not seem to have any interest in becoming a director or even involved in management.

Newhouse and Spisak conclude their article with four suggestions for senior staff to consider in order to create a more affirming work environment. The first is to support the education of the staff. Second, because library schools can only do so much in terms of preparing librarians for the "real world," some in-house training and mentoring is essential. Third, libraries should offer praise, feedback, and encouragement, thereby building employee self-confidence. Finally, senior staff should be open to ideas from the junior staff members. One author's concluding comment, addressed to senior management, is to "embrace change" (p. 26).

At almost the same time as the Newhouse and Spisak article appeared, Rachel Gordon (2004) published an article that contained many echoes of the former's survey results. Gordon wrote about the "nextgen" librarians (those twenty to thirty years old with several years of experience). Many of the concerns were similar; however, all the respondents had in fact become part of management. The primary point of the article is that young managers and leaders found it difficult to get older staff members to see the need for change, at least when the need was articulated by the younger person. Again the sense for younger staff was that the library was not an affirming work environment.

Check This Out

Richard Sweeney's 2005 article "Reinventing Library Buildings and Services for the Millennial Generation" (*Library Administration and Management* 19, no. 4: 165–175) provides useful insights for thinking about generational differences for the newest group to join the workforce.

We believe there has always been some tension between recent graduates and more senior staff. However, it would seem that changes taking place today in the environment and in generational differences make it crucial that there be more collaborative leadership that actually does empower individuals.

Effective collaborative and empowering leadership will help, especially when one accepts the notion that everyone can be a leader. However, that idea means it is necessary for most of us to learn how to lead. Kouzes and Posner (2002, p. 386) make the following point: "It's not the absence of leadership potential that inhibits the development of leaders; it's the persistence of the myth that leadership can't be learned." The balance of this chapter will help you decide if you want to become a leader as well as outline steps to take if you do decide this is something you want to do.

Do You Want to Become a Leader?

Before going off to a leadership training program, if you are not already functioning as a leader, it is worthwhile to give some serious consideration to the question "Do you want to become a leader?" Moving up in an organization to a managerial or leadership role normally brings with it an increase in salary. (The differences between being a manager and a leader are discussed in chapter 1). Such an increase may or may not be highly attractive when one is at an entry level. Accepting such a position does, however, bring with it responsibilities and obligations that otherwise may be overlooked.

As we saw in chapter 2, there is no single comprehensive list of what it takes to be a leader, at least not one that everyone agrees is complete. However, there are some factors that do arise very often and therefore deserve some thought.

Visioning appears on almost every list as something an effective leader must do. Think about how comfortable you are with not just thinking about the future but also developing a plan to meet an uncertain, changing environment. Although you may be comfortable engaging in such an activity for yourself, as a leader you must do this for many people, both inside and outside the organization. That means the stakes are substantially greater whether the plan succeeds or fails. This is a fact of leadership that you should ponder with care and honesty. Do you want to handle that type of responsibility and pressure?

We have made the point that *empowerment* is a requisite behavior for the 21st-century leader. Further, empowerment, like delegation, requires giving up some power and control. Again, assuming one engages in meaningful empowerment, there will be a number of people involved, especially in a team setting. Questions to ask yourself include "How trusting of other people am I?" and "How strong is my self-confidence?"

Being a manager, and even more so for a leader, calls for a *high energy level* and a willingness to work longer than the organization's official work week. A serious issue for managers and leaders is *maintaining a balance* between work and personal time. Factors such as family obligations require careful thought. Too often individuals in such positions have difficulty taking personal time off. Cell phones, e-mail and text messages, and fax machines make it relatively easy for the workplace to "stay in touch, just in case," even during vacations or other time off. (The need to stay in touch may be a sign that the person has not been willing or perhaps able to delegate to other staff members the responsibility of temporarily handling issues. Another possibility is the person does not want to develop such capability.) Not having a balance between work and personal life is a guaranteed way to develop burnout. The bottom line is, you need to accept that becoming a leader will take some time away from your personal time. So, a question to consider is "Can I be an effective leader and also have a meaningful personal life?"

This question becomes even more complex and important when it comes to dual-career situations. Add into that the prospect of having a family, with all that entails, and the question becomes very difficult to honestly address. As Bill George (2003, p. 45) writes, "To find that delicate balance, it is essential to set clear boundaries between work and home life."

Check It Out

The American Library Association's web page for Librarians' Associations of Color provides links to a number of ALA-sponsored organizations that support ethnic librarians: www.ala.org/ala/olos/libassocofcolor/librariansassociations.htm (accessed May 1, 2006).

Camila Alire (2001) raises some other issues for people of color to consider when considering a leadership role where they are not the majority. One of the added burdens for a leader of color is to dispel (and also overcome) stereotyping and a higher burden of self. Today such leaders have what she terms "a two-pronged leadership agenda—leading in a predominately white society and the need to lead (model) other people of color" (p. 98). Her essay is worth reading by anyone, not just people of color, thinking about the question "Do I want to lead?"

If, after pondering the questions posed so far in this chapter, the answer is "Yes, I want to be a leader," it is time to engage in some serious self-assessment. To some degree, just making the decision, yes or no, is the start of your personal assessment.

Assessing Yourself

Bennis (2003, pp. 115–119) identifies four areas you should examine when making a self-assessment:

- The first test is to know what you want, knowing your abilities and capacities and recognizing the difference between the two.
- The second test is to know what drives you, knowing what gives you satisfaction and knowing the difference between the two.
- The third test is to know what your values and priorities are, know what the values and priorities of your organization are, and to measure the difference between the two.
- The fourth test is—having measured the difference between what you want and what you are able to do, and the difference between what drives you and what satisfies you, and between what your values are and what the organization's are—are you able and willing to overcome those differences?

These tests appear to be straightforward, and they are, but they require careful and honest self-reflection. Thinking about what you want from a career is relatively easy compared with having an accurate self-understanding of your abilities. (It is interesting to note that in our survey, our respondents listed more strengths than weaknesses. This is a typical result because most of us have difficulty seeing our weaknesses. Nevertheless, when doing a self-assessment, gaining a clear picture of weaknesses is important. Successful leaders understand their weaknesses and spend time trying to overcome them.) One way to cross-check your self-assessment is to ask some friends or colleagues to give you feedback—read more about such feedback later in this chapter.

Bennis's third test, comparing your values and priorities with those of the organization, is in some ways easier and also more complex than the first two tests. It is easier in the sense that the organizational priorities should be readily accessible from the organization's mission, vision, goal, and objective statements, as well as other documents. Organizational values may be more difficult to determine because not many organizations commit their values to a document—although priority statements will provide useful clues. Keep in mind that there can be significant differences between stated and actual priorities and values (see chapter 5 for a discussion of organizational culture). Essentially, Bennis's fourth test is the source of information that can ultimately help you decide if you want to be leader. Again, honest reflection as to your abilities compared with what may need to be overcome is essential. Careful thought is called for to accurately answer the question "Am I willing to try to overcome the shortfalls?" Bennis's tests are useful for both existing and potential leaders; existing leaders ought to undertake the assessment every few years.

EMOTIONAL INTELLIGENCE

There is another issue you should think about long and hard—your "emotional style." We have all had one or more work experiences where a colleague's emotional style or behavior has had a significant impact on everyone. "Look out for X today, he is having a bad day," or at least a variation on that theme, is heard all too often in the workplace. It is unfortunate that people having a "good day" don't have as much impact on work behavior, or do they and we just don't remark about that fact? There is a tendency to think of emotional behavior as having a negative impact; however, a person with emotional maturity and an understanding of others' emotions can have a very positive influence. Leaders need to have or develop such maturity. Setting a positive tone encourages such things as self-confidence, initiative, collaboration, and teamwork. For information work, particularly given its service orientation, the need for emotional control as well as an understanding of others' emotional states is paramount for everyone on the staff, not just the leader.

As noted in chapter 2, research on emotions as a factor in intellectual functioning goes back a very long time. However, it has only been since the early 1990s that there has been significant research on the concept as a workplace factor. As is often the case with new areas of interest, the terminology is varied— *emotional intelligence, emotional literacy, emotional quotient,* and *personal intelligence* are some of the most common labels for the concept. Lack of a single accepted term also means there is a lack of clarity and acceptance of a definition of the concept(s). We prefer emotional intelligence (EI) as the label because it appears most frequently in the popular literature.

EI, if one follows and believes the popular literature, is the "magic bullet" for modern management. That is clearly too strong a claim, but there is no question that EI is an important element in a successful service organization. The concept draws on psychological and management research. There is evidence that EI affects such workplace behaviors and activities as commitment, teamwork, innovation, developmental activities, and quality of service, as well as customer loyalty.

Perhaps the most widely used definition of EI appeared in 1990 (Mayer and Salovey, p. 189). EI is "the ability to monitor one's own and others' emotions, to discriminate among them, and to use the information to guide one's thinking and actions." This fairly broad definition encompasses most of the elements various authors and researchers include in their work, regardless of the label they use for the concept. It is also one of the first efforts at defining the concept.

There are two primary models of what constitutes EI—mental ability and mixed (Zeidner, Matthews, and Roberts, 2004). The mental ability approach is led by John Mayer, while Daniel Goleman has led the popularized mixed approach. Mayer and Salovey divide EI into four broad areas—accurately perceiving emotions, using emotions to assist in thinking, understanding emotional meanings, and managing emotions. Meanwhile, Goleman and his followers employ a five-category approach—identifying one's emotional states and the links between emotion, thought, and action; managing one's emotions; entering emotional states related to the drive to achieve and succeed; reading, being sensitive to, and influencing others' emotions; and entering into and sustaining satisfactory interpersonal relationships. Both approaches clearly relate to the definition just given—knowing one's and others' emotions, understanding those emotions, and employing that information in a positive manner.

Check These Out

Compare and contrast the two models of EI by visiting John Mayer's website, www.unh.edu/emotional_intelligence (accessed May 1, 2006), and Daniel Goleman's website, www.eiconsortium.org (accessed May 1, 2006). Another site worth visiting is David Caruso's EI Skills Group at www.eiskills.com/index.php (accessed May 1, 2006).

You can see the potential value of understanding workplace emotions, especially your own, along with the ability to use those feelings in a positive manner. Being able to effectively (positively) influence others based on an understanding of their emotions is a major plus. Either model provides guidance for developing such abilities. Understanding your emotions, much less those of others, is a complex process. Emotionally intelligent leaders usually have a greater sense of well-being, stronger relationships, employees with higher morale, and overall greater success. You cannot become an expert on emotional competencies by attending one- or two-day workshops or from reading a book, although both will help develop the abilities. A highly effective method is to create a strong support system through a mentor, coach, or peer group that works together on the process and provides honest feedback. A host of websites can help you assess your EI (a recent Google search for "emotional intelligence tests" generated more than 1.2 million hits).

Check These Out

A popular book on EI is Daniel Goleman's *Working with Emotional Intelligence* (New York: Bantam, 1998). Goleman's chapters on "Collaboration, Teams, and the Group IQ" and "Taking the Organizational Pulse" are of particular note, as is the appendix covering "Further Issues in Training." Another popular resource is David Caruso and Peter Salovey's *The Emotionally Intelligent Manager* (San Francisco: Jossey-Bass, 2004). Their work is based on exploring four key emotional skills of EI:

- Identifying emotion
- Using emotion
- Understanding emotion
- Managing emotion

One EI test can be found at www.queendom.com/cgi-bin/tests (accessed May 1, 2006). Another site worth reviewing is at http://psychology.about.com/library/bl/bleq_onlinetests.htm (accessed May 1, 2006).

Prospective leaders will also benefit from a careful reading of Rooke and Torbert's (2005) essay on leadership. One of their main points is that it is "action logic" that differentiates one leader from another. Action logic describes how leaders "interpret their surroundings and react when their power or safety is challenged" (p. 67). Their second major point is that leaders can improve their skills when they make an effort to understand their action logic; the organization also gains from this process.

Rooke and Torbert identify seven action logics based on their research—opportunist, diplomat, expert, achiever, individualist, strategist, and alchemist. Essentially, the seven categories are a scale of leadership from least to most effective. The following characteristics are drawn from a chart in their article (p. 69). *Opportunists* win in any way possible; they are power oriented, self-oriented, and manipulative. *Diplomats* avoid conflict as much as possible; they are group oriented, with a high need to belong, and keeping things "smooth" is a major operational goal. An *expert's* primary actions are guided by logic and expertise, and there is a strong focus on rationality and careful planning. *Achievers* place their focus on meeting goals, especially strategic ones, while also emphasizing teamwork and being very action oriented. *Individualists* are fully aware of the potential conflicts between their values and those of the organization—a reminder of Bennis's test discussed earlier. They view this conflict as both a source of tension and creativity, while others in the organization frequently view the individualist as a "wild card," or unpredictable. *Strategists* are transformational at both the individual and organizational level; they are adept at creating visions people relate to. *Alchemists* are sources of social transformations; they excel at integrating material, spiritual, and social factors into useful transformations.

According to Rooke and Torbert, only 5 percent of the people in their studies fell into the opportunist category, and only 1 percent were what they label as an alchemist. Thus, more than 90 percent fell into the midrange categories, which are the ones most commonly found in libraries and information centers, in our opinion. We believe the goal of information professionals should be to strive for the strategist level. Rooke and Torbert provide some suggestions for a how a leader can move from one level to another, and their work is worth reviewing.

TOOLS FOR SELF-ASSESSMENT

Potential leaders, as well as existing ones, can benefit from a variety of self-assessment steps and tools. A primary step is to devote some time to thinking about and understanding where you are as a person. An individual who acts as himself rather than acts the role of leader is much more likely to be successful in gaining the support and commitment of others. Knowing the difference between "who you are and who you want to be from what the world thinks you are and wants you to be" (Bennis, 2003, p. 48) is an important if highly complex process. Being yourself is not always as easy as it would seem.

Beyond thinking about yourself, there are some tools that assist in assessing various aspects of leadership. There are also instruments that can help you gain a sense of who you are. Some forms are available in books on leadership. Many are freely available online, while others have fees associated with them. Often those with fees are from organizations that provide leadership training and coaching.

A reasonable question to ask is how valid, useful, and reliable such instruments are. The answer is that it varies. Every psychometric measurement has some limitations. The more abstract the area being measured, the greater the limitations for the instrument. Leadership, with its hundreds of definitions, is obviously an abstract concept. The greater the number of people who use a particular instrument, assuming there is someone monitoring and modifying it, the greater the likelihood of reliability. If the results are cross-checked with actual leadership performance in the real world, the greater the likelihood that some validity exists. Certainly no single instrument is going to provide the definitive data about potential and actual leadership abilities. We strongly recommend using a number of tools, particularly ones that assess a variety of aspects related to leadership.

It may be too obvious to comment on, but the most significant factor in how useful the tools will be is *you*. You must respond to the questions in an honest manner. Many of the instrument questions are worded in such a way as to make it clear what the "leader's" response is likely to be. For these tools to have value, the test taker must truly want to understand her limitations as well as her potential, and thus only honest answers are useful.

There is one way to cross-check your self-assessment and help avoid the danger of wanting to look "good." Many of the instruments can be used by people who know you and are in a position to assess your leadership abilities. Such assessments can be a form of performance appraisal—similar to a 360-degree appraisal. Although data from an instrument designed or employed as a performance appraisal form can provide information for self-assessment, you need to be cautious because the data was collected for a different purpose. There are 360-degree instruments designed just for self-assessment purposes.

The bottom line is to use multiple instruments, be totally honest and realistic, and if possible, use cross-checks from colleagues or a mentor. The results are meaningful only to the degree the process is undertaken with the goal of gaining self-understanding. What follows is but a sampling of what can be found on the Internet by searching "leadership assessment." (Such a Google search produced more than 19 million hits in early 2006!)

One starting point for online leadership assessment sites is the Leadership Learning Community's website at www.leadershiplearning.org. (accessed May 1, 2006). Among other things, this site supplies links to other sites that have assessment instruments.

The Learning Center offers a thirty-point "Leadership Assessment: Personal Satisfaction Survey" (www.learningcenter.net/library/leadership.shtml, accessed May 1, 2006). Some of the areas covered include "making and communicating decisions promptly," "involving others in planning actions," and "believing in and providing training that teaches leadership, teamwork, and technical skills." The test taker responds on a five-point scale from very satisfied to very dissatisfied, with a "neutral" midpoint.

A site we like because it offers multiple tools is from Robert Gordon University (Aberdeen, Scotland). The site provides links to eleven assessment instruments, covering a variety of leadership issues (www.rgu.ac.uk/hr/leadership/ page.cfm?pge = 9421, accessed May 1, 2006). The first instrument covers the values ("Envision, Enable, Empower, and Energize") of a leader, along with some suggestions for how to improve in this area. Another test—the "Assessment of Leadership Qualities and Skills"—should prompt an introspective look at your leadership qualities and skills. (This is a form you might want to have some friends or colleagues fill out in terms of your qualities and abilities.) An interesting link looks at the current environment ("Are You Ready to Manage in the 21st Century"). The last of the eleven items is the familiar Myers-Briggs self-assessment form.

As we stated, there are thousands of sites you can explore as part of your self-examination. Many of the sites are from organizations that also provide in-person and online assessment and training services. One such site is the University of Maryland University College's National Leadership Institute (www .umuc.edu/prog/nli/nli.html, accessed May 1, 2006). The institute offers a six-week program, half of which is devoted to testing and assessment, followed by two weeks of online classes and one week of personalized coaching. (The cost, as of early 2006, for the online program was $2,200, while the fee for the in-person resident program was $7,200.)

In the United States, the federal government has created a leadership development program called the Leadership Assessment Program. It is a five-day program designed for persons who recently moved into leadership positions (www.leadership.opm.gov/content.cfm?cat = LAP, accessed May 1, 2006). Like many similar development programs, this one contains both self- and 360-degree assessments while also making use of case studies, with trained observers providing feedback. (The cost of this program was $4,800 in early 2006.)

One organization that has been in the business of leadership assessment and training for some time is the Center for Creative Leadership (CCL) (www.ccl .org, accessed May 1, 2006). CCL provides a wide range of assessments and training, both online and at locations in many parts of the world—the United States, Belgium, and Singapore, plus "associates" in Australia, Canada, Japan, and Mexico. An example of its broad coverage is its 360-degree assessment, where there are tracks for senior-level leaders and managers, midlevel leaders and managers, and "prospectors" (high-potential individuals).

Developing Yourself

Having secured information from the self-assessment activity, whether done via paper and pencil or online, you can make decisions about what areas to concentrate on in your development program—assuming you still wish to be a leader.

(Although even if you find you have no desire to become a leader, it is still worthwhile to work on those areas identified for improvement, since some individuals find leadership "thrust upon them.") Bennis (2003) provides some sage advice about how to start a self-development process. He suggests there are four key areas to think about—self-motivation, taking responsibility, having self-confidence in the ability to learn, and thinking about your experiences. He, like almost every other writer on the topic of leadership, believes a key factor in long-term success is a commitment to lifelong learning.

Without self-motivation, learning is not likely to take place. As noted in chapter 1, experience is one of your best teachers, assuming you thoughtfully reflect on those experiences. In essence, or as Bennis suggests, you are your best teacher. You must assume responsibility for your learning. This is important because many if not most information services have limited funding for staff development and training activities. Using such limitations as a reason for not learning means you are not taking responsibility for your own growth and development. Kouzes and Posner (2002, p. 381) suggest, "Self-confidence is really self-awareness of and faith in your own powers. These powers become clear and strong only as you work to identify and develop them."

Everyone accumulates experience and information about the workplace on a daily basis—what happens, how it happens, who makes it happen, why it happens, and so on. The longer we work for an organization, the larger our "database" of information becomes. Most of us draw on that information without thinking about it. A trait that most successful leaders make use of is *reflection*. Reflecting on the contents of their experience "database" often distinguishes leaders from nonleaders. They take time to ponder the successes and failures, the whys and wherefores of those occurrences, with the purpose of gaining useful insights and lessons.

After you have identified individual needs, it is time to address them by developing an individual development plan that focuses on those areas through learning opportunities. The modes of learning can be divided into three broad categories—self-, one-on-one, and group learning. We strongly believe lifelong learning is a hallmark of the successful leader. Further, as mentioned in chapter 1, we believe learning is not a one-shot process.

SELF-LEARNING

Three of the most common self-learning modes are observation, experience, and reading. We begin learning through observation almost as soon as we are born and continue to do so throughout life—if we make an effort to learn from the observations. After entering the workplace, the combination of experience and observation can be a powerful learning tool for a leader. Individuals who put time into thinking about the meanings and implications of their observations tend to be the most successful. Almost every one of our survey respondents made reference to experience as a part of their leadership development.

Reading, and doing so widely, is something that effective leaders must make time for. Throughout this book we make reference to how essential it is to monitor the environment, both internal and external. Engaging in a wide-ranging reading program geared to monitoring activities pays dividends. Dipping into leadership as well as professional literature is an excellent method for maintaining development activities.

Check This Out

Bennis, Warren, and Joan Goldsmith, *Learning to Lead: A Workbook on Becoming a Leader* (New York: Basic, 2003).

ONE-ON-ONE LEARNING

One-on-one learning can take several forms; we will cover three of the most common—coaching, mentoring, and modeling. (Note that in addition to being learning modes, they are also behaviors of successful leaders. Because of that, we devote more attention to these topics.)

Coaching, mentoring, and modeling are interrelated to some degree. A coach is often modeling while engaged in coaching and thus has an influence beyond the one-on-one coaching activity. A mentor can be, and often is, both a model and a coach. As Hudson (1999) says, coaching is not about advising, nor is it about fixing things or problem solving. Rather it is about establishing a trust relationship with the goal of improving or developing a skill or ability. Likewise, mentoring is also about trust and respect. Modeling is directed not at a particular individual but rather at demonstrating a behavior or value that others can copy. Nevertheless, only a person who is trusted or respected is likely to have his actions or values modeled by others.

Coaching plays an ongoing role in the management of any information service as a normal part of the control process or performance appraisal program. However, the type of coaching of interest here is not the "corrective" type but rather is developmental in character. As such, the coach for a leader may not necessarily be a member of the organization. Many of the firms that offer leadership development programs make available one-on-one coaching services. (Coaching at the senior level in both the for- and not-for-profit sector has become a small growth industry.)

Coaching for "success" is what the leader's goal should be. Most people have a desire to succeed, and activities directed toward improving success (e.g., faster, easier) are welcomed, especially when the source is trusted and respected. Striving for ever-greater success means coaching is not a one-time event. The process should be a "philosophy" rather than a job for the leader. Underlying values of such a philosophy follow:

- Respect for the existing knowledge, skills, and abilities of all members of the work group
- Belief that individuals should be free from controls that limit the initiative and innovative behaviors of group members
- Recognition that coaching is a partnership in which both partners have responsibilities
- Knowledge that the process is more about motivation and relationships than it is about power and control
- Recognition that listening more and talking less can be a powerful element in successful coaching
- Knowledge that feedback, especially positive comments, is a key to successful coaching

Because coaching as well as mentoring is one on one, it should be clear that the "one size fits all" approach is not very effective. Tailoring the approach to the individual is what works best, but it calls for the coach to have a high degree of "people sensitivity." Working on developing or improving "people sense" is a worthwhile activity. When the work group includes a range of generations, a different approach is more appropriate. (An example is when to use e-mail as part of the coaching activity. "Nextgens" would probably find an e-mail not only reasonable but probably preferable, while veterans are likely to find it too impersonal.) A tailored approach also requires the coach to keep in mind that the coaching process in itself will not change the coachee. What coaching can and should do is motivate the coachee to want to change (a personal "transformation").

Timing is of course an issue in coaching, mentoring, and modeling. At the right time and place and under the proper circumstances, the process has a high probability of being successful. When one or more of the elements are wrong, the odds for success drop quickly. What this means is that coaching and mentoring cannot always be planned ahead. Coaches and mentors need to develop a sense of when a person is motivated or receptive to coaching or mentoring. It also means being ready to stop doing whatever you are doing and start the coaching or mentoring process at the drop of a hat. Needless to say, planned coaching is desirable but not always possible.

We believe a useful coaching process involves several elements. Just as leadership development begins with self-assessment, so does coaching in the sense of assessing what issues should be addressed. What are the priorities if there are multiple issues? After establishing the issues and priorities, you can then identify some short- and long-term goals for the coaching sessions. In setting goals, it is crucial to consider the interpersonal relationship with the coachee and take whatever steps may be necessary to achieve the best possible relationship. Taking the time to think through what activities will most likely motivate the coachee to want to change or develop before starting will pay dividends in faster, more useful coaching. Providing support and meaningful feedback during the process increases the chances for success. As is true of most activities, a postactivity assessment of what was and was not effective can be a learning activity for the coach.

Check These Out

A number of coaching resources exist, including online resources such as the website of the International Coach Federation (www .coachfederation.org/eweb, accessed May 1, 2006) and Coach U (www.coachinc.com, accessed May 1, 2006) and print resources such as Nicholas Nigro's *Everything Coaching and Mentoring Book* (Avon, MA: Adams Media, 2003) and Ruth Metz's *Coaching in the Library* (Chicago: American Library Association, 2001).

Although there are similarities between coaching and mentoring, there are also important differences. *Mentoring* is based on a different one-on-one relationship. A mentor—someone with more experience, knowledge, or skill than the mentee—is committed to giving support and advice. Very often the mentor is older and in a more senior position, although that is not always the case. Part of the mentor's role is to be a helper and confidant. Frequently part of the mentor's helping activity involves career development and advancement.

Leaders, at least those viewed as being very successful, engage in mentoring. (Note: this is not always seen as a leadership requirement. Mentoring can be very time consuming, plus there may not be anyone the mentor believes will benefit from the process.) Mentoring is not the same as networking. Networking is an on and off activity for a longer or shorter time, usually involving a number of people. Mentoring is one on one, long term, and generally regular in character. The most successful mentoring appears to be of the informal type (i.e., it develops between two people without any organizational involvement), although professional organizations and libraries do create formal mentoring programs. Here mentors and mentees (often recent graduates) are paired by the organization based on a limited amount of information about the individuals. The success of such programs is variable because the matching process does not always have enough information to create pairs that will "mesh." One of our survey respondents offered the following comment on formal mentoring program experiences: "I have experienced quite a mix, from absolutely zero response to several overtures initiated by me to my mentor, to very satisfactory. However, none of the formal mentor components turned into networking relationship nor outlived the formal required time frame."

Our respondents had a good deal to say about mentoring, most of it very positive: "They had a very strong influence. They were instrumental in advising, job choices, educational degrees, and professional service strategies." "I don't think my mentors ever thought of themselves as mentors, but I was greatly influenced by them." "Mentors have been very important in each of the positions I have held." "Some of the best mentors I have had are true intellectuals who read widely and worry about the intellectual depth of the collection." "Mentors have had an overwhelming positive influence on my career." "I had only one really great mentor, though I also have had great colleagues and friends who I felt I could seek advice from occasionally. My mentor later became a very good friend in life, and to this day we still bounce around ideas on emerging trends."

Several of the respondents commented on the need for a leader to be a role model and mentor: "The best managers go with the strengths of subordinates and build their confidence." "I think leading by example, whether formalized or not, is quite powerful." "Mostly I observed their management styles and learned a lot."

Check These Out

For more information on mentoring programs, visit the Marriott Library Librarian Mentoring Program at the University of Utah (www.lib.utah.edu/mentor/mission.html, accessed May 1, 2006), Cornell University Library Mentorship Program (www.library .cornell.edu/pdc/Mentor.html, accessed May 1, 2006), the Society of American Archivists Mentoring Program (www.archivists .org/membership/mentoring.asp, accessed May 1, 2006), and the Medical Library Association Mentoring Program (www.mlanet .org/mentor, accessed May 1, 2006).

Mentors assist mentees in a number of ways. If both work in the same organization, as is often the case, the mentor may be able to provide the mentee with a challenging or developmental project to work on, or the mentor can often provide insight into organizational policies and procedures. Related to challenging assignments is the mentor's role in encouraging and providing assistance in problem solving. An obvious role is providing career advice. In addition to career advice, the mentor can, and frequently does "nominate" the mentee for a desirable leadership position. Encouraging lifelong learning and taking advantage of educational opportunities is something most mentors do for their mentees.

Modeling is something every manager and leader engages in every day, often forgetting that they are doing so. The model may be good or bad, but a model it will be—and staff do observe the behavior. Saying something but acting in a contrary manner is quickly spotted by the staff, and the person's influence frequently drops as a result. Two of our survey respondents made the following points when commenting about mentors: "I mostly learned from bad examples," and "Every other role model was an example of how not to do it." Most of us, at least those with some years of experience, can think of one or more instances where we learned from observing what one should *not* do in the workplace as a manager or leader. Managers and leaders should remember that they are always modeling something, for better or for worse.

What are some behaviors a leader should model on an ongoing basis? Exhibiting confidence in the team's ability to perform at a high level is one such behavior. Demonstrating and reinforcing organizational culture and values is another, because it assists in building organizational commitment. For the information professional, there is probably no more important behavior than emphasizing the critical importance of what excellent user service means. Leading in ways that illustrate good work habits, especially by getting your "hands dirty," will build team motivation. Showing respect for organizational policies and rules, even when you don't agree with them, will assist in building organizational loyalty. Other key modeling behaviors include handling your disagreements in one-on-one sessions with senior managers. Further, you should not use your team members as "sounding boards" for your disagreements with organizational issues. Showing people what it means to be "professional" is, if nothing else, simply appropriate. (Too often in information services there is an unfortunate tension between professionals and support staff. Generally this is the result of poor modeling of true professionalism.)

GROUP LEARNING

The self-assessment process is indeed individualized, but developing leadership skills need not be a solitary activity. A number of group learning opportunities are available, ranging from commercial programs, such as those mentioned later in this chapter, to one-day workshops offered by professional associations. Engaging in a mix of self- and group learning is probably most effective. Self-study has the advantage of addressing just those areas you decide are important. Group study presents opportunities to interact with others who may provide insights you may miss when working alone.

As noted earlier, a quick Internet search identifies thousands of sites from commercial sources of formalized leadership development. However, we will discuss only those programs offered by library and information science organizations. A 2004 *Library Trends* article by Mason and Wetherbee identifies thirty programs, held annually or biannually. Most of the programs listed are in the United States; there is one in Australia and one in Canada. Two library schools (the University of California, Los Angeles, and the University of Missouri, Columbia) started offering programs in the early 1980s, an indication the field has recognized the need for formal leadership training for some time. Another long-term program is available through the Association of Research Libraries (ARL) Office of Leadership and Management Services (OLMS). ARL's program is offered for established managers in two parts—focusing on the manager and the organization separately. ARL also offers programming on other aspects of administration, such as project management skills and leading change.

Check These Out

Information on several of the previously mentioned formalized leadership programs can be viewed online, at the ARL Library Management Skills Institute, with information available from the ARL OLMS office (www.arl.org/training/index.html, accessed May 1, 2006), ARL Leadership and Career Development program (www.arl.org/diversity/lcdp, accessed May 1, 2006), UCLA Senior Fellows program (is.gseis.ucla.edu/seniorfellows, accessed May 1, 2006), and University of Minnesota Libraries, Early-Career Librarians of Color (www.lib.umn.edu/about/news/release.phtml?id=39, accessed May 1, 2006). In addition, regional library associations also sponsor leadership development programs, such as the Maryland Library Leadership Institute (www.mdlib.org/leadership, accessed May 1, 2006). Information on other library leadership programs in the United States and Canada may be found at www.cjrlc.org/leadership.htm (accessed May 1, 2006) and in Mason and Wetherbee's article.

Mason and Wetherbee found that most of the programs that were residential in character lasted about five days. For most of the residential programs, participant selection was on a competitive basis, and the individuals selected needed to have library work experience. In most cases, there was "social" time that was viewed as part of the learning experience. Workshop programs, on the other hand, were "open" in that anyone could register, up to the limit of the course size. Most were one-day programs and included no planned social activity. Given the workshops' limited time frame, it is not surprising that they tended to focus on one or two aspects of leadership, unlike the broader coverage of the residential programs. The authors conclude it is "clear that the package of required leadership skills for librarians and other workers is not a one-size-fits-all list. In fact, there continues to be considerable variety in ideas about an appropriate library-related set of leadership skills" (p. 214).

Check This Out

An article describing a leadership development program for public libraries is Donna Nicely and Beth Dempsey's "Building a Culture of Leadership: ULC's Executive Leadership Institute Fills Libraries' Biggest Training Void," Public Libraries 44, no. 5 (2005): 297–300.

Common Areas for Development

As mentioned earlier, some of the obvious areas leaders want to develop or maintain are empowering behaviors, visioning, becoming an effective change agent, and problem-solving behaviors. Our survey respondents listed twenty-seven personal weaknesses; presumably they are working on these areas. The five most frequently listed weaknesses are not being patient enough, saying yes too easily, being overorganized, not allowing for enough personal time, and needing better speaking skills. Some of the less frequently mentioned areas relate to people skills, setting priorities, and self-confidence. All these issues can be effectively worked on; some take more time and effort than others, but all are "doable."

Empowering staff, as noted a number of times, is one of the most important activities for the 21st-century leader. Empowered people tend to be more productive and highly motivated, thus both the leader and staff gain. John Maxwell (1993, p. 113) suggests, "The more people you develop, the greater the extent of your dreams." Before you empower or develop people, you must value and respect them, as well as have a high level of confidence in their abilities (trust). Working on, developing, and maintaining these values is a lifelong process.

Visioning is a skill all leaders must develop, for without a sound vision the organization and work units tend to drift aimlessly. Useful visions are based on an assessment of past performance; a knowledge of the current environment; an assessment (best guess) of what the future will hold; a statement, in broad terms, of what areas to work on; and plans for meeting future challenges. Each of these areas calls for different skills, many of which can be worked on alone; others will benefit from the input of a good mentor.

Almost every vision statement carries with it the prospect of change. Even without the vision implications, an effective leader is a change agent. There is a body of literature and research on the nature and process of change in organizations. The first step for a leader is to explore that literature and gain a sound understanding of the change process and how it affects people. One title mentioned in chapter 2 but worth mentioning again is Susan Curzon's *Managing Change*. The second step is to stay current with developments in the field. Obviously, this is a good area for self-development.

Problem solving is something every manager and leader must do on a regular basis. Again, there is ample research and application literature on this topic, making it a likely candidate for self-study. When available, group analysis of case studies can also be an effective tool for sharpening problem-solving skills.

Leaders tend to be energetic, action-oriented individuals. Such individuals tend to move forward quickly on projects and frequently have the same expectations for team members—perhaps even higher expectations than they can deliver themselves. Having realistic expectations or an accurate understanding of team capabilities will help address the lack of patience leaders may have. Another element in gaining patience is experience—often it is the less experienced leader who identifies patience as an area for improvement. Experience was certainly important for one of the authors of this book. Early in his career, patience would not have been listed as one of his strengths. Time and experience, plus having a fine mentor, helped address this issue. A good coach can also assist in pointing out the virtue of being patient with people.

A saying in the United States is "If you want something done, ask the busiest person you know to do it." There is more than a grain of truth in that statement. Busy people usually have very good time management skills and set effective and realistic priorities. They also have confidence in their ability to get things done. Speaking for ourselves, we know from personal experience that saying yes is, to a degree, giving something back to or advancing the profession. Such a motivation tends to make one say yes more often than not. That in turn leads to overextending oneself. The result is the project or work is finished and generally on time, but at the cost of personal time, which should be very precious to the busy person. Mentors are good at helping you sort out what to say yes to and when the answer should be a regretful no.

Building up and maintaining self-confidence is essential for a leader. When something goes wrong, it is natural to do some soul searching to see if there was something you could have done to avoid the problem. At the same time, a small amount of self-confidence is chipped away. Replacing that chip and building up more self-confidence is important. There are at least two things you can do in this area. Having a good mentoring relationship is probably the greatest help. Since a good relationship is based on trust and respect, the mentor's assessment, even from a distance, will be helpful. You can also consider undertaking an occasional 360-degree assessment; it is essential that this be done outside the organization's normal performance appraisal process in order to receive the most useful data. Feedback from staff indicating you are doing a good job is always satisfying, as well as being a confidence builder.

Summary

We provide some food for thought in this chapter. The key question we have asked you to consider is "Do you want to be a leader?" That question deserves careful pondering, and it is a decision you should not take lightly. There are some questions and suggestions for assessing yourself, which may in turn influence your leadership decision. With the information from the self-assessment, which will identify strong and weak areas, you need to create a plan for building on strengths and working on weaknesses. We presented some information on how to go about implementing such a plan, but we do also wish to remind you that even if you decide that formal leadership may not be for you, it is still worthwhile to address those issues raised in your self-assessment, because you never know when a leadership opportunity may arise inside or outside the organization.

You can learn to be a good leader or become a better one. However, it takes time to learn and refine the requisite skills, and you must commit to making this a lifelong process in order to be successful.

References

Alire, Camila, "Diversity and Leadership: The Color of Leadership," *Journal of Library Administration* 32, no. 3/4 (2001): 95–109.
Bennis, Warren, *On Becoming a Leader*, rev. ed. (New York: Basic, 2003).
Berry, John, "Be Not Afraid of Greatness," *Library Journal* 127 (March 2002): 8.
Curzon, Suzan, *Managing Change*, rev. ed. (New York: Neal-Schuman, 2005).
George, Bill, *Authentic Leadership* (San Francisco: Jossey-Bass, 2003).
Gordon, Rachel S., "Nextgen Move Mountains," *Library Journal* 129 (September 2004): 42.
Hudson, Frederic, *The Handbook of Coaching* (San Francisco: Jossey-Bass, 1999).
Kouzes, James K., and Barry Z. Posner, *Leadership Challenge* (San Francisco: Jossey-Bass, 2002).
Mason, Florence, and Louella Wetherbee, "Learning to Lead: An Analysis of Current

Training Programs for Library Leadership," *Library Trends* 53, no. 1 (2004): 187–217.

Maxwell, John, *Developing the Leader Within You* (Nashville, TN: Nelson, 1993).

Mayer, John D., and Peter Salovey, "Emotional Intelligence," *Imagination, Cognition and Personality* 9, no. 3 (1990): 185–211.

Newhouse, Ria, and April Spisak, "Fixing the First Job," *Library Journal* 129 (15 August 2004): 44–46.

Online Computer Library Center, "Library Landscape: Staffing," in *2003 Environmental Scan: Pattern Recognition*, edited by Alane Wilson, at www.oclc.org/reports/escan/library/ (accessed May 1, 2006).

Rooke, David, and William Torbert, "7 Transformations of Leadership," *Harvard Business Review* 83, no. 4 (April 2005): 67–76.

Zeidner, Moshe, Gerald Matthews, and Richard Roberts, "Emotional Intelligence in the Workplace: A Critical Review," *Applied Psychology* 53, no. 3 (2004): 371–399.

Part 2

DEVELOPING LEADERSHIP SKILLS

CHAPTER 4

Creating a High-Performing Team

This chapter focuses on the following:

- What teams are and why they are a valuable component of an information service center
- How to create sound teams
- How to build and support teams
- How to avoid some common pitfalls when working in teams
- How to handle being the "leader in the middle"

Teams in the workplace have been with us for a long time, in one form or another. They are not a new concept; however, they are playing an ever-greater role in how organizations get things done. Over the past twenty-some years, organizations including libraries have undergone a "flattening" of their structures, resulting in fewer layers of management. In many cases, they experienced downsizing or at least received no increase in staffing even with increased workloads. As a result of these events, the staff must be more productive, be flexible, learn new skills, and take on more responsibilities. So far, the 21st century has placed additional pressure on organizations and their personnel to be adept at handling rapid change. All these factors place a premium on flexibility and having a knowledgeable workforce that is more capable of working independently than in the past.

Leaders must get the best possible performance from their existing followers, and they must depend on team members to operate and problem-solve, often on their own. (Fewer supervisors are available, and if work is to progress in a timely fashion, team members must act without waiting for assistance from higher-level personnel.) Although the management fundamentals—decision making, planning, organizing, and so on—remain unchanged, there is a shift in who engages in these activities when true teams exist.

Some of the differences that exist between a true team environment and the traditional workplace are significant from a leadership point of view. Teams call for consensus rather than command and control. They require acceptance of the idea that conflict (both positive and negative) is a normal part of team operations, and those conflicts must be addressed in an open, honest manner. Although not every difference of opinion that occurs in a team will result in negative conflict, time will still need to be spent in meetings to resolve problems or make decisions. Reaching decisions in a team setting tends to be more knowledge based than when done on the basis of one person's opinion. In teams, more emphasis must be placed on the "whys" than on the "hows." Essentially, the leader must engage in a collaborative process with the team members in order for the team to succeed. It should be noted that in this discussion, the word *leader* refers to the higher-level manager rather than to the team leader. We use the term *leader, sponsor,* or *coach* to represent the higher-level leadership (you), but it should be remembered that teams may and often do have their own internal leader or chair.

The Whats and Whys of Teams

Writers and people in general use the term *team* in a variety of ways, even when referring to a workplace concept. One definition of a workplace team that appears to capture today's environment follows: "A work group [that] is made up of individuals who see themselves and who are seen by others as a social entity, who are interdependent because of the tasks they perform as members of the group, who are embedded in one or more larger social systems, and who perform tasks that affect others" (Guzzo and Dickson, 1996, pp. 308–309). Perhaps two more elements ought to be part of the definition—team workgroups develop a shared commitment to one another, and the group is empowered to make decisions regarding their work activities.

Keep in mind that there are important differences between teams and committees. John Lubans (2003, p. 144) identifies five significant differences:

- Team members are equals, while committees may have an implicit pecking order or hierarchy.
- Conflict in teams is normal and addressed, while committees may labor under unresolved, often historic, conflict.

- Teams seek high trust, while committee members may have turf issues and hidden agendas.
- Teams strive for open communication, while committee members may be overly cautious in discussions.
- Team members are mutually supportive, while committee members may work independently and represent factions.

Leaders should keep these factors in mind to make sure they create a team and not a committee by another name.

The literature is filled with labels for teams—project teams, self-managing teams, quality circles, cross-functional teams, virtual teams, and production groups are some examples. Whatever the label, successful teams, be they permanent, temporary, or virtual, share some common elements. Although our interest is in long-term teams, all effective teams share a commitment to a goal or purpose. There is a recognition that interpersonal relationships play a role in the team's success, and members work on these relationships in an open manner. Additionally, all teams should be empowered. This concept is discussed later in this chapter.

When an organization employs teams, especially self-managing teams, it should be beneficial in several ways. First, overall performance ought to improve, especially when teams work directly with users. Being able to make a decision on the spot, beyond enforcing rules and regulations, generally results in service that better meets the customers' needs and time frames. Second, there ought to be more "learning" and greater flexibility for both the organization and the staff. This occurs, in part, because teams can and do experiment as well as engage in innovative approaches to challenging situations. Third, staff commitment to the organization and its goals tends to be higher. Greater commitment results in higher retention of staff, which in turn reduces personnel costs (recruitment and training). Finally, more committed and motivated people are more productive as well as more willing to change as circumstances change.

Without a doubt, teams can be and are highly effective and beneficial for an organization; however, teams do not always live up to their potential. One problem area that comes up is using *team* to refer to what is actually committee work in the mistaken effort to appear "current." Such usage quickly leads to staff disillusionment and sometimes gives the concept a bad name within the staff. Probably a bigger problem is trying to employ teams too quickly without carefully thinking through all the start-up issues. When teams are struggling, in many cases it is because one or more start-up issues were not fully addressed in the rush to establish a team environment. Yet another area that does not get very much attention in the literature is personnel changes, both within the team and the organization. Many of the start-up issues must be addressed with newcomers, either to the team or the organization, on a one-on-one basis. This is often forgotten for newcomers who are not going to immediately join a team, which may cause problems. The remainder of this chapter discusses both the start-up and maintenance issues for effective team usage.

Before You Start

Teams require thoughtful leadership and support in order to realize all their benefits. Thus, implementing teams does not reduce an organization's need for leaders and managers. What follows is guidance for making teams a key component of an information service's primary mode of operation.

The decision to employ teams—temporary or permanent—is not one to make lightly. Teams and time go together like bacon and eggs. They require thoughtful planning, a careful assessment of staff capabilities, and an assessment of the organization's ability to adjust to team operations *before* starting the selection of team members. Teams require careful, ongoing nurturing from the time they are created until they are disbanded. They also require a different and rather complex assessment process to ensure sound and proper accountability.

Time spent in preparing and thinking about creating teams will pay off in better long-term performance, or in extreme situations, success or failure. The questions to be addressed fall into three broad areas—organizational, team, and individual team member. Taken together, the answers form an assessment of the organization's readiness for true teams.

ORGANIZATIONAL ISSUES

Perhaps the most basic question is whether the organization is completely committed to using teams. This may be one of the weakest links in team usage. The "let's try it and see how it works" approach contains the seeds of trouble; there is no complete commitment to the concept. The question takes on increased importance when thinking about implementing self-managed teams. Being committed to this endeavor will entail modifying some of the existing underlying organizational structures and systems. One example of where fundamental changes would be key to team success is assessing and rewarding team performance. Team assessment is very different from individual performance appraisal. (Although teams are becoming increasingly common in information services, the performance appraisal and reward systems for teams are still in their developmental stages.) Another area that might require change is access to information by staff. Teams often need more in-depth management information to function properly than the level the organization currently shares with personnel.

A related question is how committed the senior staff is to making the shift toward a team-based organization. Successful team implementation seldom occurs in organizations where one or more senior staff members have doubts about the concept. Such individuals can, even without thinking about their concerns, cause delays or otherwise impede a team's progress or activities. A more subtle factor can be behavior on the part of doubters that suggests, or makes clear, that they do not support the concept.

Resources are always an organizational issue, and they are almost always not as plentiful as everyone would like. It is the rare case where the decision to move to a team format is accompanied by additional resources for implementation. That naturally results in a reallocation process, with one or more units losing something—people, equipment, funds—in order to provide for the team(s). Since the usual process requires finding the necessary resources from what already exists, the question is, does the organization have sufficient resources to implement teams without undue hardship or loss of productivity, and is there agreement about where they will come from?

Another resource the organization must allocate is time, which some people may view as expended partially on nonproductive activities. Forming teams for the first time in an organization calls for staff training and development regarding just what the team concept means. Both team members and the other staff will require this type of orientation if the organization wishes to avoid conflict, open or covert, between team and nonteam staff. Traditional workplace behavior, at least in the United States, has a strong element of competition and a low emphasis on cooperation. Team-based work calls for just the opposite behavior; it takes time to develop this change in focus for team members. Taking time to develop needed team skills usually limits productivity during the developmental period; that in turn can cause resentment among nonteam staff due to a lack of understanding about team processes. To address this issue, the organization may wish to consider whether or not teams can be established throughout the entire organization, thus eliminating the "team versus nonteam" mentality. All teams would not need to be established simultaneously—as long as there is a "master plan" for team establishment, this may alleviate concerns over "us versus them." Regardless of the extent to which teams are to be implemented, a critical question to ask is whether the organization has the necessary time and training capability to develop a proper team environment.

Most information services are part of a larger organization with a number of management systems in place that all subunits utilize. (The systems are generally outside the control of the senior information professionals, but it is possible that they can influence how the system operates within their unit.) Human resources or personnel services is one such system, which only the very largest of information services has as part their organizational structure. (Even where there is a unit-based personnel office, its activities are normally guided and constrained by the parent body's system to a large degree.) To foster a team environment that is conducive to success, some significant adjustments must be made to the traditional personnel system. Teams will fail without such changes. The two primary areas of concern are the appraisal process and the compensation system. So, the question is, is the overall personnel system willing to work with the information service to make modifications for team-based work activities?

Other questions include the following: Are team goals and anticipated results clearly articulated? Have the team-management information-sharing systems been thought through? Has a team monitoring and support structure been developed? As you can see, all these questions are substantial in character, and the decision to go with teams, just at the organizational level, requires thought and planning; beyond that there are team and team member issues to consider.

TEAM ISSUES

Turning next to the team level, there are fewer issues to address, but there are still significant questions to think about nonetheless. An obvious question is whether the team is temporary or permanent. Certainly the answer may have an impact on the ease of getting agreement on resource reallocation. Often forming a temporary team creates more challenges than does a permanent team because the "disruptions" may be twofold, once during the formation of the team and again during the reintegration of team members into their former units. Another issue is whether the temporary team will in fact truly be a team—or just another committee by a different name.

Identifying the appropriate team resources should be part of the planning process rather than finding them as needed; there will be enough unexpected needs to keep the organization "on its toes." Preplanning in this area may identify one or two resources that are not readily available from existing sources. Knowing what those sources may be provides some lead time for securing them or, if resources are not available, rethinking team goals.

Effective teams exhibit a high degree of coordination and communication between team members as well as with nonteam work units. Knowing what those activities are and what skills are required will help ensure success. That knowledge will also play a major role in selecting people for the team. A factor to keep in mind is that although a relationship exists between team goals and requisite skills, empowered teams can and often do come up with approaches to achieving the desired goal(s) that call for unanticipated skills. Thus, the planning process seldom is the final answer to what will be needed.

TEAM MEMBER ISSUES

At the individual level, there are several questions to ponder before starting the selection process. A common feature of teams is cross-training of members. Although cross-training does take place in nonteam environments, it is not that common. Thus, few individuals have experience with the process and its purposes. Gaining acceptance of the value of cross-training on the part of individuals new to the idea can take some time. Two rather common suspicions are that the idea is just a management ploy to "give me more work without any benefit" or to off-load some of the work of low performers without addressing the nonperformers' behavior(s). The question to consider is, will the staff be receptive to cross-training, if needed? If there may be resistance, are there resources available to help change the staff attitudes?

There is little doubt that a key question is whether the prospective team members have the necessary personality characteristics. One personality characteristic for team membership is the preference for and ability to handle a high degree of autonomy. Another desirable characteristic is a preference for social interaction as opposed to solitary activities. Being receptive to new ideas, concepts, and approaches to problem situations is also a fitting attribute. A desire to grow in one's work is a trait good team members have. Additionally, having a willingness to address differences of opinion in an open, straightforward manner is essential for team members. They also must understand that differences and conflict are a natural part of the team environment, and resolving the issue(s) is a must for successful team operations. (Again, conflict can be viewed both negatively and positively, and efforts should be made to be sure the team understands this.)

An area where team-based work differs from the traditional workplace is accountability. At least in the United States, most workers are accustomed to being individually responsible for their work outcomes. Group accountability may be one of the most difficult concepts for team members to understand and accept. Teams *must* be accountable, and success or failure is a *team* responsibility. Accepting that "my performance assessment" may be negatively affected by someone else's actions often does not sit well. (An important feature of self-managing teams and their accountability is that the team must be allowed to address member performance on an ongoing basis rather than have the external leader handle any problems.) The question becomes, are there staff who already have a sense of team accountability or appear capable of accepting the concept?

Team accountability raises the question of performance appraisal. Do prospective team members have the maturity levels to engage in meaningful peer evaluation? The answer to this question is likely to be difficult to determine. For a great many employees, experience of peer evaluation is nonexistent or exceedingly limited at best. Peer evaluation in information service centers is rather uncommon, especially for the support staff. There is some use of peer evaluations for professionals, primarily in academic settings. Lack of experience with the process, as well as concerns, doubts, or fears about the fairness of the process and its impact on interpersonal relationships, usually creates a situation where some serious training and development of staff is required. Also, as noted earlier, the team should address performance issues, up to and including dismissal of team members.

Check This Out

For more information about team performance appraisal, see G. Edward Evans, *Performance Management and Appraisal* (New York: Neal-Schuman, 2004).

Creating the Team

Information gathered through assessment of the aforementioned planning issues allows leaders to make informed decisions about forming teams and who on the staff are likely candidates. Assuming the decision is positive, the organization can now set about creating the team (composition and size), creating the right environment (empowerment and support), establishing the initial activities and processes (interdependence and goals), and creating a plan for training and development. Teams do require support and monitoring, and leaders play a primary role in those processes.

Before starting these activities, a leader is wise to engage in some self-assessment. The assessment revolves around the need to recognize that the purpose of teams should be as much about developing team members as it is about getting things done through people. Effective staff development, whether team related or not, rests on some basic principles and assumptions about people and work that leaders hold.

STAFF DEVELOPMENT AND TEAMS

John Maxwell (1993) suggests some principles on which to base a staff development program. Every good manager and leader knows that, at its most basic level, management is about accomplishing things through people. Most successful long-term organizations *value* people. They recognize staff as much more than a cog in the organizational machine. Part of valuing is having a *commitment* to people. Commitment involves developing an individual's abilities. In most successful organizations, that process goes beyond the skills required for the person's immediate job responsibilities. Basing a development program on clear and well-understood *standards* as well as on the vision for the future also helps create a successful organization. Two interrelated principles are *integrity* and *influence*. A leader must have influence over people in order to motivate their desire to learn and develop. Although most people have the desire to grow, even in the workplace, they take their cues from the leader's attitude and positive or negative influence regarding developmental activities. A key factor in influencing behavior is integrity. Without integrity, which builds trust, a leader's behavior is more likely to be viewed as negative rather than positive.

To a large degree, development is all about motivation. This is not the book to address the complex issues of workplace motivation beyond that of how a leader's actions influence it. In terms of basic management training—or Worker Motivation 101—and the discussion of worker motivation, McGregor's (1960) Theory X and Theory Y motivators deal with assumptions about people's willingness to work. Using this theory, where a leader's assumption lies along the continuum between X and Y, will significantly influence any development program. The closer a person is to the X end (lack of willingness) of the scale, the fewer development activities are undertaken, and those that are have low expectations for positive outcomes. When employees appear to be unmotivated to perform, much less develop skills, the chances are high that the problem lies with the manager or leader rather than the staff. Assuming the vast majority of people want to learn and develop is a key factor in effective development programs.

Related to a general willingness to work and learn is the fact that people want to feel worthwhile. Again this goes back to Worker Motivation 101, as exemplified in Maslow's (1943) needs hierarchy; self-worth, or self-esteem, is a basic human need. Part of a person's self-esteem arises from feeling or knowing her work performance is good. Acting on the assumption that employees want to feel worthwhile pays dividends that go far beyond development activities.

One means of building up self-esteem is to give feedback and encouragement on a regular basis. Too often the manager or leader waits for some especially noteworthy performance or idea before giving feedback. Certainly such occasions call for feedback; however, providing ongoing positive support and encouragement generally creates a more productive environment and a committed staff. While operating on the assumption that encouragement is good, you should be aware of two dangers in implementing this approach. Giving encouragement in private is not nearly as effective as public recognition or support; however, there are potential problems with the public aspect. If not everyone is likely to deserve public recognition, at least occasionally, there may be serious performance problems for those who do not receive the support. So, consider the situation carefully. A second danger, and one often overlooked, is failing to provide equitable support or recognition. The appearance of "favorites" on the part of the leader or manager can offset any gains from assuming people desire support and encouragement. It will actually undermine trust and some peoples' sense of the leader's integrity. (It is important to note that encouragement and support are not necessarily the same as praise.)

A related assumption about employees is that everyone needs assistance with work activities, at least occasionally. Very few of us are perfect in everything we do, nor do we have all the desirable work skills. At the very least, we have some skills that could use further development. We are not talking about corrective assistance, but rather the coaching that develops a person's work attributes. Good coaching draws on a person's desire to succeed; it also can effectively build self-esteem. Employees who view the leader as actively helping them grow become more committed to the leader's vision and to the organization.

Most of us have the motivation to learn somewhere within us, even if it is not always readily apparent. That motivation may be deeply buried and difficult to bring to the surface, but it is there nonetheless. Great leaders and coaches are able to bring out that desire and use it for the benefit of both the individual and the organization. A host of factors can enhance motivation—making and having recognition of a significant accomplishment, having a sense of being a true peer, having meaningful involvement in decisions about work, and having a sense of providing a significant service to people, to name just a few. Leaders build on those types of motivation to persuade staff to "buy into" the concept of lifelong learning.

As we have noted several times, behavior is a key to a person's success or failure as a leader. An articulated but unexecuted leader style (e.g., saying empowerment is important, but not allowing it to take place) accomplishes little beyond building doubts about and lessening trust in the leader. Doubts or lack of faith in the leader quickly transforms the workplace into a poorly performing unit. Only when a leader has the trust and respect of the staff do leadership characteristics come into positive play. A leader may be able to develop a realistic, viable vision of the future for the unit and even articulate it in a dynamic manner, but without the trust of the people who are to implement it, the vision goes nowhere. Thus, another assumption is that leadership starts with the person and then moves to "style."

Remember, development takes time, especially when it comes to team building. Modeling appropriate behaviors, values, and goals is essential for successful leadership, whether in a team setting or not. Caring for people and developing their abilities will build strong work groups. With this in mind, you can start building the team(s).

THE TEAM CHARGE

The *charge* (or charter) is the purpose or primary task of the group as assigned by the group's sponsor, coach, or external leader. The charge tells the group what is expected of it and when it is expected to be performed (particularly if it is a temporary team). Although not every organization uses charges when creating teams, they can be useful to give the team a sense of its parameters, responsibilities, and resources. Scholtes, Joiner, and Striebel (2003, pp. 2–12) note that a well-crafted charter can be useful in helping the team understand the following issues:

- What the problem is
- Why it is important to customers and the organization at this time
- Any boundaries or limitations, including time and money
- The beginning and ending dates of the project, as well as key milestones for review
- The key measures related to the problem or process under study
- The scope of the authority, for example, calling in co-workers or outside experts, requesting information normally inaccessible to them, and making changes to the process
- Who the core team members are and the amount of time allocated to the project

When discussing its charge, the group can then create its mission. (Creating mission statements is covered in chapter 6.)

Check This Out

Scholtes, Joiner, and Striebel (2003) include a Charter Worksheet (p. 14) in their text, which provides useful guidelines for creating a charter, or charge.

TEAM SELECTION

The two critical factors in team selection are abilities and personal characteristics. Some examples of abilities on a database management team are knowledge of databases, knowledge of networking, knowledge of database contracts and licensing, and fiscal management. On the personal characteristics side, such things as having self-direction, being sociable, being comfortable with group processes, being trustful of others, and having strong communication skills are desirable.

In many ways, identifying desirable abilities and characteristics is the easy step. Finding the right people is generally the big challenge. As noted earlier, it is the rare case where moving to a team-oriented environment brings with it additional resources—be they human, equipment, or funding. Even when everyone on the staff is "in the selection pool," the process is complex. Some suitable members may be in positions that are critical to other operations, and moving them to a team would be highly problematic. A common circumstance is having to select team members who lack one or more of the desired abilities or characteristics, which in turn means finding training opportunities in the lacking area(s). Another challenge is assessing the personal characteristics of potential team members, as some of the desired capabilities may not be apparent in the current working environment. The process becomes less challenging as the organization gets more and more experience with teams and collaborative work projects. However, it arises periodically as people resign and new employees are hired.

Team size is a variable that is decided on a case-by-case basis. A team must be large enough to handle the assignment(s), but not so large as to create coordination problems. If there is a team size rule, it is to make the team no larger than absolutely necessary to accomplish the established goals.

Creating the Team Environment

Creating the best possible team environment can be easier than putting the team together. Needless to say, it is only easier when senior management fully supports the concept. One critical element in the environment is ensuring that the team, and the entire staff, receives the requisite training; this is particularly true when first moving into a team environment and staff have little or no experience with team processes. As noted earlier, when an organization shifts from a traditional to a team-oriented workplace, everyone must understand how teamwork differs. Without such an orientation, staff who are not on a team often develop resentments toward team members. One of the most common reasons this happens is that teams do spend more time in meetings (gaining consensus, resolving conflicts, establishing priorities, and so on), especially during the start-up period. Nonteam members often view such meetings as not constituting "real" work, thinking the team is getting paid for doing nothing.

The person selected to monitor the team—the external leader or sponsor—is another very important element in the team environment. Research suggests that leaders who understand team design factors (e.g., goals, resources, personnel, size) most strongly affect team performance. They are also skillful in assessing team weaknesses and taking prompt steps to correct any problems (Wageman, 1997).

A team has a much greater chance of success when it starts with a clear set of directions and goals; if those can be inspiring, even better. As noted earlier, the most basic piece of information when creating a charge for the team is why the team exists and what is to be accomplished. Keeping the focus on the whys rather than the hows, especially for the direction, improves the chances for successful team outcomes. If the leader thinks of the direction (or charge) as akin to a team's mission statement, this helps keep the focus on broad issues rather than on details that limit the team's initiative.

Related to clear goals and directions and the "right" team environment are the tasks the team is to perform. The leader must be certain the tasks *require* teamwork. A common mistake, especially in first-time team environments, is creating a team in name only (tasks, yes, but not requiring teamwork). What happens is an appearance of teamwork, but in reality it is just individuals doing their own independent work. Making this mistake quickly leads to disillusionment. Another fairly common mistake is assigning tasks that only occasionally call for teamwork. Although there will likely be times when team members need to work independently to produce a product that is shared by or ultimately benefits the entire team, assigning too many individualized tasks to the team risks sending a mixed message and does not take advantage of the benefits of a team-based structure. This creates a pull on team members, making it difficult to build a team commitment.

One element of the environment where the leader may not have as much control or influence as might be desirable is team rewards. The leader will need to work closely with the HR department to develop a true team reward orientation. Such a system will ensure that a vast majority of rewards are equally shared by team members. Although some individual rewards can be employed in a team system, they should make up a very small percentage and be clearly related to the team's activities. Another approach is to allow the team to decide how, if, and when differential rewards should be distributed. A system that bases reward distribution as low as 50 percent on an individual basis sends a mixed message about the importance of teamwork.

TEAM EMPOWERMENT

Empowerment is a widely used word, and it is apparent that many people want to be "empowered" in the workplace. Just what does empowerment entail? We have stated that empowerment is a form of delegation or sharing of power, with the leader retaining most of the responsibility. Perhaps *the* key element to empowerment is an environment of high trust. This means trust that goes in both directions. The leader must trust that the followers will perform at high levels, and the followers must trust that the leader will let them perform without undo interference while being available to provide support as needed.

Leaders may need to address several personal barriers when it comes to empowering others. One such barrier is a concern about one's position—"If I empower, what may happen to my position? Will I no longer be needed?" When empowerment brings positive results, it actually enhances the empowerer's position. Leaders of high-performing groups have little to fear when it comes to their position and the fact they empowered others. Another internal barrier, more for managers than leaders, is a dislike of change, especially when there are no apparent problems with what is taking place. In an empowered environment, change and experimentation are fairly common. Leaders by the nature of the role should be leaders of change, so this should not be a significant barrier for them; however, it is something to keep in mind should a leader begin to hesitate about increasing the amount of empowerment he has given. Individuals with low self-confidence, or whose self-worth arises largely from their power position in the workplace, have substantial problems with empowerment activities. Such individuals often talk about empowering and even think they have engaged in doing so, but what they don't do is actually relinquish any real power.

There are also organizational barriers to empowerment. It is easy to say that a leader should empower her followers; however, it often proves to be more difficult in actuality than one might expect. Besides personal hurdles, senior management can also be a barrier. This may happen because empowerment is not seen as important enough to devote adequate time, effort, and money to make the process meaningful. Sometimes empowerment requires that the organization provide training for staff members, training that requires both time and funding in most cases. Perhaps the greatest senior management barrier to empowerment is a lack of commitment to the concept. The lack of commitment is not so much a function of the age of the senior managers as it is a matter of management philosophy. Assessing senior management's views and commitment to empowering activities is something a leader at lower levels in the organization should undertake. Even if a person is committed and willing to engage in an empowering process, he will not succeed without top management support.

At the operational level, frontline personnel can also be a barrier, at least during the early phases of the process. Past negative experience with managers and leaders who only talked about empowerment can create a situation of "prove to us you mean to do it." Particularly in this case, leaders need to "walk the walk" rather than just "talk the talk." Beyond wanting proof, some staff members will have concerns about what skills or knowledge may be required if they are empowered, since empowerment usually means some change(s) in activities. When staff have questions about their abilities, which are often not fully expressed, this is where a leader's ability to build self-confidence, offer encouragement, and provide coaching come into play.

Senior managers, if they truly desire effective leadership at all levels of their organization, should do the following:

- Undertake some self-study or training in empowering activities
- Provide this training to all other managers
- Create an environment in which everyone can be a leader
- Recognize that empowerment will require staff development and organizational resources in order to be effective.
- Reward superior performance in the new activities—remember, rewards can be other than financial in nature

---

Check This Out

For a number of suggestions for how to recognize and reward employees, consult Bob Nelson's *1001 Ways to Reward Employees*, rev. ed. (New York: Workman, 2005).

What are some common areas for empowering others? Underlying all empowerment is the authority and responsibility to succeed or fail due to one's own efforts, actions, and behaviors. This fact is often not fully understood by a newly empowered person, especially when it is that person's first experience with the process.

In a team setting, a leader must address the following areas if the team is to properly function as a unit. First and foremost, team members must be able to make *decisions* about their activities. Certainly the leader or sponsor should be available to support the team's efforts (e.g., providing information or making suggestions), but she must be careful not to make the decision for them. Although the organization and leader must set the overall goal(s) for the team, the team should have the power to *set internal goals and targets* (way markers) for how to achieve the ultimate goal(s). Related to setting way markers, a team needs to *set work standards* if it is to be self-managing. Having the freedom to *experiment* with work processes goes with establishing standards and way markers. It also follows that team members have the power to allocate *assignments* as they see fit. An area of shared power is *monitoring performance*—the team monitors members' performance and the leader monitors the team's progress toward the ultimate goal(s).

Another area where team members need freedom to operate is in *allocating team resources* as they think appropriate. Effective empowerment leaders are careful about *when* they intervene in team activities, especially when it comes to problem solving; having the latitude to *resolve problems* on their own is something effective teams have. Perhaps an area in which leaders have the greatest difficulty timing their intervention is *conflict resolution*. Jumping in too quickly when team conflict develops, or at least before the team requests assistance, is something good leaders avoid. When a team works through a conflict on its own, it tends to become stronger. A team that has all these powers is indeed empowered to succeed or fail as a result of its performance.

Worth Checking Out

A good book on empowering library staff is Connie Christopher's *Empowering Your Library* (Chicago: American Library Association, 2003). The ideas presented are useful in almost any information service environment.

TEAM RESOURCES

An obvious factor in a proper team environment is having the necessary resources to achieve the ultimate goal(s) as well as the internal team-generated goal(s). It goes almost without saying that lacking the required resources, a team cannot act in a timely manner, be proactive, or even be semi-functional. There is more to it than just receiving the resources; it is a matter of receiving them at the time needed. This can be a problem for both the leader and the team, particularly when senior management is not fully committed to team processes. There is also the danger that a leader may be slow in providing necessary materials to a struggling team due to thinking, "They have not made good use of what they had." Generally, this is a mistake that will only lead to further difficulties for the group, and it is likely to decrease team members' commitment to the team process. This is the time for the leader to intervene to help the team determine what is causing the group to struggle.

TRUST

Trust is a key element in sound team environments. There are three areas of trust to think about—the leader's trust of the team, the team's trust of the leader, and the team members' trust of one another. Trust underlies effective collaboration, and collaboration is a keystone for effective team performance. It is clear that without trust and collaboration in all three areas, the chances for the desired outcomes diminish.

Trust is built on interpersonal skills that apply equally to all involved in the team process. One essential skill is listening and doing so with empathy. (There is a difference between listening and listening effectively.) *Effective listening* is a developed skill and one that most of us need to actively work on to more fully develop or maintain. People can hear and understand words at a much higher rate than most people speak (approximately four times faster). This means that up to three-quarters of our "listening time" is available for other thoughts, and this is what often happens.

There are some steps you can take to improve the quality of your listening time. Starting with the assumption that the speaker is saying something new, important, or unknown will help you focus on the message's meaning and keep the mind from wandering too much. Two mistakes in listening are thinking you "know" the person's message and starting to formulate a reply prior to the speaker's being finished. In team settings, it is crucial to listen for details; thinking only about the "big picture" can be counterproductive in problem solving and decision making. The most important factors frequently lie in the details, and not grasping these details often leads to poor results.

We also tend to "filter" what we hear. Being aware of the common filters helps us become more effective listeners. Researchers have identified three major types of filtering—leveling, sharpening, and assimilation. *Leveling* drops elements out of the message, thus changing its meaning. *Sharpening*, as the label suggests, involves giving certain elements of the message greater emphasis, thereby changing the sender's meaning. *Assimilation* retains all the elements of the message but adds other elements, which results in a different meaning.

Finally, accurate feedback is crucial for effective listening and for ensuring that the sender's and receiver's understandings are the same. Feedback is also related to building trust in that group processes require people to engage in "give and take." Accurate feedback must, at least occasionally, reflect the fact that we do not agree with something. Timing of such feedback is very important in building trust. Just hearing negative feedback, such as "That is a bad idea," or "What in the world makes you think that?" will create distrust in the group. Using less evaluative terms tends to encourage people to continue to contribute. Trustful team environments have people who are open to ideas and feelings, committed to a shared set of goals, willing to explore alternatives, and satisfied with team-based work.

GOALS

Setting realistic but challenging goals is another aspect of creating the ideal team environment. The leader or organization must set the ultimate goal(s) while allowing the team to set the internal goal(s). Striking the right balance between realistic and challenging goals can be a challenge in itself. An impossible goal will rather quickly destroy team morale and the willingness to engage in team processes. On the other hand, easily achievable goals will not bring out the maximum benefits of developing a team environment.

One way to think about this activity is to differentiate between purposes and goals. Although interrelated, they are different concepts. *Purposes* should be broad directions that a team is to strive for; very often purposes are never fully achievable because they draw on the larger organizational mission and vision statements. *Goals* are more specific and often contain a time element. Starting with the team purpose(s) is a good way to begin to strike the balance between too easy and the impossible.

When setting the purposes and goals for the team, it is a good idea to make the goal(s) specific, but not so limited as to leave little or no room for the team to develop internal goals. In other words, leaders should avoid prescribing the what, who, when, and how. Sometimes the useful step of discussing the goals with team members gets overlooked. Spending some time discussing goals and coming to a mutual understanding is well worth the effort.

COACHING AND SUPPORT

Group discussions about goals are likely to elicit information about team concerns, both for the team and for individual members. Many of those concerns will relate to resources and skills required. For first-time teams, there will be worries about team processes, whether or not they are articulated.

Check It Out

One resource to consult in order to find suggestions to support team activities is Michael West's *Motivate Teams, Maximize Success: Effective Strategies for Realizing Your Goals* (San Francisco: Chronicle, 2004).

With the input from group discussions as well as independent judgment, the leader can begin to plan what training and development activities are appropriate. One challenge may be finding the resources for conducting the training, at least in a timely fashion. Following are some of the typical areas where coaching or development will be required:

- Group decision making
- Group problem solving
- Meeting management skills
- Conflict resolution
- Peer performance assessment

Maintaining the Team

Having created the team(s) and the best possible team environment, the leader must now turn to the activities that support and maintain the team(s). Remember, all the elements that went into creating the environment remain as ongoing issues. However, in addition to these elements, the leader must address motivation, communication, feedback, and accountability.

MOTIVATION

The basics of team motivation do not vary much from that of individual employees. An underlying factor in everyone's motivation to work is self-interest, if nothing more than working as a legal means of securing the money one needs to live on. It is of course far more complex than that, but self-interest is a factor. Thus, the first difference in the team environment is the need to keep self-interest to a minimum. Another difference is the team will likely have members from different "generations" who may be more or less inclined toward teamwork (see chapter 3).

Monitoring team activities is an essential role for a leader. When a team exhibits morale or productivity problems, the leader must intervene. If the poor morale is arising from a performance problem as a team, assisting the team with its problem solving in an attempt to isolate the issue may lead to a solution. That will not resolve the poor morale by itself, but it will stop the problem from "feeding" the morale issue. It may be as simple as the timing of resources for teamwork. On the other hand, the issue may be a nonperforming team member. When that is the case, the team may be hard pressed to resolve the matter on its own.

One weak member can and will create significant problems for the team. There are really only two options when it comes to a weak team member—train or replace. In the best of circumstances, it is just a matter of the team member needing the requisite training rather than unwillingness to learn. When it is not a training issue, often the team is not empowered to replace the person, which is something the leader must undertake. Failure to take action will have disastrous consequences for the team. Poor morale will increase as other team members' resentment festers and grows. Resentment and poor morale almost always translate into exceedingly poor team performance. Another negative outcome of failing to act is that the team will begin to doubt and lose trust in the leader.

When morale is just starting to decline (moderate to low morale), there are several things the leader can do. One step is to model behavior that is positively geared toward success. If the leader can identify coachable areas in need of improvement, it is probably a good time for some serious coaching. Helping the team find one or two small and quick successes almost always boosts morale. Having a team meeting and discussing the vision and its positive values may also make a difference for the better. Demonstrating commitment to the vision and modeling that commitment will help team members "buy into" that vision. Such discussions may also lead to revelations about what may be causing a decline in morale, assuming the leader is an effective listener.

COMMUNICATION

Everyone knows the importance of communication for an organization and its success. Although employees working independently must and do communicate with one another about work, the level and frequency of those exchanges are rarely as crucial as they are between team members. Effective communication—speaking, writing, and listening—is the glue of successful team functionality. Group commitment, decision making, problem solving, conflict resolution, and accountability all rest on the quality of the communication that occurs in the team.

Team members who understand and follow four communication rules find themselves, more often than not, on great teams. Rule one is to be open and honest with one another, and that leads to vulnerability. These factors almost always lead to greater commitment to one another. Rule two is to be clear and concise. Trying to "show off" one's vocabulary tends to turn off listeners as well as make the real message harder to identify. Being long-winded does little but eat up valuable team time. Rule three is to maintain consistency. Maintaining consistency does not mean being unwilling to compromise or to admit to being wrong about something. However, constantly changing views or positions raises doubts about a person and may lead to less trust. Rule four is to be civil and courteous as well as to show respect for others and their views. Teams that follow these rules in their communication with one another, with the leader, with other units or teams, and with the public are likely to achieve great things.

FEEDBACK

As location is to real estate, so timing is to feedback. At the right time it can work wonders; at the wrong time it can cause a surprising amount of damage. As noted earlier, feedback is crucial for establishing trust within a team. Getting feedback timing right takes a good deal of practice and careful thought on the leader's part. One aspect of managerial and leader feedback that seldom receives enough attention is that it can be positive as well as corrective in character.

For feedback to be useful, it must be based on accurate information. Leaders and managers collect their data from several sources—reports and documents; observations; and thoughtful listening to comments from staff, the public, and other units. It's important to bear in mind certain issues about feedback, particularly in a team setting. Ideally, feedback should

- Be face to face, not a memo or e-mail
- Be specific—which is essential when it is corrective in nature
- Allow for a response from the recipient
- Occur as close to the time of the event as possible
- Focus on behavior rather than personality
- Be carefully thought through before being given
- Be based on the leader's information, not secondhand data
- Be honest

ACCOUNTABILITY

Developing a sense of group accountability in the team is absolutely essential for the organization. This will take some time, particularly in cases where teams and their accountability are a new concept. (Although the use of teams is growing, the overall majority of information services, at least in the United States, still does not make extensive, if any, use of the self-managing team concept.) Once the team internalizes accountability, it is relatively easy to maintain, because peer pressure to achieve the best becomes high. Individual members become resolved not to let their teammates down. Teams will be quick to respond to a person who slacks off, and even make up for the lapses for a time, if the team believes there is good reason for the lapse and it will not be a long-term issue.

One area of concern for a leader, at least in most U.S. organizations, is the organizational reward system. As mentioned earlier, when the system is focused on individuals, problems can arise in a team environment. Even small rewards such as "employee of the month" can be detrimental to team functioning. Reviewing the organization's reward system is a worthwhile activity very early on when developing a team environment. Although it is not exhaustive, Crow (1995) lists ten potential "problem areas" for maintaining effective teamwork and a sense of group accountability:

- Institutional performance appraisal system that rates individuals numerically and is used for ranking people
- Institutional performance appraisal system that employs forced distributions (a system wherein a certain percentage of appraisals must fall into a "needs improvement" category, and only a small percentage can receive high ratings)
- Pay for performance (individually based)
- Employee of the month/year programs
- Contests between units, individuals, departments
- Internal promotion policies based solely on individual achievements
- Ranking of units from best to worst
- Use of individual quotas, piece rates, and so on as the basis for rewards
- Identifying units as profit or loss centers
- Managing "by the numbers"

Working with the organization to address issues such as these, or any other practice that emphasizes individual work rather team-based work, is vital for the long-term success of teams and their sense of group accountability.

While teamwork is the desired outcome, the fact remains that individuals make up the team, and they do perform at different levels of effectiveness. Thus, a leader must engage in some level of individual appraisal. How does a leader do this without damaging the group? LaFasto and Larson (2001) provide some useful guidance. They suggest two categories of factors that distinguish the successful from the less successful team member—working knowledge and teamwork. They include two factors in the working knowledge category—experience and problem solving. Within teamwork they identify four factors—openness, supportiveness, personal style, and action orientation. Collecting information about the teamwork aspect takes observation, and when that activity has some structure it produces better, more accurate assessments. One way to get ideas for how to structure the observation is the team evaluation form that appears in an article by Mealiea and Baltazar (2005). Other useful articles to consult on the process of evaluating group contributions include those by Phipps (1999) and Zigon (1998).

Senior Management Teams

Almost everything covered in this chapter so far can apply to senior management teams, executive teams, or what the literature refers to as top management teams (TMTs). If anything, having high trust in such teams is even more critical than for teams at other levels. Perhaps one of the most significant dangers for TMTs is "group thinking," especially in cases where the leader or CEO has strong views on an issue.

Check These Out

Two good sources of information about "groupthink" and how to avoid it are Paul Kowert's *Groupthink or Deadlock* (Albany: State University of New York Press, 2002) and Rupert Brown's *Group Processes*, 2nd ed. (Oxford: Blackwell, 2000).

Just what are TMTs, and do they really exist as teams? One of the various labels for senior management teams is often employed to look "current" or collegial when in fact true teams do not exist. As Michael Roberto (2003, p. 120), of Harvard Business School, writes, "Beyond disagreements over how to define the TMT, some scholars have questioned whether CEOs actually employ teams at the top at all." He also notes that "the CEO and his/her direct reports often refer to themselves as a team, but typically, they do not behave as such." A recent study (Smith et al., 2006) reports on a survey of fifty-one top management groups and teams in hospitals. They note that almost all the CEOs were the most "powerful" persons in the groups labeled *team*. While that is what one would expect, they also note that organizational effectiveness, as they define it, was strongest in teams in which there was a substantial power sharing and collaborative activity.

Some years ago, Peter Drucker (1992) wrote a piece for the *Wall Street Journal* about teams, especially at the executive level. In that article, he uses a sports analogy to suggest there are at least three types of teams—baseball, football, and tennis doubles. His point is that executive teams more often than not function like a baseball team, where there are fixed positions that rarely are interchangeable, and "plays" seldom involve more than two or three individuals. There is a great deal of independence in how individuals perform the plays as long they accomplish the tasks at hand. For Drucker, a better model is a football team, where positions rarely change but everyone must be effectively involved in the plays if the team is to succeed. His preferred management configuration resembles a tennis doubles team. Although in doubles each player has a general area to cover, it is essential that each move from position to position and cover for one another's weaknesses. He also makes the point that as the need for flexibility increases, team size should decrease.

Leaders of TMTs should think about Drucker's team variations and make a conscious decision as to what type of team is appropriate for the existing environment. Each type can be successful; the challenge lies in selecting the best model.

Information Profession Teams

Information services do make some use of teams, and it seems highly likely that the usage will increase over time. However, currently there are not a great many institutions where teamwork is the primary organizational pattern. Perhaps the best-known team-based information service with the longest operational experience in the United States is the University of Arizona Library. It has received a substantial amount of publicity. Two good articles about the Arizona model are Laura Bender's (1997) "Team Organization—Learning Organization" in *Information Outlook* and Joseph Diaz and Chestalene Pintozzi's (1999) "Helping Teams Work" in *Library Administration & Management*. Other academic institutions that employ the team concept include Emory (web.library.emory .edu/about/reorg, accessed May 1, 2006), Indiana University-Purdue University Indianapolis (IUPUI, www.ulib.iupui.edu/libinfo/teams.html, accessed May 1, 2006), and the University of Maryland, College Park (www.lib.umd.edu/PUB/ documentation.html, accessed May 1, 2006). An interesting article discussing the team concept in a public library setting is Betsy Bernfeld's (2004) *Library Trends* piece titled "Developing a Team Management Structure in a Public Library."

Summary

Teams are becoming the preferred way to structure the workplace. They can achieve great things when the environment is right; they can cause more harm than good when things are not right. This chapter attempts to show that "getting things right" is a complex task. A library should carefully think through the requirements for effective team operations before starting down that pathway. The journey is worth it, but it must be undertaken with a full knowledge of what will be involved.

References

Bender, Laura, "Team Organization—Learning Organization: The University of Arizona Four Years into It," *Information Outlook* 1, no. 9 (1997): 19–22.

Bernfeld, Betsy, "Developing a Team Management Structure in a Public Library," *Library Trends* 53, no. 1 (2004): 112–128.

Crow, Robert, "Institutional Competition and Its Effect on Teamwork," *Journal of Quality and Participation* 18, no. 3 (1995): 46–53.

Diaz, Joseph, and Chestalene Pintozzi, "Helping Teams Work: Lessons Learned from the University of Arizona Reorganization," *Library Administration & Management* 13, no. 1 (1999): 27–36.

Drucker, Peter, "There's More Than One Kind of Team," *Wall Street Journal*, 11 February 1992, A16.

Guzzo, Richard, and Marcus Dickson, "Teams in Organizations: Recent Research and Performance Effectiveness," in *Annual Review of Psychology*, edited by James Spence (Palo Alto, CA: Annual Reviews, 1996), 307–338.

LaFasto, Frank, and Carl Larson, *When Teams Work Best* (Thousand Oaks, CA: Sage, 2001).

Lubans, John, "Teams in Libraries," *Library Administration & Management* 17, no. 3 (2003): 144–145.

Maslow, A.H., "A Theory of Human Motivation," *Psychological Review* 50 (1943): 370–396.

Maxwell, John, *Developing the Leader Within You* (Nashville, TN: Nelson, 1993).

McGregor, Douglas, *The Human Side of Enterprise* (New York: McGraw-Hill, 1960).

Mealiea, Laird, and Ramon Baltazar, "A Strategic Guide for Building Effective Teams," *Public Personnel Management* 34, no. 2 (2005): 141–160.

Phipps, Shelley E., "Performance Measurement as a Methodology for Assessing Team and Individual Performance," in *Proceedings of the 3rd Northumbria International Conference on Performance Assessment in Libraries and Information Services* (Newcastle upon Tyne: Information North, 1999), 113–117.

Roberto, Michael, "The Stable Core and Dynamic Periphery in Top Management Teams," *Management Decisions* 41, no. 2 (2003): 120–131.

Scholtes, Peter R., Brian L. Joiner, and Barbara J. Striebel, *The Team Handbook*, 3rd ed. (Madison, WI: Oriel, 2003).

Smith, Anne, Susan Houghton, Jacqueline Hood, and Joel Ryman, "Power Relationships between Top Managers," *Journal of Business Research* 59, no. 5 (2006): 622–629.

Wageman, Ruth, "Critical Factors in Creating Superb Self-Managing Teams," *Organizational Dynamics* 26, no. 1 (Summer 1997): 49–60.

Zigon, Jack, "Team Performance Measurement," *Journal for Quality and Participation* 21, no. 3 (May/June 1998): 48–54.

CHAPTER 5

Honing Political Skills

This chapter focuses on the following:

- Organizational politics
- Organizational culture and climate
- Networking and visibility
- Decision making and negotiation
- Partnerships, alliances, and coalitions
- Managing change and conflict

High-performing teams operate at their optimal level when their leaders demonstrate that they have the skills and experience to participate *effectively* in the politics of the parent organization. All organizations and work teams revolve around internal politics—it's a fact of life leaders quickly learn to accept, even if it takes a little time to understand.

Why Organizational Politics Matter

Internal politics play a part in resolving the disagreements and differences in viewpoints that emerge in any group of people having diverse needs and a vested interest in the allocation of scarce resources. Each leader or group within an organization uses political tactics to ensure they gain their preferred outcome when resources are being allocated. To do this they employ political tactics (e.g., by influencing decisions or building coalitions). Organizational politics can be used to good effect when they are employed to resolve disagreements informally and in a noncoercive way. The skills are learned through experience, basically by winning some points and losing others. So the leader needs to build up an understanding of how the political game is played within the organization so that control can be gained over resources, decisions are influenced, and coalitions built. No two organizations function in exactly the same way.

Remember

Political tactics are used in decision making to gain support, deflect resistance, and win the argument.

Within any organization, politics operate at all levels, from the governing body down to the information service. Politics are often evident within work teams when someone wants to push his own needs above those of others. Sometimes the individual has his own circle of influence, both within and external to the service.

So the effective leader learns how to play the game in the unique setting in which she is working. Our experience indicates not only that no two organizations function in exactly the same way but also that how they function will change over time. People come and go, and it is the people element that influences the way organizational politics are played out, not the formal decision-making process of committees and boards.

We stress from the outset, in discussing organizational politics, that leaders use their political skills for the benefit of their team and the community they serve. Political power should never be used for personal gain. (There have been some poor role models among leaders in business and politics who have used their power to gain personal reward). So a new leader needs to look carefully to select an appropriate role model. That model should be someone who has demonstrated a sound moral and ethical approach to his position.

Politics are sometimes viewed in a negative light. Words and phrases such as *manipulation, backstabbing,* and *keeping his cards to his chest* spring to mind. However, it is perhaps not surprising that the terms used to describe political action within organizations are emotive. People spend a large proportion of their lives at work, and this means there is likely to be an element of self-interest. All employees want the best for their information service, and they may feel aggrieved, for example, if sometimes theirs is not the winning department when resources are allocated.

Leaders need to learn the political game if they are to be successful. More particularly, in wanting to be successful, they are anxious to play the game for the benefit of their service. Leaders need the support of their immediate colleagues. If they can create the conditions in which the service is seen to be successful, it first and foremost results in a sense of pride within the staff. In healthy organizations, this feeling should run throughout the workplace. By contrast, a staff that lacks pride is probably an unhappy staff lacking in confidence and not performing at an optimal level. Dissatisfaction and unhappiness will set in, with the result that work time becomes polluted with discussion about "the problem." When this happens, works slows down, output is lowered, and the morale of the staff sinks even further. It's a downward spiral. Users sense what is happening—and a growing number will find alternative ways to meet their information needs. The second reason is simply that any leader wants to be seen as performing well. This enhances the leader's confidence and is also infectious.

One essential political skill is the ability to balance the best interest of the service with that of the organization. The staff will be in closer daily contact with the leader than with the governing body, and they will know the level of resources they perceive are needed to operate the service. At the same time, the governing body is charged with making decisions in the perceived best interests of the organization as a whole. No organization is likely to have the level of resources to meet all requests, and so some decisions made by the governing body may well not be to the advantage of the service. The leader faces a difficult challenge in balancing both viewpoints. The challenge is to adopt a strategy that will enhance the competitive advantage of the service. This will benefit both the service and the staff, without alienating either group or, more important, the governing body. It's a balancing act that needs a strategy based on experience, sound up-to-date information and data, and an understanding of power and authority. Power and politics are closely linked, and Drummond (2000, p. 169) makes this point succinctly: "Power rests in the *ability* to achieve intended purposes. Politics concerns *how* capability is mobilized in order to achieve results." (Refer to chapter 2 for a discussion of power and authority.)

The Expert

"You don't empower other people. You don't give other people their freedom. You don't legislate self-esteem. You begin with yourself. You cannot give to others what you have not claimed for yourself. Claim your autonomy, your vision; declare the organization you wish to create. Live that out at every moment. Then, and only then, make it easy for others to do the same. . . . Stop enrolling, start embodying. Enrollment is soft-core colonialism." (Block, 1987, p. xv)

Handling these challenging situations starts with empowerment—first, the leader's empowerment, which enables her to have control over her actions and the environment in which she is operating, and second, the empowerment of the staff. P. Block (1987), writing about positive political skills, discusses empowerment and describes ways to handle situations that are helpful for anyone new to the cut and thrust of organizational politics. He emphasizes the need for the individual to empower himself.

Empowering yourself takes courage. Confronting the unknown and working in a new situation where there can be a sense of uncertainty may produce a feeling of fear. In a sense, professionals in a leadership role may, sometimes, be at a disadvantage in confronting their fear. In an information service, there are always professional tasks waiting to be done, papers to be written, and so on, and it can be all too easy to take refuge in these actions. But they may not be the most appropriate actions to take. Leaders who bury their heads in the sand may feel they are doing something. But it may not be the most urgent action. Reflection should help them realize that their professional training has equipped them with skills, such as interpersonal skills, that will help them overcome the problem. Managerial or supervisory experience will have honed financial and team skills. Together these provide a strong foundation on which to build the skills of organizational politics and self-confidence. Self-confidence develops empowerment, and reflection is an aid to deciding the priorities for action.

So empowerment strengthens the courage to tackle the difficult situations, building support across the organization and gaining influence. Negotiation skills develop. The leader learns when to tackle problems head-on and when being patient may be the wiser tactic.

Remember

A fact of life quickly learned is that a difference of viewpoints and opinions can, and will, emerge from any level in the team and organization—from the bottom to the very top.

Establishing Good Working Relationships

Creating good working relationships is the first action anyone takes when moving into a new post at any level. For a leader, it is vital, starting from the first minute on the job. Internal promotion can be an advantage if there is a group of loyalists who can, and are willing to, provide information and support. There will already be awareness of how the organization works, in general terms, and who the key personnel are. A word of caution that this might be a disadvantage, for information gathered about individuals and departments might have been gained secondhand, be colored by the judgments of others, or be out of date.

Assumptions should be tested. It may be sensible to put this information aside and consider every person or situation in a fresh light.

Incoming leaders may, in a sense, have an advantage, for they start with no, or few, preconceptions about the organization, the department, or their staff. They have a steep learning curve, however, for it takes time to get used to the culture. The textbooks used to say up to two years, but very few today have that luxury. It is more like two months at the most. Even the "honeymoon" period newcomers used to enjoy is shorter or nonexistent today as organizations face rapidly changing situations and often have a suggestion or two for expected (often as soon as possible) actions for the new person.

First impressions leave an image in the mind. They are important. But every new leader comes with a reputation gained from her previous role within the organization, or through the professional grapevine if it is an external appointment. It's often trickier for the leader who comes from an information profession, because the network is comparatively small and lives up to its "information" label. Reputations travel ahead of a new senior colleague. Impression management is the key word. Moving into a new role means the question of image becomes important. Taking into account the organization and its public image, clues picked up during the selection process, and careful thought about the message the new incumbent wants to give out helps in identifying an appropriate image. If it is a promotion from within, the new leader may well feel the need to look just a bit more formal in some way. As a new recruit, it is probably better to be just a little more formal than to be seen as being casual or informal. Dressing down later, if this is appropriate, is easier than going formal. We live in an age where image is important. Meeting the boss and the team on a first day can be daunting, but when the new person knows he looks good, then this makes him feel more comfortable and helps him relax—just a little.

The new leader needs to get people on side as soon as possible. Making time to talk with team members one on her one provides useful insights into matters such as outstanding challenges and the relationship between time spent on work activities and the perceived priorities (sometimes the two do not match up). Meetings with individuals supplement group meetings. Together they help the new leader establish her ideas. The key is to enthuse, inspire, and motivate—both the boss and the work team—while working out strategies for development. Giving out the right signals, by the way she dresses and the responses she makes, is vital. People watch for any hint of intentions. The staff will want to know something about their new leader, and how he likes to work in a short general meeting, before talking with him on a one-on-one basis. Their views need to be heard and assessed. It is vital to know what they feel strongly about, and it's a rash person who forgets the golden rule: Don't make any promises before you understand what you are promising. People remember them.

The leader builds up loyalty and trust from her work team. In any political situation the trust and support of team members is vital. An incoming leader needs to be aware that the team will have developed its own grapevines and networks before she arrived. Their opinions can influence the perceived power of the leader.

The community served must be central to the thinking of the leader. Showing the flag at the earliest opportunity gains the support of users; asking them what they like about the service and getting them to talk provide sound first impressions. Again, it is sensible advice not to make rash promises to users; they will have some ideas about the future and can offer important input regarding forward planning. It is human to feel that a new person will probably provide a better service. At the outset it is an information-gathering exercise on the part of the new leader, talking with the community served to inform impressions. But it also needs to be a regular part of the routine. Good advice is to get to know the users, as they can be the best allies. It is also not good politics to neglect to identify the ex-users and nonusers and talk with them. People in the community will be members of committees and can champion the service. And they will almost certainly be providing feedback to the top levels of the organization. Their support is essential in fighting for resources because they have a strong vested interest that may be weaker for other departments. The new leader ensures that the community knows he has arrived and has the interests and needs of the community at the core of planning. Visibility matters.

Meeting the person, or group, the leader reports to takes careful preparation, particularly if it is to a governing board. Clearly a good impression must have been made during the selection process. Matching this with information gained during the appointment process, and given time to gather more information, the leader can formulate a message to give to the governing body. It should certainly be a message they will want to hear, but the astute leader ensures that expectations are not set too high. It is better to underpromise and overdeliver at a later date than vice versa. The leader needs to encourage the trust of members of the governing board, be honest in dealings with them, and give reassurance that they made the right decision when the appointment was made. The leader needs to listen carefully to the message she is giving. Sometimes it may not be what is expected, so the leader should make sure the message has been heard correctly, with all the nuances understood, and that lines of communication and preferred methods of reporting are clear.

A trickier group to get to know is the peer group within the organization. Members of the peer group will sit on the same committees as the new leader, and sometimes they will be rivals when resources are allocated. Building a friendly relationship at the outset gives a little breathing time to observe them in meetings or committees and to catch up with internal minutes and other documents. Time spent doing homework and preparation can gain dollars later.

Among the constituencies the leader needs to make contact with is the profession at large. Members of the profession are likely to sit on advisory boards and can be good political allies. It is possible that they may sit on state or federal committees that control grants. They may be people the leader can talk with when he needs friendly advice.

It takes energy and enthusiasm to make real contact with the large number of people who play different roles that affect the daily work of the service and the parent organization. And it takes time—and there is not a lot of it. A great deal of information will need to be absorbed and analyzed, both for immediate and future use. Good communication skills, particularly listening and reading body language, are essential. And information may have a short shelf life, so setting up a system to gather data from internal and external sources is essential for becoming a successful politician. The causes that should be supported within the organization, the profession, and the community at large should be identified. The leader has time limitations, so causes should be selected carefully. Interests can always be expanded, but cutting back is not a smart idea.

Remember

Effective leaders gather information in order to monitor the external operating environment. This is a vital input to the planning process.

Gathering Information

A considerable flow of information comes from people within the organization. The good politician invests time and energy in gathering information from people within the department, the governing body, and across the organization. Being in contact across the organization is perhaps less easy than it was in the days when structures were hierarchical. Flatter structures generally mean there are more people who are in a position to influence the political climate. Gathering accurate and useful information is vital, and managers and supervisors play a role in ensuring that data concerning the operation of the service is up to date and readily accessible to the leader. It helps to accurately read the behavior of other people who are in influential and decision-making roles. Recognizing the hidden agendas and how to operate effectively within the formal and the informal decision-making processes must be quickly learned.

Taken together, the external and internal information flow informs strategy and decision making—one is of no value without the other. The successful leader knows the contribution that information makes to political game playing. And information professionals also recognize the problems of information overload and the importance of organizing information effectively. They therefore have an advantage in handling the flow of "soft" information they receive. It is a challenge that has increased with the growth of e-mail, e-groups, voicemail, cell phones, blogs, wikis, and, no doubt, the newer approaches that will have been introduced by the time you read this text. The range of sources and the immediacy of reaction that is expected add to the complexity of the politics. Being up to date is vital. And this increased flow of information is in addition to internal planning documents and budgets; briefing papers and agendas for meetings (and their subsequent minutes); keeping up with the professional literature and the management literature; and scanning newspapers, journals, and correspondence. Forming sound judgments based on this information takes time. We read of executives who dare not travel on holiday without their mobiles and laptops. But this isn't a healthy way of life. We all need to get away to recharge our batteries. The savvy politician knows that time away is essential, but it doesn't stop him from thinking when sitting on a long-distance flight. And there is probably less human administrative support than in the past. Not everyone has a highly skilled personal assistant to relieve some of the load, but there may be enthusiastic young interns who can provide valuable support.

Time management and speed-reading are vital skills. Taking a refresher course as part of a continuing professional development commitment is a good investment and pays dividends.

Remember

As well as gathering information, consider the public relations and marketing aspects of the service. Giving out information helps win arguments and debates. A skillful PR and advocacy campaign among stakeholders pays dividends. Check out general texts. One written for information professionals is Lisa A. Wolfe's *Library Public Relations, Promotions, and Communications: A How-to-Do-It Manual*, 2nd ed. (New York, Neal-Schuman, 2005).

Organizational Culture and Climate

Understanding how an organization works informally forms a steep learning curve for a new recruit to an organization who is moving into a leadership position. Even if the new recruit possesses good people and professional skills, it is understanding the organization's culture and climate that is a key determinant of the success or failure of a leader, and therefore of the information service. It is an aspect of the new role that isn't fully carried over from a managerial or supervisory position, since at this level the tasks are likely to be centered on matters internal to the service. The leader works across the organization, and in some situations it can be like swimming with sharks.

During the 1960s, writers on management turned their attention to one of the softer aspects of management, the culture and climate of U.S. organizations. In the 1980s the issue emerged again when Peters and Waterman (1982) wrote about the concept of the excellent organization.

Parallel to the research on culture being carried out in the United States in the 1960s, Geert Hofstede, in the Netherlands, developed the concept of culture as being "the software of the mind." He employed the analogy of how computers are programmed, with patterns of thinking, feeling, and acting mental programs forming this software of the mind. "A person's behavior is only partially determined by his or her mental programs(s): he has a basic ability to deviate from them, and to react in ways which are new, creative, destructive, or unexpected" (1997, p. 4). Hofstede formulated the view that culture is a collective phenomenon "because it's at least partly shared with people who live or lived within the same social environment, which is where it is learned. *It is the collective programming of the mind which distinguishes the members of one group or category of people from another*" (p. 5). This concept can be carried over into organizational culture and climate, thereby illuminating the ways people behave.

Check This Out

See Geert Hofstede's *Culture and Organizations: Software of the Mind* (New York: McGraw-Hill, 1997) for a deeper understanding of organizational culture and diversity, as well as www.geert-hofstede.com (accessed May 1, 2006).

Picking up the nuances of the organizational culture is essential. Some early clues emerge from the image presented in publications such as the annual report or the organization's website. More understanding is gained when being interviewed for a position. The way the recruitment process is organized, what is said and not said, and the nature and depth of the questioning all yield impressions. Other factors come to light during an induction program, or the sessions at which a new leader is introduced to their peers, and committee meetings. Listen for the way that members of the peer group address the boss and members of the governing board—is it formal or informal? But learning "the way we do things here" takes a little time and comes through osmosis—observing, listening, and reading. Gaining an understanding of the informal characteristics and interactions within the complex world of both the parent organization and the information service within that organization makes it possible for the leader to operate effectively. The leader can't know or begin to understand the workings of any organization without being aware of both its formal and informal characteristics. And as they change almost imperceptibly over time, staying aware of these changes increases leader effectiveness.

Understanding the culture of an organization presents challenges because it is derived from three sources. The first source is its history—its foundation and the beliefs, assumptions, and values that build up over time. The second source is the learning experience of the staff as the organization evolves. Finally there are the beliefs, values, and assumptions brought in by new members. Together they produce the three dimensions of culture that Schein (2004) defines as follows:

The assumptions: the ingrained views in our subconscious of human nature and social relationships

The values: the preferred outcomes and how they can be achieved

The artifacts: the rituals, traditions, and myths

All organizations have their unique unwritten and unspoken approaches to how they operate. This is generally articulated by longstanding staff members as being "the way we do things here."

The Expert

Sannwald (2000, p. 9) defines organizational culture as
- Who we are as an organization, or "Us"
- How we became "Us"
- What makes us "Us" and not "Them"
- How we recruit new members and socialize them to become "Us"
- How we perpetuate "Us"

The organizational culture has four functions (Sannwald, 2000):

- It gives members of the organization identity.
- It provides a collective commitment to the organization.
- It builds social stability, which is the extent to which the work environment is perceived to be positive and reinforcing.
- It allows people to make sense of the organization.

There is likely to be another variable in the organizational culture that revolves around the different departments. Although networked organizations have broken down many of the previous historical barriers, some still exhibit the silos of the past. Each department may form a silo, and sometimes information does not necessarily pass between the silos. Within the departments, the staff will have their own culture, which can resemble a tribe with its own customs, terminology, and ways of operating. This is not surprising if you consider the information professions. They consist of archivists, knowledge managers, librarians, record managers, and other specialists, with each group having its own traditional practices and terminology. Historical development and conditioning during professional training create their unique identities. They probably talk more easily with members of their own professional groups than they do with other professional groups within the organization, such as accountants or lawyers.

Remember

Two of the crucial success factors for leaders center on the organizational culture. The first factor is whether it is easy to quickly identify the key features of the organization that are necessarily unrecorded (i.e., the soft side). The second factor is that introducing change requires an understanding of the organizational culture—the hows, the whys, the whos. It's a major challenge.

You might reasonably assume that moving between organizations in the same sector makes it easier to settle in. Experience indicates that this is not necessarily so, and it is dangerous to assume that it will be. It can be tricky to instantly spot any differences in culture between two organizations in the same sector, since it is easy to make assumptions based on earlier experience. Leaders need to consciously unlearn all that they learned about their previous organizations. Globalization produces a good example in the legal sector, where one legal firm may have its foundation in an English practice and another have its roots in the United States.

Lory Block (2003) examined the connection between leadership and culture, commenting that there has been little research into the relationship between the two. However, some tentative conclusions have emerged from research:

- The impact of leadership on an organization's performance is mediated by the organizational culture.
- Contextual factors such as organizational culture have an impact on the emergence of specific leadership styles.
- Leaders use their knowledge of organizational culture to effect change.
- The behaviors of leaders influence the perceptions of organizational culture among followers.

Block comments that there is a surprising degree of consistency among these proposed conclusions.

The organizational climate changes more frequently and is easier to understand than the culture. It is more visible, since the climate reflects the ways in which an organization handles its environment and its people. Examples are the decision-making process, the managerial style, and the attitudes that pervade the organization. The climate consists of shared perceptions; the culture consists of shared assumptions.

Central to the culture are the values that are embedded, and generally indicated, in the organization's mission statement. This will demonstrate its approach to the community it serves, to employees, and to the wider community at large. Values are unlikely to change to any great extent over time.

The climate reflects the ethical stance adopted at an organizational level. What is ethically correct behavior, and how should ethical issues be handled? We have noticed how this has become of increasing importance in the past decade as a reaction to the unethical behavior uncovered in some large corporations. *Openness, trust, personal accountability*, and *responsibility* are words to be found in a statement of ethics.

One issue that service providers may face in the information sector lies in a potential conflict between professional ethics and organizational ethics. This might, for example, revolve around who can be provided with a service or under what conditions a person may have access to external databases. There may, on occasion, be conflicts with external agencies (e.g., in terms of some requests from law enforcement officials).

Culture and climate clearly affect how internal politics are played out. Without an effective involvement in organizational politics, the leader may be less successful in gaining resources and is unlikely to bring about change. Raising the morale of the team, meeting internal competition, increasing internal communication, and overcoming noncooperation and feelings of powerlessness all bring success. If the leader fails to play the game effectively, the productivity of the team will fall, and this moves into a downward spiral as people become demoralized and lose focus.

Understanding Governance and Knowing Where the Power Lies

We discussed power in chapter 2 and now turn to formal power in relation to governance. (Refer to chapter 2 for a description of the theoretical bases of power and authority.)

Governance represents the explicit chain of control and authority within an organization. It generally consists of a structure of a governing board, with members drawn from senior executives and representatives of stakeholders. This will be supported by one or more committees at a lower level in the hierarchy, such as department heads and managers. It is structure specific, having rules and procedures set down for decision making, together with the rights and responsibilities of the members of the boards and committees. In this way the organization has a structure within which objectives can be set and performance monitored.

In terms of governance, there are four terms that relate to control. These are authority, accountability, responsibility, and power.

Definitions

Authority is ``the capacity to invoke compliance in others on the basis of formal position and any psychological rewards, inducements, or sanctions that may accompany formal position'' (Presthus, 1962, p. 123).

Accountability and responsibility are not identical. A person is always completely accountable, but responsibility has a dual character. Responsibility is always shared. An individual or unit has the responsibility or obligation to do something, but the individual or unit assigning that responsibility always retains a portion of responsibility (Evans, Layzell Ward, and Rugaas, 2000, p. 201).

Power is the judicious use of influence to get things done through people (Kotter, 1977, p. 135). Kotter's definition can be more colloquially expressed as ``You scratch my back, and I'll scratch yours.''

The more difficult question is to determine where power lies. Where are the decisions really made? Who controls the agenda?

Power is another term like *leadership*—it is more easily recognized than described. In the days when there were more tiers of management in large organizations, power was most likely to reside at the top level. With flatter organizations and a more highly educated workforce, any individual can exert power more easily now than in the past. Power can be acquired informally and exercised without authority. Remember that old but accurate saying: Knowledge is power.

Rereading Machiavelli (1961 edition) shows that many aspects of power haven't changed over the centuries. If a leader has the resources she can stand alone, but if this is not the case, then she needs to strengthen her position and gain allies.

From the viewpoint of the staff of the service, their leader acts as a liaison and a bridge to build strategic alliances within the organization or the wider community. This brings strength when power politics come into play and helps anticipate the next move. It is essential to recognize that power struggles are a fact of life and that a leader must have the capability and skill to produce the desired outcome. In developing the winning strategies, leaders should keep the following in mind:

- Holding the loyalty of the staff is vital—they have their futures at stake and their own grapevines that carry useful information.
- Understand who holds the power behind the throne.
- Identify the key players—know what the power brokers are saying and doing, both publicly and behind closed doors.
- Check facts and the grapevine—and evaluate the source and the origins of this information.
- Be present at the places where decisions are made—both at the formal meetings and at the informal social events.
- Cultivate the art of making points where and when it matters, and do so cogently.
- Ensure others know, and understand, your viewpoint and position on an issue.
- Take care not to lose your cool or put someone down at a meeting or in an e-mail—and that's easier written than achieved when the going gets tough.
- You can be devious, but be underhanded only as the very last resort and in exceptional circumstances.
- Prepare champions and supporters if they are in positions of influence— ensure they are well briefed in adequate time—and pay attention to external members of the governing board.
- Prepare, think, gather words, and then speak. If necessary, prepare cue cards before a meeting and clip them on your notepad—and listen carefully to the response and feedback.

Remember

The reality of organizational life and power is very different from that displayed in an organizational chart. Organizational charts should be seen as mapping relationships, rather than as being a representation of reality. And the real world changes over time even if the chart doesn't. People come and go, alliances form and break up, and changes happen that can make any department "flavor of the month."

Power can reside in a number of places within the service or the organization, and it may not be in the obvious places. Symbols often provide a clue (e.g., who has their own office or PA). (At one time the British civil service laid down standards for office furnishings. The style and color of your chair denoted your grade, for example—people were clearly labeled. It was very useful when visiting offices in other departments or locations, and perhaps a motivator for promotion.) More commonly today the symbol is likely to be the allocation of a parking bay and where it is located. Benefits such as interstate or overseas conference attendance can be symbols of rank, another indicator of power. Among the stakeholders, those who are active in trade unions or representatives of other employee organizations will have a degree of power.

Some people will shape their image to indicate how they perceive their power. At one extreme is the very smart executive who selects designer gear, and at the other is the executive who chooses to dress very informally, giving out the message "I don't need to look good." They are both playing politics.

Aside from indications that are given by symbols, identifying the power brokers comes from listening—hearing the talk around the watercooler and what the staff and colleagues are saying; listening to the grapevine and what is said, or not said, at meetings. It is essential to attend all meetings of all relevant committees. Carefully reading the briefing papers and minutes of meetings pays dividends.

Social contacts build good relationships with the people above and around you, with the staff of the service, and within the community served. Picking up useful information at social events and work-related networks outside the office adds to the picture of the power base within the organization.

Uncovering the power base is vital for new leaders. They need to identify the core group who can either help or make life extremely difficult (Kleiner, 2003). Krackhardt and Hanson (1993) make a useful suggestion. They indicate that power in organizations can be harnessed by diagramming three networks: the *advice network*, which reveals the people whom others turn to for advice; the *trust network*, which indicates who shares delicate information; and the *communication network*, which shows who talks about work-related matters.

One visible indicator of power is a degree of control over resource allocation, particularly of finance and space. The size of a budget controlled by one department, in the eyes of other departments, places them in a pecking order of power. However, high-spending departments may be vulnerable to raiding, particularly if there is an alliance of smaller departments that are perceived to be successful. (We recall the expected power of university science departments that need large budgets for equipment, compared with the power of alliances between arts and social science departments.) Increasingly, services in the information sector also draw external funding to add to that allocated from central sources within the organization. Grants are obtained from external agencies, and an income may be derived from services paid for by users, such as photocopying, printing, and coffee bars. Donors or "friends" may provide endowments, or make annual or one-time payments, to publicly funded services. Generally, these external funds are spent at the discretion of the service. Even though the allocated budget for the information service may not be as large as that of other departments, the entrepreneurial leader can enhance his status and power by gaining external funding. Governing bodies and committees see this as strength, as does the team, if it is earmarked funding skillfully deployed.

The space occupied by the information service can also be an indicator of its power and influence. Location may be more important than the size of the space. The quality of the fittings and furniture is another indicator. (Some special libraries in government departments are now less visible than they were in the past when more users had to visit in person, but the libraries in some large law firms have been fitted out to be a prestigious space.)

Leaders also gain power in less visible ways. Building dependency is another route. In the information sector, the service should be core to the parent organization. Examples include government and business, which need an efficient records management center to serve as their organized memory as well as knowledge management, which is a key service in the private and health care sectors. In the public sector, the community at large wants their local authority to provide archives and library services. School and education libraries are at the center of learning. This creates a built-in dependency, and stakeholder support that can be drawn on when arguments are being made for resources. The nature of the information sector also adds another significant element of power. Experts who operate in this field have an understanding of information skills, emerging technologies, management, and the subject field of the organization. Leaders and their staff should be, and must remain, well informed.

Another aspect of power that can be employed is psychological dependency. Being present, being well informed, being a good communicator, and presenting the right image can link with interpersonal skills to ensure the leader is invited to major events within the organization, the profession, and the community at large. Demonstrating these competencies means that invitations for public speaking flow in. The governing body's respect for the leader grows, knowing she can be depended on to represent and promote the interests of the organization.

The more times the leader wins, the more loyalty flows from the staff and the more influence is gained within the peer group. Peers do not necessarily see information professionals as being a threat. However, having the support of their users and a range of transferable and professional skills of value to other departments means they can be good allies. Being visible, but possibly less threatening than others, builds alliances.

Just a word of warning—one professional trait that can emerge is that of being "too nice." We can give power away to those around and above us and perhaps find it difficult to be direct. It can be a challenge in very competitive and macho cultures.

Networking and Visibility

Gathering information is supported by networking. Networking makes the connections that create a web of contacts. The higher up the ladder, the more vital the contacts. Not just any contacts, but the right contacts. Networking also brings relationships with those who have similar interests. An effective network should include people at the same level in the organization, in the constituencies served in the wider community, and in the profession. All can yield information or opportunities—for the organization, for the service, and for the leader. The network helps determine the views of the peer group, because it is likely to meet casually (e.g., at receptions, social events, and before and after business meetings). It provides a means to lobby for support and to get to know key people informally ahead of formal meetings. Networking in the professional community can bring news of opportunities for the service (e.g., grants and awards). It may bring awareness of possibilities for further advancement. Leaders know that getting out of the office is essential, as is the need to socialize. Leaders must be aware of what colleagues and team members are thinking. They lobby supporters. Not all the information sought may be found, and some in the network won't play fair. But over time the leader comes to realize who can be trusted by their actions rather than their words. Being a valued member of a network is important, and this is achieved through the following:

- Treating others as you would like to be treated
- Ensuring that you give as much as you take
- Keeping in touch with the network rather than using it only when you need something (e-mail makes it easy to maintain contact)
- Helping others make connections in the network
- Being unselfish and giving time without expecting a return
- Expanding your network—as interests change, so should your contacts
- Remembering networks should be of mutual benefit to all members—trust and reciprocity are vital

Two benefits will emerge. The first is integration into the organization, and the second is a high level of job satisfaction.

Some of the most enjoyable and rewarding networks we have experienced have been in the management and business sectors, which often meet over breakfast. Going out for breakfast makes a good start to the day. There is usually an interesting and informative speaker, an opportunity for an informal exchange of ideas and information, and the chance to meet newcomers to the community.

At one time the issue of networking surfaced for women and ethnic minorities who were in leadership roles. Breaking through the glass ceiling was said to be difficult because of limited opportunities to network—the old story of the men's locker room. But the situation changed as new networks emerged to meet new needs. With a wider awareness of diversity issues coupled with a greater sharing of family responsibilities, this question now emerges less frequently. And networks have developed among women and ethnic minorities.

Decision Making

Making decisions is an everyday action. Making them in a leadership role presents greater challenges. Balancing the immediate needs of the service, which may be short term, against the longer-term needs for the future can be tricky. Decisions are influenced by organizational politics. Nondecisions are a subtle form of power.

Decisions can be divided into two types. The first is easier to handle, for it consists of the structured decisions that can be resolved from known rules (e.g., overseeing the preparation of the annual budget). The more challenging are the unstructured decisions that can't be solved by using rules. One example to consider is forward planning and formulating the vision of what the service will look like in, say, three years' time. In theory, decision making involves six steps:

1. Define the problem and analyze the constituent parts.
2. Clarify and prioritize the goal.
3. Consider all the possible ways to achieve the goal.
4. Evaluate all the options, considering what would happen if . . . ?
5. Compare the consequences of each option with the goal.
6. Select the option with the outcomes that most closely match the goal.

But that is in theory; in practice it is likely that a limited number of options are selected. The one that is chosen is the one that "will do," an action Simon labels "satisficing" (Drummond, 2000, p. 173). In the real world, a crisis can precipitate a decision, while longer-term and perhaps more important problems get forced to one side for the moment. Risk enters into the process, and Bazerman (2002) describes prospect theory, which infers that the manner in which a problem is formulated determines the behavior of the decision maker.

Another myth of decision making is that decisions are based on "good" information. But our experience indicates that information may be selective, may be partial, may come from an unreliable or undocumented source, and may be incomplete. Sometimes information may be brought forward at a later date to justify an earlier decision. It can depend on the organizational politics at the time. And sometimes the leader can be fed inaccurate data.

Having considered these points and worked through the process of making an important decision, the best one, in the judgment of the leader, may well be the one that is not acceptable to the majority of stakeholders. Introducing a change may not always appear to be acceptable at the outset (e.g., a change in the hours of service or the introduction of a new technology). In the longer term the change may bring benefits for staff or users, but at the outset it could be unpopular. If the outcome would bring savings in the budget, the changes could be very acceptable to the governing body and so win some brownie points for "a good decision." There are also some decisions that are made on grounds of expediency.

The skills of the lobbyist come into play in gaining acceptance for decisions. Identifying the key decision makers in the group, listening to the grapevine, sounding out people who will be affected by the outcomes, and talking up the issue will yield feedback on likely reactions to the issue under consideration. Sometimes this may mean that the nature of the decision must be modified to be acceptable to the majority. Possible opposition may well come to light, requiring that political tactics be formulated to deflect this and win the debate. On occasion it may be found that others have similar thoughts, and so an alliance can be formed and their support encouraged. Perhaps a coalition is built from departments having similar interests and views. Notice how lobbyists get active around the time that the annual budget is set. Good listening skills coupled with the ability to make clear proposals, in a relaxed manner, are assets of the lobbyist. Being realistic and at the same time persistent in gathering reactions shapes the tactics for a win.

The Expert

"It's time to acknowledge that it's impossible for any individual to make fully informed decisions about running vast entities like large firms and nations. Leaders do, of course, have a role to play—inspiring the troops, building teams, representing the organization. But when it comes to organizational decision making, maybe America's national motto, *E pluribus unum*, can be used to new effect: From many voices, one better decision." (Prusak, 2005, p. 22)

Working at the service level in a team environment, or with a peer group at an organizational level, reveals the impact people have on the decisions to be made.

Status differentials can affect interaction within the group; this is the level at which people place themselves within the group. In an open climate few people are likely to hold back, but generational factors can intervene, and new members of the team may be more hesitant or, by contrast, eager to make an impression. There are also the group norms to consider: what the group sees as acceptable and unacceptable. The culture of the group is paramount. Groups will be swayed by each other's contributions to discussion, and some members will have louder voices than others; some will have a stronger vested interest if the decision affects their work more than it does for other members of the team. Over time "groupthink" may emerge, where there is an involuntary suppression of individual thinking. The emergence of groupthink is a warning sign for leaders.

Not everyone will agree with the final decision, and there will always be disagreement based on how individuals are personally affected by the intelligence that informed the decision, the interpretation of that intelligence, and the differing preferences and values they hold. Political tactics help to win the situation. Winning depends on providing accurate information that stands up to scrutiny, building up support within the team or peer group, knowing where the resistance is likely to come from and deflecting it, and presenting the case lucidly and knowing it so well that it can be effectively defended in debate. The aim is to achieve a win-win outcome.

Remember

A major influence on decision making is the organizational culture the service operates in. New leaders must work hard to understand how the organization works. Organizations operate in explicit ways (e.g., making decisions through committees) and also have informal ways of influencing decisions by lobbying key decision makers (some will carry more weight than others). Organizations are multifaceted, and identifying the facets is essential, even if it is not an easy task. Without this understanding, the leader will be less effective in this role.

Learning about politics from a professional politician is a great experience. One respondent to our survey had a politician as a mentor, who taught the library administrator to understand the essential questions that should be asked when making decisions.

Negotiation

Negotiation follows from decision making and lobbying. And while everyone likes to win, experience indicates that it may be better to yield ground sometimes on the less important issues in order to win the more important points. This applies within both the team and the peer group. It is good advice to lose a few battles to win a war or two, but a leader must know exactly how much ground she is prepared to give. A wise leader has a contingency plan and a fallback position, and she is flexible and prepared to change a position quickly after some fast thinking about the potential outcomes. Sticking to an opinion all the time, every time doesn't help to develop and maintain good working relationships, and any allies will quickly melt away. This affects the staff of the service, who may shy away from providing feedback if their leader's influence appears to be lessening. It is disastrous for anyone in a leadership position to lose feedback.

The Experience of Being Mentored

''I did have an influential mentor when I was an administrator in Canada. He has influenced my work in library administration. This individual was on the board to which I reported, and was a senior leader in a transportation union, and was a member of the Alberta legislature. He showed me the value and function of protocol and helped me to ask the ''protocol'' questions related to decision making that fostered optimal ways to interact with others inside and outside an organization. More specifically, he brought to my leadership style a clear focus on the nature and role of the ''political'' dimension of administration. Protocol and political questions I now ask include: Who needs to be consulted? Who needs to know? What conversations need to occur, and with whom, and where? What is the best time frame for decision making, and what are the timelines that need to be followed? How does the decision or action look to others? When do you stand your ground, and when do you seek compromise? There are many other questions, but these are some of the key ones.'' (survey respondent)

But it isn't easy for a new leader to strike a balance between winning and losing while, at the same time, coming to grips with the organizational culture. If the negotiation fails, then the leader must be prepared to engage in damage limitation.

In negotiation, the skills to influence people come into play. The leader wants people to see his point of view and gain support for it, or perhaps persuade them to come around to his viewpoint. It requires an understanding of the differing views and positions gained by listening, and then developing an argument for a change in the other person's stance on the issue. A good working relationship is a start, especially if the affiliation doesn't depend on being called on only when something is wanted. Reciprocity forms a backbone to a relationship. Gathering information in order to be able to appreciate the other person's viewpoint backs this up. Being able to talk in a relaxed atmosphere, listening carefully, and knowing the issue so well that it can be articulated clearly and logically helps the negotiation. Perhaps that is why serious negotiation often starts over lunch or a coffee. Truth and honesty are vital when working within an organization, as any digression can return to haunt at a later date. Being positive, pointing out the benefits that can be gained without exaggeration, and being prepared to encounter disagreement helps the process of negotiation. One essential trait is having the ability to enthuse and inspire, and another is to ensure that the other person leaves feeling good. This helps win people over.

There is good sense in Ertel's (2004) advice to shift from the mind-set that concentrates on making a deal to one that shifts to implementing it. Given the range and size of the contracts that an information service enters into today, his five approaches will be useful when entering into negotiation:

1. Start with the end in mind. Imagine the deal twelve months out: What has gone wrong? How do you know if it's a success? Who should have been involved earlier?
2. Help them prepare, too. Surprising the other side doesn't make sense because if they promise things they can't deliver, you both lose.
3. Treat alignment as a shared responsibility. If your counterpart's interests aren't aligned, it's your problem, too.
4. Send one message. Brief implementation teams on both sides of the deal together so everyone has the same information.
5. Manage negotiation like a business process. Combine a disciplined preparation process with postnegotiation reviews.

Try This

Go back to chapter 2 and reread the discussion on influence tactics. Consider the types of manager that Kipnis and his colleagues describe, then reflect on your own managerial or supervisory experience. Which type best describes you—and be very honest. Which influence tactics do you need to develop?

Kipnis et al. (1984) differentiate between four types of people based on the way they use different influence tactics. *Bystanders* rarely use any influence tactics, have low organizational power, have limited personal and organizational objectives, and are frequently dissatisfied. *Shotguns* use all the influence tactics all the time, have unfulfilled goals, and are inexperienced in their job. *Captives* use only one or two "favorite" tactics, out of habit and with limited effectiveness. *Tacticians*, however, make high use of rational appeal and average use of other tactics, are successful in achieving their objectives, have high organizational power, and tend to be satisfied in their work.

Buchanan and Badham (1999, pp. 63–64) draw attention to influence tactics identified by Kipnis et al., which are summarized here:

Assertiveness. Order the person to do it. Point out that the rules demand it. Keep reminding him about what is required.

Ingratiation. Make the request politely and humbly. Act friendly and complimentary before asking. Sympathize with any hardship that may result for the person.

Rational appeal. Write a detailed justification. Present relevant information in support. Explain the reasoning behind your request.

Sanctions. Threaten to get the person fired. Threaten to block her promotion. Threaten with a poor performance evaluation.

Exchange. Offer an exchange of favors: mutual backscratching. Remind him of the favors you have provided in the past.

Upward appeal. Get higher-level management to intervene on your behalf. Send the person to speak to your boss.

Blocking. Threaten to stop working with the person. Ignore her and stop acting friendly. Withhold collaboration until she does what you want.

Coalition. Get the support of colleagues. Make the request in a formal meeting where others will support you.

Try This

Think about the influence tactics shown previously. Which are likely to be the most appropriate for anyone in a leadership role?

Partnerships, Alliances, and Coalitions

Creating effective partnerships, coalitions, and alliances is an essential political skill. Think about the way political parties operate. Political parties set their priorities based on their beliefs, which have developed over time. Each party has different causes that it debates. This process sharpens views, which in turn improves the quality of decision making on behalf of the people. It is echoed within organizations, and often within the information service, when different approaches to desired outcomes emerge. When space and budgets are allocated, the process often surfaces. Everyone party to the debate will bat for his own team, and this is natural. Participation in the formal debate at meetings is a given, but discussion also takes place behind closed doors, where alliances may

be formed. It is a tricky area for newcomers, and it follows closely behind learning where the power resides and identifying the power brokers.

Investing time and energy in developing working relationships, at all levels
within and across the organization and in the wider community, is very worthwhile when emphasis is placed on *working* relationships. They need to be continuing relationships. This is when well-honed communication skills, based on
reading people and situations, come into play. Drawing on relevant information;
observing people meeting in both formal and informal situations; and hearing
what they are, and are not, saying helps identify potential partners in the relationship. And, too, it is essential to bear in mind the hidden agendas that usually
exist. The information service has to flourish if it is to support the needs of the
parent organization. This means that other people are likely to have a vested
interest in the health of the information service. The leader needs supporters
and, more important, champions. But what may be good for the department
may not be good for the organization as a whole. The leader has two loyalties
to balance in a complex situation.

The type of relationship matters, and using the right term defines the nature
of the relationship. A *partnership* indicates a common shared interest. An *alliance*
is stronger since it indicates an agreement between one or more partners. The
most formal and strongest relationship is the *coalition*, where a number of parties
with a mutual interest form a temporary agreement to further that interest.
Moving beyond a working relationship where common interests may be discussed and information shared is rather akin to considering marriage, not to be
lightly entered into.

In many instances the archives, information service, library, or records center has low costs compared with other departments. It lacks the power of having
a large budget. It is a service, and not all information services are revenue generating. So it may be beneficial to form a liaison with another department to
maximize strength at the bargaining table (i.e., the committees and places where
decisions are made). The nature of the liaison will depend on the issue, the
organizational culture and climate, and the level of trust that exists in the relationship. In the case of alliances and coalitions, binding agreements need to be
set out before tactics are discussed and put in place. Agreements that are not
binding may well turn out to be unstable.

Partnerships, alliances, and coalitions come into play most commonly in
the work of committees that generally form the decision-making bodies within
the organization. Committees exist at different levels, from those within the
team to the highest level of governance. They are the public face of politics.
Learning to work with committees comes with experience and probably a few
bruises along the way.

Gaining a benefit from a committee involves making a decision on a set of issues. For each issue placed on a meeting agenda, there will be a number of possible courses of action and outcomes. No course of action is likely to be supported by all the committee members. The leaders know what they want, but they also try to establish what others want by using working relationships, networking, the grapevine, observation, and so on. However, when every member of the committee knows what each of the others wants, then saying what you think and doing what comes naturally is probably the easiest way to lose the argument. It is easy to be outsmarted, since the other members will take your probable action into account when they make their moves. The leader needs to think about what the others are likely to do, and which members are taking into account what the leader is likely to do, ad infinitum. . . .

Remember

Leaders work to gain maximum benefit for their team while bearing in mind the well-being of the total organization. This is not always easy to achieve.

No leader is likely to have reached his position without some experience of the ways in which committee work can be manipulated. Being nominated as the chair of a committee can bring both disadvantages and advantages. When it comes to voting, the chair will have only a casting vote. He cannot propose motions. His influence lies in deciding the agenda and the order of items on the agenda. When observing committees at work, we have noted that the higher on the agenda an item is placed, the more likely it is that it will fail since more time may be allowed for discussion at the start of a meeting. The lower the item on the agenda, the more pressed the committee is likely to be for time, and so a decision may be passed more easily. The chair has control of the meeting and so selects or rejects speakers or curtails discussion. He can wield this considerable influence while being perceived as neutral.

Committee members will be free to form partnerships, alliances, and coalitions ahead of the meeting. Watching the body language around the table can sometimes identify the relationships, as can a careful scrutiny of the minutes of earlier meetings and an awareness of who is talking to whom in the lunchroom or canteen. Committee members can raise items for the agenda and provide briefing papers. At the meeting they can make proposals or second proposals; speak to motions; propose amendments; and use procedural motions such as a motion for recess or, in extreme cases, a vote of no confidence in the chair. If information needs to be revealed to the committee, then skillful members will ensure that it is hard to interpret accurately or to be verified on the spot. An excellent training ground for leaders is university politics, and the older the university the tougher the politics. Powerful coalitions emerge that influence the allocation of resources or decisions about sensitive matters such as the appointment of vice-chancellors.

On the surface, coalitions may appear to be useful groupings, but playing politics at this level requires care. People join a coalition because they want something that is important to them. The parties need to agree on a common goal and on what they want to achieve if the coalition is to be successful. It may be agreement about the allocation of resources or benefits that could flow from a certain person being appointed to a position of power. In terms of resource allocation within universities, there may be a coalition of science departments, or perhaps arts departments. Think of a vice-chancellor and consider that an appointment of someone from his own academic discipline may be seen as desirable to a group of departments.

Each member of the coalition will push her coalition partners toward the agreed decision, but if someone pushes too hard, she may not be considered as a favorable member when the next coalition is formed. Working with a coalition brings advantages and disadvantages, some of which have wider implications. If the leader is seen to lose, then this reflects on her service. So the best interests of the service, and the organization, need to be carefully considered. Leaders do not have the luxury of inaction—it's just not an option in the real world of organizational politics. Consider trust and its implications as well.

Check This Out

Curtis, Susan, "Lies, Damned Lies and Organizational Politics," *Industrial and Commercial Training* 35, no. 7 (2003): 293–297.

Heery (1998) explored the question of how librarians can win financial resources from their parent organizations, stressing the importance of political skills. His tactics will be of interest to other information professionals who face funding challenges.

To this point, working relationships have focused on those formed within the organization, but many of the issues that affect internal relationships and committee work can emerge in extramural situations. In general terms, professional committees are often not benign, despite the public image of the information professional. Within any of the professions there will be vested interests, perhaps based on sectoral issues. Some interests will be influenced by left or right wing political views or by larger or smaller services. All professionals need to develop their political skills, and many do this by joining local professional committees working through regional, national, and perhaps international committee work. An excellent form of continuing professional development, these skills can be applied in the workplace. Contributing to extramural committees brings greater recognition and publicizes the team and the leader's work to a wider audience.

A newer form of partnership within the information professions has emerged as a result of action by national governments. That is the establishment of cross-sectoral bodies that cover archives, libraries, and museums. In the United States, the grant-making Institute of Museum and Library Services promotes innovation and change, and in England it is the Museums, Libraries and Archives Council.

Handling Change and Using Political Skills

Since no organization is ever in a steady state for any length of time, the leader functions as a change agent. We agree with Buchanan and Badham that a change agent who is not politically skilled will fail. Change agents have the ability to take an active part in the political process, pushing their agenda for change, influencing decisions, watching for criticism and challenges, and handling any resistance. Leaders need to be successful when introducing change and also to ensure their reputation is not damaged. Buchanan and Badham (1999, p. 19) carried out a survey focusing on the politics of organizational change, and among the responses the following have particular relevance for information services:

- Change intensifies the politics.
- Managing change is about using interpersonal influence to manage stakeholders who will be affected by changes in different ways and to different degrees.
- The change agent needs well-developed negotiating, persuading, and influencing skills.
- Employees at any level can be influential players in the politics of the organization.

New leaders generally find that their political skills need to be sharpened if they are to operate as effective change agents.

Handling Conflict

Negotiation doesn't always end in success, no matter how much we try using the skills that information professionals learn in order to avoid conflict. In a leadership role, conflict is likely to emerge. Introducing change within the team can produce a disagreement with someone who will be affected by, for example, the introduction of a new procedure or an upgrade in technology. This person may have been comfortable doing a task in her own way, but change is necessary. On other occasions, a team member may have a valid reason for questioning change. Understanding his viewpoint, and the reasons for his resistance to change, is essential as a step toward arriving at an agreed solution. Conflict also arises at an organizational level, perhaps in the allocation of resources between departments, or with the governing body.

Talking and, more important, listening to the other party in a quiet, neutral place may lead to a solution. This may be easier under the following circumstances:

- The discussion is constructive and doesn't get personal.
- The discussion focuses on the problem.
- Facts are obtained.
- The other person's viewpoint is understood (where she is coming from and what impact she sees).
- Effort is made to limit any escalation of the situation.
- There is a sincere intention to avoid a win-lose outcome; instead a win-win solution is sought.
- The value of persuasion, rather than coercion, is kept in mind.

If an agreed way to proceed emerges, this is beneficial. The problem hasn't escalated, both viewpoints have been heard, and a way to proceed has resulted. Both parties can feel there is a win-win situation, and a backlash will have been avoided. Sometimes there may be agreement to disagree if it is recognized that no further action needs to be taken. Conciliation and a way to proceed that is acceptable to both parties should be the preferred outcome.

If this doesn't work, then mediation may provide a solution. Mediation involves a person external to the situation. The mediator may be someone from within the organization that has the necessary skills and experience and is respected by both parties. For example, in a university a counselor may act as a mediator; in other situations the human resources department may provide a trained person. If this fails then the matter should go to conciliation, which means moving into the paralegal field. Problems that may need resolution at this level can emerge from personnel decisions: salary and benefits, promotion, diversity, and so on. Arbitration is the next stage that moves the process outside the organization. The final level of resolution is reached after all other processes have failed and the issue must go to litigation. Aside from personnel matters, issues needing resolution can include questions of copyright, which is becoming more complex in the digital age, and contracts with suppliers.

Getting involved in any form of conflict is time consuming and can incur visible costs. But there is also the invisible cost of the damage it can do to the team and the organization. Think of the cases concerning sex and racial discrimination that have been brought against large corporations and the damage this has done to their reputations. Following bad publicity, the corporations may not be able to attract the highly talented employees they were able to in the past. There is also the aftermath for the leaders. Whatever the outcome, and even if the stand has been justified, there will still be comment and gossip, and time that could have been given to other important matters has dissipated. Getting early resolution helps everyone and builds confidence for the leader.

Two Essential Points

One of the best pieces of advice that comes out of the stories of successful leaders is to underpromise and overdeliver. It keeps the team and the governing body happy. At a time when targets are important to the powers that be, setting targets that can be realistically achieved provides room to create the situation in which they can be exceeded. That brings a glow of pride to everyone and motivates the leader to do even better next time. Set a target that's too high and stress quickly sets in, and if the target is missed then no one is happy. . . . Overdeliver—and you are great! That is the first essential. The second point is to ensure that the interests of the community served are at the forefront of everyone's planning and action. The users are important allies who have political muscle that can be flexed, in support of, or against, the leader's actions.

Summary

No leader can function effectively without developing and using political skills. Understanding the soft and the hard side of the organization and the way this influences how it operates is essential.

Many political skills can be learned only on the job as a leader, and they are honed over time and in different organizational settings. No two are alike. But with time come greater understanding, sensitivity to people and situations, and a personal understanding that adds to the developing skills. Having a good role model and mentor, linked with wide reading on the subject of leadership and of politics, aids the development process.

Playing politics means that being a leader is not always a comfortable situation. There are lows, but with time there will be some considerable highs. Buchanan and Badham (1999, pp. 229–230) drew up a list of political skills:

- Recognition of the value of different and competing approaches to defining and thus understanding power and political behavior in an organizational context
- Understanding of the sources and bases of power, personally and for other members of the organization
- Diagnostic capability, in "reading" the shifting politics of the organization and the changing motives and moves of other stakeholders
- Understanding of how power can be seen to be embedded in social and organizational structures and systems and in routine, everyday practices
- Ability to develop power bases through accumulating appropriate resources and expertise
- Understanding of the combination of factors that warrants political behavior in particular organizational settings
- A behavior repertoire that includes a range of interpersonal skills, such as impression management and influencing techniques
- A behavior repertoire that goes beyond interpersonal skills to include the skill and will to conceive of political strategies and tactics, and to apply these when appropriate
- An "intuitive artistry" in deploying one's behavior repertoire creatively and appropriately to fit the context
- "Positioning" ability, to take and switch roles in relation to change appropriately, to maximize personal advantage, to address opposition, and to drive the change agenda
- Understanding of the trade-offs in the turf game and thus calculating (perhaps intuitively) when it is appropriate to "lose" a play in the game in order to achieve advantage later
- Ability and willingness to construct credible accounts of behavior, if and when challenged to do so, and to refute the potentially damaging accounts of others
- Ability to construct one's reputation as a skilled political player who acts with fairness and integrity, and to maintain and develop that reputation consistently

We agree with their view that political skills involve more than the exercise of interpersonal skills, and we believe this list forms a useful checklist for new leaders.

We'll finish with a quote from Linda Holbeche, director of research and strategy at Roffey Park, which is a charitable trust in the United Kingdom that develops innovative learning approaches to enable individuals to achieve their full potential, both at work and in their wider lives.

The Expert

"Politics is a fact of life in organizations; . . . the organizational challenge is to create a culture which encourages the use of constructive political behavior rather than the negative, self-serving type." (Holbeche, 2004)

References

Bazerman, Max H., *Judgement in Managerial Decision-Making*, 5th ed. (New York: Wiley, 2002).

Block, Lory, "The Leadership-Culture Connection: An Exploratory Investigation," *Leadership & Organization Development Journal* 24, no. 6 (2003): 318–334.

Block, Peter, *The Empowered Manager: Positive Political Skills at Work* (San Francisco: Jossey-Bass, 1987).

Buchanan, Dave, and Richard Badham, *Power, Politics and Organizational Change: Winning the Turf Game* (London: Sage, 1999).

Drummond, Helga, *Introduction to Organizational Behaviour* (Oxford: Oxford University Press, 2000).

Ertel, Danny. "Getting Past Yes: Negotiating as if Implementation Mattered," *Harvard Business Review* 82, no. 11 (November 2004): 60–68.

Evans, G. Edward, Patricia Layzell Ward, and Bendik Rugaas, *Management Basics for Information Professionals* (New York: Neal-Schuman, 2000).

Heery, Mike, "Winning Resources," *Library Management* 19, no. 4 (1998): 252–262.

Hofstede, Geert, *Cultures and Organizations: Software of the Mind* (New York: McGraw-Hill, 1997).

Holbeche, Linda, *The Power of Politics* (Horsham: Roffey Park, 2004), quoted in "Managers Vote for Office Politics," *New York Times*, 21 October 2004, Careers, 2.

Kipnis, David, Stuart M. Schmidt, Chris Swaffin-Smith, and Ian Wilkinson, "Patterns of Managerial Influence: Shotgun Managers, Tacticians, and Bystanders," *Organizational Dynamics* 12, no. 3 (1984): 58–67.

Kleiner, Art, "Are You In with the In Crowd?" *Harvard Business Review* 81, no. 7 (July 2003): 86–92.

Kotter, John P., "Power Dependence and Effective Management," *Harvard Business Review* 55, no. 4 (July/August 1977): 135–136.

Krackhardt, David, and Jeffrey R. Hanson, "Informal Networks: The Company Behind the Chart," *Harvard Business Review* 71, no. 4 (July/August 1993): 104–111.

Machiavelli, Niccolò, *The Prince*, translated by George Bull (London: Penguin, 1961), 71.

Peters, Thomas J., and Robert H. Waterman, *In Search of Excellence: Lessons from America's Best-Run Companies* (New York: Harper & Row, 1982).

Presthus, Robert V., "Authority in Organizations," in *Concepts and Issues in Administrative Behavior*, edited by S. Mailick and E.H. Van Ness (Englewood Cliffs, NJ: Prentice-Hall, 1962).

Prusak, Laurence, "The Madness of Individuals," *Harvard Business Review* 83, no. 6 (June 2005): 22.

Sannwald, William, "Understanding Organizational Culture," *Library Administration and Management* 14, no. 1 (Winter 2000): 8–14

Schein, Edgar H., *Organizational Culture and Leadership*, 3rd ed. (San Francisco: Jossey-Bass, 2004).

CHAPTER 6

Thinking and Acting Strategically

This chapter focuses on the following:

- Why vision is important
- The relationship between vision, values, mission, and strategy
- How to prepare vision, values, and mission statements
- Why strategic thinking and planning are important
- The basics of strategic planning
- How to manage change
- How to make change an organizational way of life

Successful organizations know their purpose, have a sound sense of the future, and develop plans for how to achieve their goals and handle future challenges. The way they accomplish this and communicate their purpose to staff, customers, trustees, and other stakeholders is through a series of interrelated documents—a vision of the future, core values of the organization, the organization's mission, and a strategic plan. It is these documents that provide the direction and the basis for coordinated activities for an organization and, ultimately, its success or failure. Without such guiding documents, scarce resources are not likely to be put to effective use. Leaders play a prominent role in the creation of materials that guide the organization's activities.

There is a relationship between these concepts and documents. A well-formulated vision provides part of the foundation on which to build a strategic plan. Another part of the foundation is the organization's core values, which also play a part, or should, in the organization's vision. The mission statement draws on both the vision and the values to develop the third element in the foundation for a strategic plan. Taken together, these three elements provide the broad general context for developing plans and activities (strategic thinking and planning) that will achieve the broad organizational goals. All these documents carry with them the implication that change will be occurring in the organization. While it is true that all organizations change over time, the successful ones are those that engage in planned change, and the four items just identified are the keys to successful planned change. Essentially, these statements allow leaders to know when they have gotten to where they want to go. Without them there is little sense of direction.

Definitions

The *vision* is a vivid, realistic, credible, and attractive description of the future of an organization.

Core values represent the central priorities and beliefs of an organization and drive the intent and directions of planners.

Mission statements are brief, specific, and actionable descriptions of why the organization exists.

Strategic plans outline where the organization is going over a specified time frame, how it is going to get there, and how it will know when it has achieved those ends.

Why Vision Is Important

As we have noted, all effective leaders are good at developing a vision of the future for their organization or unit. They are also very good at communicating that vision to all concerned. In chapter 1, we quoted Alan Thompson's comment that a difference between managers and leaders is that leaders have a vision. We also reproduced a list of distinctions between managers and leaders developed by Warren Bennis and Joan Goldfield in which words such as *innovate*, *original*, *long-range perspective*, and *horizons* were associated with leaders. To quote Bennis (2003, pp. 31–32) again:

> The first basic ingredient of leadership is a guiding vision. The leader has a clear idea of what he or she wants to do—professionally and personally—and the strength to persist in the face of setbacks, even failures. Unless you know where you're going and why, you cannot possibly get there.

Our survey respondents also made frequent mention of vision, planning, and managing change in their responses about leadership strengths. Their comments include the following:

- Visionary, meaning I know where I want the organization to go, and sharing that vision, meaning soliciting input from others on where we should go
- Initiating and implementing shared vision through strategic planning
- An architect
- Articulate a broad vision
- Value driven
- Embrace change
- Maintain a broad vision and anticipate problems that may arise and attempt to position the library in advance to meet them
- Ability to plan for the future
- Ability to understand and articulate ultimate goals and specific objectives
- Developing visions with people and inspiring them to work toward those visions with me
- Ability to try new things
- Ability to look at the big picture
- Have the success of the organization firmly as my goal and am working to achieve that goal all the time using group planning, altering plans when necessary, and by keeping moving toward our goals
- Carefully plan by way of figuring out as many scenarios as possible for dealing with major events, problems, situations that we might face and then plan what I will do if any of them materialize

Clearly, the respondents see the need for and engage in the activities we cover in this chapter. As leaders of libraries, they understand the value of implementing concepts that are intended to help organizations handle an ever-changing environment. Their responses also suggest that not all libraries are traditional, unchanging organizations that might disappear in the near future because they could not adjust to the world of the 21st century.

Vision statements play a vital role in maintaining a viable organization. At several points throughout this book we have mentioned the pressure on organizations to respond to the varied changes in their operating environments. Like it or not, constant change is a fact of organizational life, and having an up-to-date vision is a key factor in being able to respond to those pressures.

A useful vision statement accomplishes at least three things for the organization. First, it *clarifies* or *sets* the general direction of change and the organization's anticipated future. In the absence of such clarity, the organization is likely to engage in ineffective movement or have disagreements over what is the proper direction. Essentially the statement clears away "planning clutter" and allows staff to clearly focus on what is important. Second, a well-articulated vision will *motivate* people to move in the right direction. Self-interest and being in a "work comfort zone" (lack of interest in changing work activities) will be reduced if not eliminated by an inspiring vision. It will even assist in dealing with very negative events such as major budget reductions or long-term hiring freezes. Finally, by setting a direction, vision statements make it easier to *coordinate* the work of various people and units. Alternative activities disappear, and it is easier to allocate organizational resources to the key tasks.

Bennis and Nanus (1997) devote an entire chapter to the importance of vision for the organization and its leader(s). They note that "a shared vision of the future also suggests measures of effectiveness for the organization and for all its parts. It helps individuals distinguish between what's good and what's bad for the organization, and what it is worthwhile to achieve" (pp. 84–85). They suggest that a leader, by developing and articulating a vision, is operating on the emotional and spiritual resources of an organization (emotional intelligence and values).

Given the importance of vision statements, a natural assumption would be that they are, in fact, well crafted. However, according to Bennis and Nanus that is not always the case. Although their book originally appeared in the mid-1980s, the factors they identify for poor vision statements could have been written today:

- Changing values about the importance of personal and family time
- Changing expectations regarding an organization's social responsibility
- Changing views regarding nonmajority rights
- Changing sense of the work ethic
- Changing technological impact on organizations and their personnel
- Speed of innovation
- Pressure from staff for greater empowerment

The Expert

John Kotter (1996) developed a list of characteristics of an effective vision statement:

- Imaginable
- Desirable
- Feasible
- Flexible
- Communicable

One problem for organizations and their vision statements is the tendency to think the process is over once the vision is developed. Thinking that, especially in today's environment, results in out-of-date and useless statements. Such statements will also lead to staff members' ignoring them as just useless management jargon; they can also create doubts in the minds of outsiders about how well the organization is run. To be useful in planning, a vision statement requires an ongoing process of reviewing and updating. Leaders should periodically ask themselves some of the following questions to help keep the statement current and useful:

- Is the vision still relevant to today's customers and users?
- What do our customers and users expect from us now and in the future?
- Is the document still relevant to other stakeholders (e.g., trustees, governing bodies)?
- Have there been significant changes in technology, economy, and so on that affect the vision?
- Are there significant changes in how the information service interacts with other libraries and information providers that call for changing the vision?
- Does the statement reflect the future or just current needs and desires?

Preparing a Vision Statement

Our definition of *vision* mentions several characteristics that are similar to Kotter's characteristics—vivid, realistic, creditable, and attractive. One failing of many vision statements is they not only lack the foregoing but also are so general in nature one could apply them to any number of organizations without serious modification. Striking the balance between a vision that is neither too specific nor too general is a delicate process. Leaders can follow several steps to generate a useful statement rather than one filled with empty platitudes that only the writer thinks have any utility. One piece of good news is that following these steps leads to dividends that appear later when preparing mission statements and strategic plans, since much of the information gathered can be reused.

First and foremost, a sound vision begins with a thorough examination of the environment and identifiable trends for the future. This takes time, but the results will be more useful and will provide the base for future efforts. We have mentioned environmental scanning at several points in this text but not in much detail; here we explore the concept more fully.

What is an environmental scan? It is gathering information about events, trends, and relationships in an organization's external environment that leaders employ when planning the desired future for the organization. Such scanning allows for proactive planning, assists in avoiding surprises, identifies threats and opportunities, and helps in meeting challenges from competitors. Scanning involves looking at and searching for data that may have an impact on the organization in the near and long-term future. Some of the information may be collected by the organization as part of its normal operations, while most of it must be sought out from a variety of sources.

Obviously a leader cannot scan every factor in the environment if he wants to accomplish other critical organizational tasks. He must identify a relatively small number of factors that are of highest importance for the organization's long-term viability. Although the specific factors will vary from organization to organization, some appear regularly in a great many scans. All the following factors are common and appropriate for most information services to consider in their scan:

- Technology
- Economics
- Society
- Politics
- Competition
- Regulatory and legal issues
- Transportation

Building data collected about some of the factors into the normal operations allows scans to be completed more quickly. It can also alert the leadership that something significant has changed that may require immediate attention.

Useful data can come from almost any reliable source. A leader does *not* need to engage in random sampling or other statistical techniques to acquire valuable thinking and planning information. Ordinary professional and personal reading activities can produce highly useful information for a scan if the leader thinks about what she is reading in broad terms.

Check These Out

Abels, Eileen, ``Hot Topics: Environmental Scanning,'' *Bulletin of the American Society for Information Science and Technology* 28,(February/March 2002): 16–18.

Choo, Chun Wei, *Information Management for the Intelligent Organization: The Art of Scanning the Environment* (Medford, NJ: Information Today, 2001).

Stoffels, John, *Strategic Issues Management: A Comprehensive Guide to Environmental Scanning* (Tarrytown, NY: Elsevier Science, 1994).

Given that information professionals focus on service to the organization's service population, it is no surprise that monitoring the users should be a major scan component. For many information services, this activity will already be occurring because knowledge of user needs underlies the offering of effective services. If it is not being done, then collecting information about the following will get the process under way. (Note: the list is but a sample of the types of data that might be collected.)

- User attitudes about existing services
- User ideas about desirable services
- How they might use information
- How they access information (e.g., in house, remotely)
- Types of information accessed or borrowed

The more information a leader has about existing users of the current services, the more likely he is to create a vision that will be attractive to them.

The nonusers and the ex-users in the service population should also be considered. Generally only a small percentage of the total service population makes use of the available services. Knowing what factors cause the nonuse may lead to ideas for new or changed services that will attract new groups of users.

Leaders should also look at trends in the population—demographics such as researchers, staff, children, senior citizens, undergraduates, graduates, gender, birth rates, and ethnicity. Demographic shifts are easy to overlook unless there is a plan in place to monitor trends. Early warning of serious shifts allows for proactive rather than reactive planning.

Spending some time monitoring parent organization trends should always be part of the scanning process. Being part of a larger organization does not always result in important information about overall changes, planned or possible, filtering down to all operating units. Political and economic issues may or may not have as much impact on the subunits as they do for the parent organization. Proactively monitoring potential changes can provide what may be critical lead time for planning any required adjustments. An example is that changes in birth rates have greater impact on educational systems than they do on the libraries and media centers that support the systems. However, thinking through alternative scenarios of potential consequences beforehand can make a significant difference, even for the library.

Obviously, economic issues can have serious implications for libraries and information centers. Local issues may appear most important, and they may be in the short run. However, for vision development and other uses, leaders must take a broader and long-term perspective. What happens regionally, nationally, and, in today's environment, globally, can and very often does have local consequences at some point. Reading news magazines such as the *Economist* will provide a wealth of economic information at a global and national level.

There are some other common environmental factors for information services that we will briefly note. Technology and competition are two environmental factors that require increasing attention. In many cases they are one and the same; all one need think of is Google's plan to digitize millions of books (http://print.google.com/googleprint/about.html, accessed May 1, 2006) to see the blending of the factors. Knowing where technology may be headed is important, but given its scope and speed of change, a person could monitor activities full time and still not be certain she has identified all the key trends. Staying at the top of the technology curve, not the leading edge, is the best most services can realistically hope to achieve. With technology and competition, a leader must accept the fact there will be occasional miscalculations—think about the libraries that jumped on the portable e-book reader bandwagon a few years ago.

We believe that leaders should add some internal assessment to their scanning activities. In particular, they need to think about staff skills vis-à-vis an initial vision to check on its feasibility. Creating a vision the staff cannot achieve because of ability issues is pointless—no chance of securing additional staff with requisite skills, personnel incapable of developing the skills, and so on. Also, looking back at where the organization has come from may provide useful insights about possible futures. Sager (1999, p. 288) sums up the case for information service environmental scanning: "The contribution of environmental scanning to library management and planning, therefore, is that it permits us to see our strengths, weaknesses, opportunities, and threats from many different perspectives."

Check These Out

The following are two library examples of the results of environmental scans that are worth reviewing:

American Library Association, *ALA 2000 and Beyond* (Chicago: American Library Association, 1998).

Online Computer Library Center, *2003 Environmental Scan: Pattern Recognition*, edited by Alane Wilson, at www.oclc.org/reports/2003escan.htm (accessed May 1, 2006).

After completing the scan and carefully pondering the implications of the information, it is time to produce a *draft* vision and take the next step. That step is to involve the staff in thinking about the future. Gaining such input from the staff, as several of our survey respondents noted, will improve the quality and usefulness of the final statement. Taking this step will also build staff commitment to the vision by creating a sense of ownership. Although it takes more time, the broader the staff involvement, the greater their "buy-in." Ingrid Bens (1999, p. 129) suggests that one way to involve staff in this process is to gather a group together, tell the group to imagine that it's exactly two years from today, and then have them answer the following questions, which are then shared and compared (and ideally incorporated into the vision statement):

- Describe how you now serve customers.
- What specific improvements have been made?
- What are people saying about the team (or organization) now?
- What problems have the group solved?
- What specific outcomes have been achieved?
- How are people behaving differently?

The time spent in sharing scan data and having the staff involved in the initial draft vision not only makes the discussion about the future more productive but also conveys a sense of trust in the staff and their ability to make valuable contributions to the long-term success of the organization. Although staff input is important, it does not alleviate the leader's ultimate responsibility for generating the final vision statement and what it contains.

Also Worth Reviewing

In addition to Bens's advice, Joel Finlay (1994, p. 64) published a description of how to involve staff in the visioning process, "which can effectively push a group . . . to an inspiring, rich, and beyond the present paradigm view of a positive future for their organization." His article, "The Strategic Visioning Process," *Public Administration Quarterly* 18, no. 1 (1994): 64–74, provides practical step-by-step advice.

Step three is preparing a final version of the draft for presentation to various stakeholders. The basic question to ask when beginning this process is "What is our preferred future?" In answering that question, a leader must do the following:

- Draw on the basic values and beliefs of the organization.
- Look at the existing vision, value, and mission statements and where the organization stands in terms of existing strategic plans.
- Describe what he sees as the most desirable future in positive and, if possible, inspiring terms.
- Don't make the assumption that any of today's organizational structure must carry over to the future; such assumptions will only limit thinking.
- Be open to significant changes in the organization, methods, purposes, and so on to help create a vision that is exciting and inspiring.
- Whenever possible, incorporate some degree of specificity that will demonstrate the vision is realistic.

The final and critical step is presenting the final version to any governing or advisory body. (It is courteous and shows respect for the staff if they see this version before others see it.) If some members of such bodies have not been involved in earlier steps, and even if they have, a leader must expect there will be some fine-tuning done to the "final" version. Once there is agreement on meaning and wording, the "final" final statement is ready for communicating to other stakeholders, such as users.

The statement should be brief and summarizable in two or three sentences. It should be specific, not generic in character. Having a single common purpose rather than several is a desirable goal. The final statement must reflect the core values and beliefs of the information service.

Preparing a useful vision statement clearly takes time, but almost all the effort will feed into other planning activities. As a leader, you should be aware of the factors that can defeat both the development and implementation of a vision. A few of the more common "vision killers" are tradition, leader or staff fatigue, short-term thinking, naysayers, fear of being seen as too visionary, and complacency. An effective statement generated through the process just described has a number of organizational benefits:

Vision, Value, and Mission Statements

Because these statements should be relatively brief, should be worked on at about the same time, and are interrelated, they often appear together in a single document. You can find many information service examples with a single Google search using *vision, value,* or *mission statement.* Two library examples are the University of Wisconsin-Eau Claire McIntyre Library (www.uwec.edu/library/aboutus/mission.htm, accessed May 1, 2006) and the public library in Fullerton, California (http://fullertonlibrary.org/libinfo/index.html, accessed May 1, 2006). The American Library Association website has an example of a core values statement (www.ala.org/ala/oif/statementspols/corevaluesstatement/corevalues.htm, accessed May 1, 2006). Sampling some statements available online before starting the process can be beneficial.

Two archive sites are Iowa State University's Archives of Women in Science and Engineering (www.lib.iastate.edu/spcl/wise/miss.html, accessed May 1, 2006) and Papalnk, the Children's Art Archive (www.papaink.org/papaink/home/statement.html, accessed May 1, 2006).

- Broadens thinking—more long-term future oriented
- Provides direction and purpose
- Provides a base for planning
- Provides lead time as well as awareness of the need to change

- Focuses attention on key issues
- Encourages group interest in and commitment to the organization's future
- Builds group confidence
- Creates a sense of group empowerment

Preparing a Values Statement

Vision and values statement preparation share the same basic process, except there is no need for scanning when working on values statements. As is true for vision and mission statements, leaders must avoid platitudes, which is probably most difficult when dealing with values. One way to avoid meaningless value pronouncements such as "We value trust" is to translate the value into action—"We build trust by keeping our commitments." By treating the values as themes for behavior, leaders provide staff with appropriate "anchors" for their actions on a day-to-day basis.

Try This

How would you translate the following value words into an action-able statement in an information service context?
- Competency
- Teamwork
- Integrity
- Empowerment
- Flexibility
- Dignity
- Accuracy
- Honesty
- Service responsibility
- Accountability
- Diversity
- Excellence

Practicing with these terms will help you get thinking about ac-tionable values.

What are "core" values? The simple answer is they are traits or qualities that the organization believes are worthwhile and should underlie all organizational activities. Core values define, or should define, how the staff behaves with one another as well as with customers and anyone else who interacts with the organization. They are, or should be, an accurate reflection of the organizational culture. Essentially, they should describe behaviors that reflect the fundamental values of most, if not all, of the staff members, which certainly includes the senior staff. When properly crafted, core values are strategic in the sense that they guide every organizational decision and action.

We cannot overemphasize the importance of translating vague values into actionable behavior. The problem with vague words is they have so many different meanings to different people. People not only associate different meanings with value terms but usually have a very strong sense of the meanings as well. In a staff of thirty, there will likely be at least twenty variations of what *honesty* means. Actionable (concrete) values provide a base for building an environment of shared meaning and, in time, work behavior. A leader's goal should be to have the values reflected on the floor, not the wall. Nonactionable values statements too often end up as a plaque on the wall or posted on the organization's website, promptly forgotten by all except the person who developed the statement.

An example of an actual values statement for an organizational unit (University of Maryland Libraries Technical Services Division, 2001) that provides some behavioral components is "Quality service to our primary clientele. . . . The key components of providing quality service were defined as support of customer focus (responsive service), excellence (balance of quality and quantity), cooperation and teamwork (both inside and outside Technical Services), and effective communication between units/functions and across staff levels."

The defined components are somewhat actionable; too many values statements would stop after *clientele*, which leaves too much room for individual interpretation to be useful. The statement could have been made even more actionable with only a small amount of rewording, such as "Focus on providing responsive service by listening thoughtfully to stated needs." Taking the time to make the values as actionable as possible will speed the process of moving from words on paper to desired actions in service.

After developing and getting a consensus on the values, a discussion about how to implement them needs to occur. Group discussions can be an effective means of creating the necessary shared sense of the values. Another key factor in gaining staff understanding and acceptance of the values is how well a leader models the value behaviors.

An important point to bear in mind when preparing values statements is that *values* and *ethics* are frequently used interchangeably even though they are in fact different. *Ethics* refer to a standard of conduct and moral judgment. *Values* may or may not be ethical. In fact, values can be ethical, unethical, or nonethical in character. An example of a professional nonethical value is competency, while a professional ethical value is honesty. Although drawing on various professional association ethics statements can be helpful in developing a local values statement, the ethics statements may not be fully applicable to the local situation. They also are unlikely to cover all the important core values of the organization. Thus, just adopting a broad-based ethics statement from a professional body, while valuable on one level, will not provide the planning usefulness of a locally developed values statement.

For a values statement to have a worthwhile impact on the information service operations, a leader must do the following:

- Actively involve all staff members in the development process.
- Keep in mind that values are behavior based, so they should have practical day-to-day utility.
- Make decisions based on the values in ways that demonstrate their importance.
- Model behaviors that reflect the values.
- Use the values to guide short- and long-term planning.
- Make value implementation part of the performance appraisal and reward system.
- Fully communicate the values to potential new hires so they can decide beforehand whether or not there is a congruence of values.

The Expert

Kenneth Kernaghan (2003, p. 718) has this to say about values statements: ''The successful integration of values into public service requires value-centered leadership. Leaders must serve not only as exemplary models of values-based behavior but also as skillful practitioners of the art of values management.''

Preparing a Mission Statement

Mission statements have been around for a long time, and some management writers suggest that organizations—both profit and not-for-profit—are more effective when they have a mission statement. Having a statement is not really the issue; the issue is having a well-crafted statement. Just as generic vision and values statements are basically a waste of paper and time, the same is true for mission statements.

One step a leader can take to avoid worthless mission statements is to ask the following questions:

- What is our reason for being? What is our purpose?
- What is unique or distinctive about our service?

- What is likely to be different about the field and organization in five or ten years?
- Who are, or who should be, our principal clients? Is this likely to change in the future?
- What are our principal services, now and in the future?
- What are, or what should be, our principal economic concerns?
- What are the basic beliefs, values, aspirations, and philosophical priorities of our service?
- What is our service area, now and in the future?
- What are our major strengths and strategic advantages?
- What are our primary technologies, now and in the future?

Although this list of questions is rather long, if the leader has developed good vision and values statements, the answers are readily at hand. The questions also demonstrate the interconnection between the concepts.

Try This

One simple way to create a mission statement is to have the key stakeholders complete the following template and then compare results: The mission of (name of organization or group) is to provide (who) with (what), which allows them to (action) so that (outcomes you wish to achieve).

Thoughtful answers to these questions will prevent fuzzy, nonspecific language and thinking. Focusing on the "our" aspect of the questions will make the resulting statement more specific to the information service and not easily interchangeable with any other service. The specificity of the statement should also make it easier for everyone to see how it can be implemented.

Just for Fun

For an irreverent but comical turn at creating mission statements, visit Dilbert's online "Mission Statement Generator" (www.dilbert.com/comics/dilbert/games/career/bin/ms.cgi, accessed May 1, 2006). Although the generated results are certainly not to be taken seriously, it can add levity to the process of creating a mission statement. A sample statement generated is "The customer can count on us to synergistically fashion effective intellectual capital while continuing to seamlessly facilitate innovative materials because that is what the customer expects."

When developing a statement, there are some parameters to consider beyond the basic process for vision and values statements. Mission statements tend to be widely disseminated, so some thought should go into who the *audience* is. Sometimes it is desirable to prepare different versions for different audiences. Although technical and professional jargon may be reasonable for internal use, including with governing or advisory bodies, such language would render the statement almost meaningless to most other stakeholders. (Note: this is a matter of word choice, not content differences.) *Length* is another consideration. A mission that is more than a page in length is too long; great length is usually a reflection of too little careful thought or, more commonly, slipping over into strategic planning. The *tone* is yet another basic issue. Working at creating a tone that will match the audience helps ensure a more accepting response to the document. Using "lofty" words and ponderous sentences is likely to result in a statement that few, if any, people will take seriously.

Check This Out

A good article addressing the process of developing a mission statement is Christopher Bart's "Making Mission Statements Count," *CA Magazine* 132, no. 2 (1999): 37–38.

Just as all planning documents need periodic review, so do mission statements. If the information service engages in a "rolling" long-range planning process, linking that activity with a mission statement review makes excellent sense. In fact, it is a good time to review all the documents we've discussed, due to their interconnected nature.

Why Strategic Thinking and Planning Are Important

Strategic thinking and planning are interrelated but different concepts. Henry Mintzberg describes strategic thinking as "seeing" (Mintzberg, Ahlstrand, and Lampal, 1998), a combination of viewing and thinking activities about where the organization might go. (The difference between Mintzberg's seeing and the visioning process is the latter is a statement of the preferred future, whereas the seeing process involves multiple futures.) Seeing involves looking at the environment in several ways—looking ahead, looking behind, looking up, looking down, looking beside, and looking beyond. To that mix Mintzberg and his colleagues add the need for creative thinking on the part of the person engaged in the looking. When all these are combined, one has achieved strategic thinking. In essence, strategic thinking deals with all aspects of the "big picture."

Focusing on details is the biggest barrier to strategic thought. Visioning is a form of strategic thinking.

We defined strategic planning earlier in this chapter. Keep in mind that strategic planning is just one type of organizational planning; however, because it is future based, it should underlie, or at least be congruent with, other planning activities.

A voluminous body of literature addresses the importance of conducting strategic planning. Mintzberg and his coauthors (1998) state that there is no one strategic planning approach. Rather, there are several schools of thought about the process. A reader of their book might even come away thinking there is no such thing as a strategic process, since they liken strategic formulation to the six blind men describing an elephant. "We are the blind people and strategy formation is our elephant. Since no one has had the vision to see the entire beast, everyone has grabbed hold of some part or other and 'railed on' in utter ignorance about the rest" (p. 3). However, after making that statement, they devote ten chapters to describing the schools that have grabbed hold of some part of the strategic planning elephant.

The Mintzberg, Ahlstrand, and Lampal Schools of Strategy Formation

Here is an overview of the ten schools as well as a summary comment about each one's key emphasis (Mintzberg, Ahlstrand, and Lampal, 1998, p. 5). One of their conclusions in chapter 1 is "All this leads to our final conclusion, which is that strategies (and the strategic process) can be vital to organizations by their *absence* as well their presence" (p. 18).

The Design School: strategy formation as a process of *conception*
The Planning School: strategy formation as a *formal* process
The Positioning School: strategy formation as an *analytical* process
The Entrepreneurial School: strategy formation as a *visionary* process
The Cognitive School: strategy formation as a *mental* process
The Learning School: strategy formation as an *emergent* process
The Power School: strategy formation as a process of *negotiation*
The Cultural School: strategy formation as a *collective* process
The Environmental School: strategy formation as a *reactive* process
The Configuration School: strategy formation as a process of *transformation*

Without question, their book is worth reading in order to fully understand both the benefits and limitations of the various approaches to the process. We agree with them when, in the final chapter, they write, "There are categories out there, but they should be used as building blocks, or, better still, as ingredients of a stew" (p. 368). What follows are highlights of some of the key ingredients of the "strategy stew."

The Basics of Strategic Planning

The future is uncertain and the environment seems to be in a constant state of change, all of which creates challenges for organizations and their leaders. Long-range planning (strategy) helps deal with the uncertainty and provides a sense of the desired direction for the organization. However, as anyone with work experience knows, circumstances change in unexpected ways, forcing plans to change. Even the most ardent advocate of strategic planning will acknowledge that it is the rare organization that ever achieves 100 percent of any strategic plan. There are just too many changes in the world for an organization to keep rigidly to a plan and remain viable. That does not, however, make the process worthless.

Our view is that vision and values statements should lead to the mission document, which in turn drives strategic planning. (A quick review of Management 101's coverage of planning: strategic planning [five to ten years in length] provides the base for tactical [six to twenty-four months] and operational [one to fifty-two weeks] planning activities.) Critics of long-range planning are correct when they say there is often wide divergence between where the organization hoped it would be and where it actually is at the end of a planning period. However, by engaging in a "rolling" long-range planning process (reviewing and making thoughtful adjustments every year or two), a leader keeps the vision and plans closer to reality.

What are the components of strategic planning? We covered four of them earlier in this chapter—vision, values, environmental scanning, and mission. Situational or SWOT analysis is an important component, as is gap analysis. Sometimes it is useful to engage in benchmarking as part of the process. Identifying strategic issues and programming are always key activities. Another factor in the mix is risk taking.

Situational or *SWOT analysis* should take place early in the process. In fact it can be done, and it often is, as part of the vision and mission preparation process. SWOT (strengths, weaknesses, opportunities, threats) analysis is a structured approach to assessing an organization's environment and where it stands in that environment. (Note: SWOT is also useful on the personal level, such as when thinking about career options.) SWOT analysis is an effective tool to use with groups. It fosters debate and often generates, from the group process, ideas that would not have been on any one person's independent SWOT list. In effect, SWOT analysis allows you to gain a clear picture of what the service does well and not so well, what opportunities exist for doing something better or moving into new areas, and what threats currently exist. A useful technique is to generate ideas in a group setting for capitalizing on strengths and opportunities as well as for addressing the weaknesses and threats.

Check This Out

For examples of several SWOT analysis tools used by libraries, visit the "New Pathways to Planning: Internal Library Audit" web page, maintained by the Northeast Kansas Library System (http://sky ways.lib.ks.us/pathway/audit.html, accessed May 1, 2006).

Gap analysis is a method for evaluating the differences between the organization's present service qualities and where it would like to be in the future. The point is to identify specific areas where the team can develop strategies for "closing the gap." One strategy is analyzing what customers expect against their perceptions of current services. A model for doing this (Parasuraman, Zeithaml, and Berry, 1985) suggests employing a ten-factor analysis that overlaps to some degree—responsiveness, reliability, tangibles, communication, competence, access, credibility, courtesy, understanding of the customer, and security. To conduct the assessment, the authors recommend a three-stage process—asking customers how much they expect from the factors, asking what importance they attach to each factor, and asking what their perception is of the service(s) in terms of each factor. Conducting such a survey takes time and effort, but it can pay off by providing data for more than strategic planning purposes. (For example, the information is useful for assessment and accountability activities.) One established form of gap analysis is the LibQUAL+ survey (www.libqual.org, accessed May 1, 2006), offered by the Association of Research Libraries (ARL). LibQUAL+ is designed to measure service quality, and 256 institutions worldwide registered to participate in the 2005 survey (www.libqual.org/information/participants/index.cfm, accessed May 1, 2006).

Benchmarking is a system for measuring and comparing an information service's operations, practices, or performance against the practices of other services. (Note: it can also be used within a large system such as a public library with multiple service locations.) There are four types of benchmarking: internal, competitive, industry, and "best in class." (Our only experience with benchmarking fell into either the competitive or industry categories. We can say that the data from the activity did prove useful in planning and in securing additional resources.) Benchmarking data can be useful for assessing where an institution stands in relation to the field in general (industry) or with institutions the leader or parent organization views as comparable (competitive). Such data can help identify strategic areas the leader might want to improve or be certain to maintain.

Check These Out

Two examples of benchmarking studies are those conducted by the University of Virginia (www.lib.virginia.edu/mis/benchmarking/index.html, accessed May 1, 2006) and the New York-New Jersey Medical Library Association (www.nynjmla.org/nynjnews_summer_2002_12.html, accessed May 1, 2006).

Strategic issues are areas the service identifies as crucial to address in order to effectively move toward its desired future. The process clearly draws on data developed from all the activities discussed previously. Strategic *programming* is the process of developing specific strategies (goals) thought to successfully address the identified issues. So-called SMART goals and strategies are what leaders should strive to develop—**s**pecific, **m**easurable, **a**greed upon, **r**ealistic, and **t**ime/cost bound. Such strategies are much more likely to be achieved than those that lack one or more of the SMART elements.

Check These Out

Both the U.S. and U.K. National Archives sites have examples of the completed package of documents this chapter addresses. They provide insights into how to translate ``theory'' into useful working documents for any type of information service.

National Archives (United States), www.archives.gov/about/info/mission.html (accessed May 1, 2006)

National Archives (United Kingdom), www.nationalarchives.gov.uk/about/operate/plans.htm (accessed May 1, 2006)

Strategic planning's purpose is to help address the uncertainly of the future. However, whatever steps a leader takes with strategic planning, it does *not* eliminate or even minimize risk. The process is risk filled—dangers include underachieving (planning too small), being too ambitious, and unforeseen events. What planning *does* do is allow leaders and followers to rationally choose among risk-taking courses of action. Risk is part of the environment, and the planning process should be designed so that the organization will take the right risks.

Getting to the right risks is what effective leaders do. A leader must be a risk taker. Every planning decision, or for that matter any action, carries with it some degree of risk. Risk taking is a personality trait, and everyone has a greater or lesser amount of willingness to take a risk. From an organizational point of view, being too risk adverse can be just as detrimental as taking too many risks. Today's information services probably need to engage in higher-risk actions than they did twenty or more years ago. As Kathryn Deiss (1999, p. 1) writes about academic libraries, "The requirement to be agile and innovative is the result of the acute attention paid to expenditures and performance and their relation to one another." The more agile, innovative, and responsive an information service is over time, the greater the risks are. Effective leaders understand there are significant risks, but they also know that significant gains can be had from taking the right risks. They also fully understand the consequences of failing to take risks and that unexpected events can create the need to adjust or even abandon plans as a result.

Two major factors play important roles in how much or little risk a person is likely to take—tolerance for ambiguity and openness to experience. At the end of the day, all the information from environmental scanning, gap analysis, benchmarking, input from staff and other stakeholders, and so on will create only a more or less ambiguous picture of the environment and the future, essentially an ambiguous situation. (An ambiguous situation is one that cannot be fully structured or categorized due to incomplete information.) Selecting strategic goals involves the evaluation of uncertain and ambiguous outcomes in an ambiguous future. Thus, the greater a leader's tolerance for ambiguity, the more comfortable he will be in taking the risks associated with strategy making. Highly tolerant individuals are more likely to initiate strategic changes that have the greatest potential for creating or maintaining an agile, flexible, and inventive information service for the future.

Openness to experience is another personality trait that plays into strategy making and risk taking. Some characteristics of individuals who are more open to new experiences include being more original than conventional, being more imaginative than down to earth, being as comfortable with change as they are with the familiar, and having a strong interest in trying new things and ideas. People who have openness to experience are thus likely to see the value in trying new (more risky) strategies, see opportunities where others see only threats, and offer up inventive approaches to challenges.

Essentially, the leader who has strong tolerance for ambiguity and is open to new experiences is more prone to undertaking proactive rather than reactive strategies. Such strategies are almost always higher risk because of less certainty of the outcomes. However, such strategies, when they work, can prove highly beneficial for the organization, and the organization and its leader(s) become a model for others to follow. If the information service environment is relatively unchanging, such leadership would probably be relatively unimportant. However, that is not what today's environment is like, and having leaders and staff with a high tolerance for ambiguity and openness to new experiences is crucial for long-term viability.

Strategic planning offers many benefits, the concerns of Mintzberg, Ahlstrand, and Lampal notwithstanding, if leaders are judicious in their selection of "strategy stew ingredients." Some of the more obvious benefits follow:

- More clearly defines organizational purpose through realistic goals
- Communicates those goals to staff and stakeholders
- Aids in developing a sense of ownership in the plan and organization
- Focuses organizational resources on the key priorities
- Creates a base for assessing progress and the need for adjustments
- Leads to action that should be more effective
- Provides for accountability to stakeholders

Check These Out

Bryson, John, *Strategic Planning for Public and Non-Profit Organizations*, 3rd ed. (San Francisco: Jossey-Bass, 2004).
Dougherty, Richard, "Planning for New Library Futures," *Library Journal* (May 15) 2002: 38–42.
Ladwig, J. Parker, "Assess the State of Your Strategic Plan," *Library Administration & Management* 19, no. 2 (2005): 90–93.
McClamroch, Jo, Jacqueline J. Byrd, and Steven L. Sowell, "Strategic Planning," *Journal of Academic Librarianship* 27, no. 5 (2001): 372–379.

Managing Change

Vision, values, and mission statements and strategic plans carry with them both the implication and actuality of change for the organization. Even without such documents, today's environment makes change an organizational necessity.

Organizational change involves risk. The consequences of change are usually less well known (ambiguous) than the consequences of not changing. It is clear there is a linkage between organizational change and individual risk-taking behavior. Understanding individual risk-taking behavior, strategic planning, decision making, and the organizational change process makes a leader more effective. The probability of organizational change does not depend only on the organization's performance issues. It is the outcome of several factors—the leader's risk-taking behavior, the staff's risk-taking tolerance and motivation to change, the opportunity to change, and the capability to change. Organizations are more likely to change when they have developed routines for making changes; part of that routine is developing staff that are comfortable with change. As mentioned in chapter 2, one work worth consulting on this topic is Susan Curzon's *Managing Change* (New York: Neal-Schuman, 2005).

Being able to manage change effectively and develop change-tolerant staff is something all good leaders do. Effectively managing change begins by having a sound understanding of the *change process*. For all practical purposes, it does not matter whether the change is *reactive* or *proactive* in nature; the process is the same. Some years ago Kurt Lewin (1951) developed a three-element model of the organizational change process that has served as the basis for almost all later research and study of organizational change. The three elements of the model are unfreezing, changing, and refreezing.

Types of Organizational Change

Reactive change comes about as a result of unanticipated problems or opportunities. Due to their unexpected nature, these changes are more difficult to manage because time may be a crucial factor. *Proactive change* comes about through carefully thought-out, planned processes or anticipated events. Such changes are easier to manage and should produce successful outcomes.

Unfreezing is where the leader develops among the staff the motivation to change by getting the staff to see and accept the need for change as well as working at overcoming natural staff resistance. *Changing* is the actual process of moving from the old to the new procedure, process, or behavior. *Refreezing* is making the "new way" the normal way of doing things. Throughout the process, the leader must model, coach, and mentor the staff.

Although the model of change is simple, the process of effectively executing it and managing it is rather difficult, and often mistakes are made. John Kotter (1996), whom we have mentioned several times in this book, proposes an eight-step approach to handling organizational change that should help leaders avoid some of the most common mistakes that take place when trying to manage change. Kotter builds on the Lewin model.

Because "unfreezing" is the key to successful change and is where many problems develop, Kotter suggests four steps for this phase. Before people will actively consider change—much less start to change—they must see there is a need to change. Kotter makes the point that seeing the need is not, in itself, sufficient to generate change. Getting staff motivated to change rests in part on *establishing a sense of urgency* for engaging in the change process. Without a compelling reason, the staff as well as stakeholders often see no reason to modify the existing situation. Being able to identify who will be in charge of the change (*creating a guiding coalition*) also helps demonstrate the belief of the senior management or leader that change is necessary. As people begin to sense the need for change, they want to know details of what will be involved. Having a plan (*developing a vision and strategy*) for the change to present to the staff will begin to address their reasonable concerns, such as "What will it mean for me?" As always, *communicating* openly with the staff is fundamental. Sometimes there is the belief that withholding information about the change that might be "unsettling" to staff is a good idea. Nothing could be further from the truth, in the long term. Whatever the "bad news" is, it will become apparent sooner or later, and staff trust of the leader or management will drop the longer it takes to make this news known throughout the organization. Any future change efforts will be much more difficult as a result.

For the actual change phase, Kotter proposes three steps. The first is *empowering broad-based actions*. This means giving the staff maximum latitude to act within the framework of the change plan. It means removing barriers that might impede the staff as they work to implement the change. *Generating some short-term goals* for the plan will help motivate the staff as they achieve some quick "wins." As part of this activity, it is important to recognize the wins and those people who made significant contributions to achieving them. Finally, *consolidating the gains* is crucial before the leader declares "victory." Making a premature declaration not only can be embarrassing but also can actually derail the entire process as the staff, rightly, assumes they need not worry about or work on the matter any longer.

Check This Out

Raymond Caldwell published an interesting article about how organizations need both change leaders and change managers and how they should work together: ''Change Leaders and Change Managers: Different or Complementary?'' *Leadership & Organizational Development Journal* 24, no. 5 (2002): 285–293.

The final step corresponds with Lewin's refreezing phase. Kotter calls this *anchoring the new approach(es) in the culture*. One of the dangers of premature victory announcements is that it can actually take a year or more for a long-term change to be fully incorporated into the organizational culture. To achieve "anchoring," a leader must reinforce the change(s) whenever possible. Another tactic that will help embed the change(s) is to develop some staff change leaders (persons who are comfortable with change and are reasonable risk takers).

Developing a Change-Oriented Staff

One goal for a leader should be to develop an organization or unit that is at least comfortable with change, if not eager to confront it. The greater the degree of comfort, the greater the chances the organization or unit will have a long-term track record of high productivity, flexibility, and success.

There are some general steps a leader can take that will enhance staff comfort with change; a plus for these steps is they also help create an overall positive work environment. One such step is one we have mentioned many times throughout this book—empower the staff. Empowered people know they can and are encouraged to make adjustments they think will improve their work. At first, people may not think of the adjustments as "change," but in time they will see the connection—the only difference is a matter of scale. This will help dissipate the fear or concern about dealing with change.

Of course, just because people are empowered does not necessarily mean they will make use of the power. Therefore, a leader should encourage ideas for new ways of doing things. She can do this by coaching or mentoring teams or individuals to think about what they could do differently that would make their work better. On a unit scale, staff often think—and have experienced—that asking "why," "what if," "how," and so on is taken as a sign of being a trouble-maker or "boat rocker" and thus something to avoid. Although it may take some time to overcome past negative experiences with challenging the status quo, the leader who takes that time and encourages such thinking and expression of ideas will have people who are comfortable thinking about change.

Once a leader has created an environment where staff members feel safe making changes in their work activities and suggesting ideas or questioning current practices, he needs to do at least two things. First, when a person or team has made a successful change, the leader needs to acknowledge that success as soon as possible—he mustn't wait until the next performance review cycle to congratulate or recognize the person's or team's success. A more difficult task is to accept the inevitable missteps and failures that occur as learning opportunities rather than a time for "corrective" action. This is a time for coaching the person to rebuild her self-confidence and let her take away some positive lessons from the experience. Coaching in general will help make staff more comfortable with risk taking and change.

During the early stages of building the staff's comfort level with change, another useful step is to just discuss the value of change, either one on one or in a group. One group method is to do some "what if . . ." exercises, in which the group explores alternative solutions or ideas and their possible value. By not being evaluative during this activity, a leader can encourage people to think broadly and imaginatively and to express their views. That in turn will build self-confidence and even encourage risk-taking behavior.

The leader can also employ Kotter's "sense of urgency" to help foster a comfort with change. He can do this by frequently talking about the importance (urgency) of doing better or being more efficient. This must be done with care so as not to have this come across negatively. Perhaps a better way for the leader to state the goal is that he doesn't want the staff to become complacent or so comfortable with the status quo that it becomes more difficult to generate necessary changes.

When effective work teams are in place, they can contribute to an environment where change is expected and not feared. Good teams are quick to make changes in their activities whenever there are problems. Their successful performance can encourage nonteam staff to attempt to improve their work activities.

Work groups that have a high comfort level with change are that way almost always because a leader has spent time developing such an atmosphere. Together, staff and leaders are capable of accomplishing much more than groups and leaders that lack this trait. Managing change is more about getting people comfortable with this concept and process than it is about "managing" the process. Change is inevitable and, today, almost constant; thus it is not a matter of *if* a leader must deal with change—it's a matter of how often and how well she does it.

Summary

Visions, missions, strategic planning, and managing change are very important for organizational success. They must be done correctly if they are to be worthwhile. This chapter explores these concepts and their importance. We outlined the process leaders should consider to make them useful tools in creating a viable library or information center for the 21st century. A key to remember in the planning process is that the vision, mission, and strategic plans should be regarded as dynamic documents that will change and grow with the organization. These documents do no good posted on a wall or website—they must be integrated into the activities of the organization, and they must be revisited from time to time to fine-tune them as needed.

References

Bennis, Warren, *On Becoming a Leader* (New York: Basic, 2003).
Bennis, Warren, and Burt Nanus, *Leaders: The Strategies for Taking Charge* (New York: HarperCollins, 1997).

Bens, Ingrid, *Facilitation at a Glance!* (N.p.: A joint publication of GOAL/QPC and AQP, 1999).

Curzon, Susan, *Managing Change*, rev. ed. (New York: Neal-Schuman, 2005).

Deiss, Kathryn, *ARL New Measures: Organizational Capacity White Paper* (Washington, DC: Association of Research Libraries, 21 April 1999), at www.arl.org/stats/program/ capacity.pdf (accessed May 1, 2006).

Finlay, Joel, "The Strategic Visioning Process," *Public Administration Quarterly* 18, no. 1 (1994): 64–74.

Kernaghan, Kenneth, "Integrating Values into Public Service: The Values Statement as Centerpiece," *Public Administration Review* 63, no. 6 (2003): 711–719.

Kotter, John, *Leading Change* (Boston: Harvard Business School Press, 1996).

Lewin, Kurt, *Field Theory in Social Science* (New York: Harper & Row, 1951).

Mintzberg, Henry, Bruce Ahlstrand, and Joseph Lampal, *Strategic Safari: A Guided Tour through the Wilds of Strategic Management* (New York: Free Press, 1998).

Parasuraman, A., Valaria Zeithaml, and Leonard Berry, "A Conceptual Model of Service Quality and Its Implications for Future Research," *Journal of Marketing* 49, no. 4 (Fall 1985): 41–50.

Sager, Don, "Environmental Scanning and the Public Library," *Public Libraries* 38, no. 5 (1999): 283–288.

University of Maryland Libraries. TSD Blue-Ribbon Committee, 2001. "Appendix C: TSD Mission and Values," in *Working Paper #6: Technical Services Division in a Team-Based Learning Organization*, at www.lib.umd.edu/TSD/workingpaper6_appA-C .html#appendC (accessed May 1, 2006).

CHAPTER 7

E-Leadership

This chapter focuses on the following:

- The challenges of e-leadership
- Information services and the e-environment
- The differences between virtual and face-to-face leadership
- E-leadership of virtual teams
- E-mentoring issues

It is very clear that technology, especially telecommunications, has changed the way work is done and even how we structure it (Kanter, 2001). Old approaches to doing things and thinking about work have given way to new approaches in the networked organization. The digital age calls for a new paradigm for skill development and organizational learning. Organizations are integrating management practices, leadership, and technology in ways not previously considered or needed. Part of what is occurring is learning to unlearn some of the past concepts that served the industrial age so well. We believe the fundamental requirement is for leaders to meet the challenge of thoughtfully integrating an organization, using new technologies to more closely link an organization that is physically dispersed (which can be isolating), while ensuring it remains a social system. This is particularly important in the information sector; the power of ICT (information/communication technology) brings great benefits because many services have a central service point and remote branches. Increasingly, information services draw on external bodies such as national and regional archives via the Internet. We have moved from the age of the telephone and fax to e-mail, webcams, and the Internet.

Workers can be connected in ways that only a few people imagined twenty to twenty-five years ago. This connectivity brings people into contact at a very high speed; in one sense it has brought people "closer" yet in other ways it makes them more detached. In the virtual world, the phrase *interpersonal relations* takes on a very different meaning. In the earlier workplace, employees normally had some sense of who was communicating even if they had not met the person. In a "workplace" where people work collaboratively from different physical locations, some of the e-communication flows from unknown persons based in unknown places. For some people, this appears to lead to a sense of isolation or disconnection. The term *interpersonal skills* takes on new meaning as different protocols develop. But whatever new technology emerges, the concept is still very relevant and must be a key factor in the integration of people, organizations, and technology.

Technology-mediated environments require some adjustments in leadership behavior. We believe the underlying leadership basics covered throughout this text remain valid, but there are changes in emphasis. Leadership in an e-environment calls for meeting the challenges posed by several paradoxes (some new ones and some old ones in new guises), accepting greater ambiguity, and understanding behavioral complexity.

Fundamental Considerations

Having introduced the topic, we need to emphasize that some fundamental considerations must underlie efficient and effective services. They are not unique to the e-environment but must be built into the planning process of the service.

Foremost is the question of the level of technology provided by the parent organization, since few information services are free-standing. The level of sophistication and support for ICT varies considerably between one organization and another, even in the same sector—and it may not be just a question of size of the operation. Some information services may have total control over freestanding ICT services (i.e., they budget for, acquire, maintain, and upgrade them as required—and are provided with the level of budget to do so). Others may need to depend on the parent organization, which can present its own challenges—support may not be available 24/7, and there may not be compatibility between the organization's requirements, those of the service, and those of the external agencies the service collaborates with. The leader must determine what is needed for the service and negotiate with the parent organization. The result may be a compromise. Libraries have a long record of working with vendors who can provide sophisticated, compatible, and stable systems, but this is not necessarily so in other sectors of the information profession or of the parent organization. Video and teleconferencing technologies aid virtual working, but not all parent organizations beyond those that operate on a global basis have provided these facilities.

A second consideration is that of documentation. In the virtual environment there is less opportunity to turn to a colleague to clarify a detail in a process or a policy. Hence all policies and processes need to be documented, updated as they change, and made available to all staff members and users who require them. Policies and processes affecting staff need to be available on an intranet, and those affecting potential users must be posted on the website of the service. One staff member should have the responsibility for keeping these two essential sources of information updated. And the careful leader ensures that managers and supervisors check the pages that cover their responsibilities. It is a management tool and good public relations.

The third requirement is to have a database of management information that is also regularly updated. Information services gather data to assist planning and decision making. This information needs to be made available on a need-to-know basis so it can be readily identified and easily consulted.

This brings in the fourth consideration, which is the security of the ICT systems. They must be protected (e.g., with daily backups stored off site), and it must be made clear to all staff who has access to which part of the system and under what conditions. The use of the Internet will also need to form part of the policy of the service, and guidelines must be prepared.

E-Challenges

Pulley and Sessa (2001) describe five sets of paradoxes and complex challenges for e-organizations and their leaders:

- Swift and mindful
- Individual and community
- Top-down and grass roots
- Details and big picture
- Flexible and steady

These paradoxes will exist, to some degree, for all organizations, regardless of size or profit orientation.

Is it possible to make *swift and mindful* decisions and responses in today's e-environment? While it may be possible, it also increasingly becomes a challenge. E-mail, cell phones, instant messaging, faxes, and so on make it possible to communicate quickly, in some cases to places not possible in the past. (Travelers to the more remote parts of Africa and Asia, for example, note how cell phone and satellite technology coupled with a bicycle has introduced the mobile communications vendor.) Communications technologies also make it more difficult to get away from work pressures. Senders know their message will arrive in a matter of seconds, and they often expect or hope to get back a quick response, whatever the time zone or location of the recipient. (Think back to the characteristics of generation X discussed in chapter 3.) A recognized problem with quick responses is regret—"I hit 'send' too quickly." There are well-documented accounts of "the fat finger" in the financial world that affects the buying and selling of foreign currencies or stocks and shares.

Rapid decisions usually require drawing on past experiences, with little or no opportunity to assess the situation to even determine to what degree the current environment matches the past environment(s) of decision making. They also depend on quick and easy access to current management information. Collecting, locating, and using additional data is not very compatible with speedy decision making unless appropriate systems are in place. The computer press provides case studies of the problems faced by leaders and managers when large-scale management information systems do not match the expectations of organizations and the communities they service. Unless there are well-designed and robust information systems in place, technology's speed and capabilities may drive a behavior that may not always be beneficial but can be part of the e-world. So, the issue is how to achieve a reasonable balance between making speedy and thoughtful decisions as the organization encounters a rapidly changing operating environment.

In terms of *individual and community*, there may be greater freedom and autonomy when communicating with each other and the "outside" world as an outcome of ICT. E-mail and the cell phone have generally replaced the landline telephone. (These modes of communication are preferred by gen-Xers, and even more so for the millennium generation, and they are quickly extending to the boomers and veterans). As noted previously, although technology facilitates *individual* autonomy and connectivity, it can also lead to a sense of isolation. Virtual teams and individuals, working from home or elsewhere, may not have the same opportunities to meet face to face and build the same *community* as those who are in the traditional workplace. Kanter (2001) notes that a 1999 study of more than 6,000 employees indicates that one of the top reasons they remained with their current employers was their relationships with coworkers. Certainly, almost all the research on employee motivation and job satisfaction in the 20th century shows that social interaction in the workplace is an important issue. Dependency on face-to-face communication and meeting at the water-cooler will change significantly when the boomers start to retire over the next two decades. New skills in using e-mail and video conferencing need to be acquired. Interaction with users who do not visit the service in person requires user-friendly Internet sites and well-trained staff in call centers who can handle both technology and information access issues. It requires well-trained and experienced staff with exceptional communication skills to walk remote users through their problems and ensure they are solved. But for some users and staff members, face-to-face interaction in a physical workplace is important. The challenge for leaders in the e-world is how to create a new sense of community while maintaining autonomy in a virtual environment without any face-to-face contact, in a place where people come together. No longer is the inquiry desk or the search room the only place the community visits.

The third paradox, *top-down and grass roots*, has existed for a great many years. What makes it more important today is the impact of technology and relatively recent changes in management practices. Empowering staff and the flattening of the organizational structure have been occurring for years, driven largely by economic conditions and technological developments. Both empowering and flattening (grass roots) means staff now have a much greater influence on operations than in the past. Technology makes it possible for any or all "voices" to speak to an issue, invited or not. Those voices can be heard both within as well as outside the organization. It is the unthinking leader who does not recognize the potential impact of one or more voices being heard by the outside world. Another factor favoring grass roots is that change is occurring so rapidly it is almost impossible for one person (the leader or supervisor) to absorb it all; thus, input from the frontline people becomes very valuable. Leaders must grapple with the task of maintaining control and accountability while engaging in collaborative activities and empowering behavior.

A good example is performing an Internet search, which can overwhelm a person with a large volume of information—some accurate and relevant, some useless. It takes time to sort the good from the bad. Even within the organization, the volume of information (*details*) generated every day can be beyond one person's ability to handle it effectively and still maintain some sense of the *big picture*. Although "information overload" has been with us for a long time, as well as being discussed in the management and professional literature, today the problem is becoming very difficult to manage effectively. A leader must keep some focus on the overall direction of the organization and the progress it is making toward the desired goal(s) while keeping a sharp eye out for factors that may indicate there needs to be some rapid adjustment(s). Priorities need to be set and the detailed monitoring delegated to others. The important point is to *delegate*. Many of the staff may have access to the information, but if no one has the responsibility for monitoring it, the task is likely to fall through the cracks. A related issue is the fact that details and changing directions have a tendency to cause people to think of the "now" and lose sight of the bigger picture and maintaining momentum toward the organization's vision. There is a danger of falling into a pattern of "fighting fires" and focusing on immediate issues without working toward long-term goals. The obvious challenge is balancing details against the need to take a long-range view and for the leader to ensure that managers and supervisors carry out this vital aspect of their roles efficiently and effectively.

Worth Checking Out

An article written with law librarians in mind, but which includes suggestions and insights applicable to any information service setting, is Kathryn Hensiack's "Too Much of a Good Thing: Information Overload and Law Librarians," *Legal Reference Services Quarterly* 22, no. 2/3 (2003): 85–98.

Pulley and Sessa's final paradox is *flexible and steady*. Again, this is not a new paradox for organizations. What has changed is its pervasive implications for all types of organizations. In the past, a number of organizational types—including a great many research libraries—operated in what might be termed a placid environment (limited threats, little change), and only a few functioned in a turbulent one (many threats, high level of change). Today, most organizations must be aware of changing circumstances and recognize that there may be, for the first time, serious threats. Stability, as long as it did not endanger long-term viability, was highly desired (many older people still wish for that environment) because it allowed for a clear focus and momentum toward well-established goals. For most of today's organizations, the requirement for flexibility and the associated changes makes it difficult to discern how much, if any, progress is taking place. For today's leader, a major challenge is keeping everyone focused on long-term directions while responding to a rapidly changing environment.

Paradoxes such as these five, along with other challenges, make it less and less likely a successful organization will be led by a "great person" or a "Lone Ranger." The "I am the boss, and I am in control" leadership style is, or should be, a thing of the past in most organizations. Yes, there are almost always one or more senior persons with ultimate accountability for the organization's success or failure. However, in many organizations, there is a growing use of multiple leaders and managers sharing most of the responsibility. The concepts covered in chapter 4 (team building) apply to all levels of the organization, including the senior management team. One issue in some organizations is that many of the staff still want, or hope for, the hero or heroine leader to whisk in and solve all problems so they can remain in their comfort zones. Essentially, they do not yet accept the idea that some leadership on their part is necessary. This is particularly challenging when the staff is roughly proportional in terms of generations.

Gen-Xers and the millennium generation are usually the ones who see the need for self-leadership, and they are frustrated by the fact that not everyone shares that view.

The Information Service E-Environment

Many information services continue to provide a physical place, with a large proportion of the staff working there most of the time. People (users) come there to access resources and services, although this has changed; much, if not most, of the access to e-resources is done remotely, and many other user services can be provided in the same way. In time, all access to information will probably be carried out at a distance. This may happen more quickly for libraries than for archives, where digitizing very large collections of original documents will require a considerable investment of funding. However, in the case of some types of libraries (e.g., at colleges and universities), changes in user habits have been fostered by a change in approaches to learning. Since society has moved toward working collaboratively in the workplace and the community at large, the sense of group- and team-based work has been woven into the curriculum. Students need access to small areas where they can work in small groups, and the library has been transformed into the learning center and information commons. Children's services in public libraries have expanded to provide more activities to enrich the educational and recreational process. It is in records management and information services in fields such as finance, health care, and law that remote access will be the norm. Regardless of how change is taking place, there is a need to think about how leadership of information services, now and in the future, must adjust.

For services in the not-for-profit sector, the paradoxes discussed earlier may be somewhat less pressing than they are for profit-oriented organizations. There is less pressure in the sense that their immediate survival, unlike for profit-oriented organizations, may not be in question; however, in the longer term, meaningful responses will be essential. The swift and mindful paradox is probably more of an issue at the interpersonal level in the service than it is in terms of causing organizational shifts. There is, at present, still time for thoughtful data collecting, assessment-based decision making, planning, and so on. In part, some services are insulated from the speed factor due to their being part of a larger organization. As such, the parent body's vision, mission, and strategic plans guide the subunit's activities and overall direction. Related is the fact that budgets and financial resources are set for a year or more, with limited if any opportunities to secure additional funding for making significant shifts in activities. This makes sudden changes that require funding much more difficult and less likely. Further, in many situations, the information service has very limited power to shift significant amounts of money from one activity to another. This is *not* to say the question of rapid change will not increase in the future; it will as the parent organization is forced to make more rapid adjustments to a changing environment. An information service leader must work effectively in such circumstances to maintain the existing level of funding while working to secure the funds necessary to respond to the parent institution's changing needs.

Given that many information service employees still work in a single physical facility, the problem of community is not yet a significant issue, at least due to technology. Systems with branch operations have had to build a systemwide sense of community for many years, long before technology played a major role in operations. One of the great benefits of technological change is that today's technological capabilities make it easier to create a sense of oneness than in the past. Technology, combined with some systemwide face-to-face events, creates a very strong community.

The top-down and grass roots paradox has also been an issue for services for some time, and it will grow as more of the millennium generation join the staff. As noted in chapter 3, members of this generation are completely comfortable with technology, are eager to be involved, and are generally not shy about expressing their views about issues that concern them. Information services that are engaging in empowerment activities are starting to more effectively balance the need for a collaborative work environment while maintaining a firm direction for the organization.

In the library sector, the current integrated library systems are capable of producing overwhelming amounts of real-time management information about the organization's performance and operations. The good news is that, for the moment, the pressure to address that detail almost instantaneously is still in the manageable range. There is still time to consider the "big picture" with some degree of care.

Many large services, such as national archives and research libraries, have traditionally been very stable organizations as well as bureaucratic hierarchies, but this is less true today as technology and economic constraints force a flattening of the organizational structure. This will produce a substantial pressure to exhibit greater flexibility. That will not, however, reduce the need to think and act in terms of long-term goals.

Although there may be less pressure on other information services to address these paradoxes, there are areas where e-leadership must be addressed. This is especially true for information services that operate on a global scale, with a central location and offices around the world. They share the same concerns of their parent multinational corporations in terms of the e-environment, particularly in terms of managing diversity, cultural, communication, and language questions.

At the more typical level, information services are becoming partners in e-services organized either nationally or regionally (e.g., 24/7 reference services). Other areas where e-projects are set up with growing frequency are consortial activities such as group acquisitions or research; technology makes it possible for even the smallest service to play an active role in governance and projects. Naturally, there are collaborative projects and professional association responsibilities—internationally, nationally, regionally, and locally—that are partly or completely handled electronically. Professional publishing activities are now more truly global as a result of technology allowing for rapid information sharing.

Internally, virtual teams increase staff involvement in operating the service as former barriers such as shift differentials present fewer hurdles to team membership. We already mentioned technology's potential in terms of branch operations and building commitment. Finally, there is increased potential for teleworking, where staff may not come to the service on a day-to-day basis. A wide range of expertise can be drawn on by pulling in freelance staff (e.g., in marketing, public relations, and web management) to complete projects. We will explore teleworking later in this chapter.

All these developments call for adjusting the leadership approach in order to take technology into consideration in a serious manner. Some emerging areas indicate what the adjustments should be. We will explore several of these areas now.

Worth Checking Out

Karen Schneider outlines the challenges and benefits of managing the "virtual workplace" in her article "Managing the Virtual Workplace," *Library Journal NetConnect* (Winter 2003): 24–25.

Virtual versus Face-to-Face Leadership

Leadership is about convincing people that the organizational direction (vision) is exciting, realistic, and doable. It is about inspiring people and getting them committed to the organization. It is about giving them confidence so they can achieve the organizational goals. It is about coaching and mentoring them in their career development activities. In a face-to-face environment, employees interpret more than just the words a leader uses; they draw on a variety of visual clues in making their assessment of the words. Lacking visual clues, people depend on tone of voice and the nature of written words in e-communication, unless there is wide use of videoconferencing and webcams within the organization. Leadership in the e-environment may call for some new skills, especially technological in character, but it primarily changes the emphasis and timing of leadership behaviors and events, with technology serving as the "wild card."

Interest in *e-leadership* is relatively new, although there has been interest in virtual teams and collaborative projects in an e-environment for a number of years. An Internet search produces a fair amount of information on moving into e-commerce. However, research on a serious basis into the subject of e-leadership is really just beginning, and the literature is "thin," especially in comparison to leadership in general. One area where work is needed is in gaining a better understanding of how technology changes people's behavior in organizations, vis-à-vis both one another and the organization. We all, to a greater or lesser degree, use technology, but we have more to discover about its impact on staff dynamics. What follows is a synopsis of ideas about e-leadership and virtual teams from the past ten to fifteen years.

A number of authors have made some broad-based statements about e-leadership. Pulley, McCarthy, and Taylor (2000, p. 3) for example, make three points about e-leadership:

- Electronic leadership is hyperlinked rather than hierarchical.
- E-leadership can come from anywhere within the hyperlinked system.
- The language of the Web is dialogue—authentic conversations in which people realize that behind the technology are human beings.

We agree with Pulley and her colleagues, as well as almost everyone writing on this topic, that communication plays a crucial role in e-leadership. More precisely, at least at present, it is *written* communication that will make or break the e-leader. In time, as Pulley, McCarthy, and Taylor note, an e-leader will need to be fluent in all existing and developing communication technologies, which may allow for better and more cost effective visual capabilities.

Being an effective writer has always been an asset for a leader; however, in an e-environment where so much of the interaction is through e-mail and various online postings, the skill becomes paramount. A leader cannot treat e-mail in the casual manner that so many people seem to do. A hastily worded e-mail to someone you have never met face to face, or only briefly once or twice, can create a long-term trust or confidence issue. In face-to-face situations, you get visual clues and cues about how the recipient took your message, and you can quickly attempt to correct any faux pas. Even in a telephone conversation, the listener may be able to glean cues from the speaker's tone of voice (sincerity, urgency, sarcasm, disinterest) and use that to help interpret the message. Lacking such feedback in the e-environment, your only indication of a problem may come through slowly by what seems to be an awkward work relationship.

Electronic communication is wonderful in a great many ways, but it also poses some serious challenges, at least in the workplace, such as developing collaborative work relationships and building trust. An e-leader should not treat e-mail and other electronic communication as something between a telephone call and a formal letter. Treating it in the casual way so many of us do, especially when you add in the need, real or imagined, for a speedy response, often leads to ineffective or, worse, damaging communication. We also tend to forget that in some ways it is a more permanent form of communication than hard copy. Despite deleting a file from your PC, even when the recipient(s) also deleted the file, copies likely still reside in cyberspace, on hard drives, and on backup tapes. It is also extraordinarily easy to forward messages, not to mention routing them to the wrong person(s). As the saying goes, "Don't say anything in an e-message that you wouldn't want to appear on the front page of the newspaper." We believe this should be the motto of the e-leader.

Worth Checking Out

A number of e-mail etiquette (or "netiquette") articles and web-sites exist. Two worth reviewing are Judith Kallos's "Business Email Etiquette," available at www.sideroad.com/Netiquette/email-etiquette-business.html (accessed May 1, 2006), and Gary Smith's "Twenty Tips for Communication Etiquette," *Intercom* 52 (September/October 2005): 18–19.

Although effective written communication is the key element in e-leadership, other behaviors also play a role. One scenario involves the leader interacting with some followers face to face and with others primarily through technology. Very often the members of an e-group believe that the face-to-face group members have greater influence with the leader than do those remotely located. Naturally, that can influence their attitudes and morale in a somewhat negative way. Leaders of such groups must work especially hard to create a balance. They can do at least two things to achieve that balance. First, when communicating with the e-group, leaders should make the messages longer than they might normally do in a face-to-face situation, in a manner that conveys caring, support, and understanding. For example, instead of "Thanks for your comment," a more appropriate message is "Your comment is interesting. I'd like to hear a little more detail. I look forward to discussing this further." In a face-to-face situation, the first response could be sufficient when nonverbals accompany it. A second tactic is to reinforce the initial message with a follow-up message along the same lines. Such an approach, when done properly, does not necessarily indicate agreement with or acceptance of the content, but it shows appreciation for the input and encourages further contributions. However, leaders should remember that culture may affect how e-mails are crafted in different parts of the world. This can be noticeable in postings to international e-groups—some can be very brief and others are more expansive.

"Reach out and touch someone" is a company motto introduced several years ago that achieved a degree of popularity and remains familiar to many in the United States. It has some relevance for e-leaders. In face-to-face relationships, there are opportunities for one-on-one and informal group encounters where the leader can offer a word or two of praise and encouragement, share a passing thought about something work related, or just engage in small talk. Such encounters can create a stronger relationship and sense of trust in one another as well as nurture a sense of being involved in organizational affairs. To achieve something similar in an e-environment, a leader can and should be an initiator as well as a responder in terms of communication. Certainly one needs to strike a balance between too little and too much communication; however, in the e-environment there can be a tendency to underestimate the need for leader-to-follower communication and basically just be a responder. Individualized messages, whenever possible, will help create a sense of belonging and that there is a caring human being at the other end. Putting out regular e-newsletters that contain more than just basic work announcements, such as "Thoughts to Ponder," staff news, events, and so on, can also help develop a more personal feeling and reduce the sense of isolation that remote staff may have.

Some other ways to create a positive e-environment include having chat rooms, wikis, and online bulletin boards where staff can interact. Limits often need to be put in place on these activities in order to keep work flowing; however, time is spent on such activities in the face-to-face environment, so why not for e-workers as well? There are pros and cons to allowing anonymous postings, and clear rules about what is and is not allowable should be in place before going down this path. Using electronic polling, when such polls are called for, for all the staff—on site and remote—also creates a single group sense of community. Information can be gathered by creating simple web-based surveys or by using services designed for online collaboration.

Employees have always needed to understand a leader's intent and goals; however, in the virtual world it becomes imperative. Several factors make this so important. First and foremost, e-workers must, by the very nature of the work, operate more independently and make decisions on their own. They also often need access to data at times outside of the face-to-face operational hours. (Note: there are concerns in the e-environment about data integrity that require careful thought and planning to ensure validity.) Thus, an e-leader must make a greater effort to make sure intent and goals are clearly understood.

Avolio and Kahai (2003, p. 333) summarize what they see as the major issues for e-leadership in the early 21st century:

- Leaders and followers have more access to information and each other, and this is changing the nature and content of their interactions.
- Leadership is migrating to lower and lower organizational levels and out through the boundaries of the organization to both customers and suppliers.
- Leadership creates and exists in networks that go across traditional organizational and community boundaries.
- Followers know more at an earlier point in the decision-making process, and this is potentially affecting the credibility and influence of leaders.
- Unethical leaders with limited resources can now impact negatively a much broader audience of potential followers.
- The amount of time and contact that even the most senior leaders can have with their followers has increased, although the contact is not in the traditional face-to-face mode.

We would add, although it could be subsumed under their first point, that written communication and trust have become increasingly important in the virtual workplace.

Some years ago, Charles Handy (1995, pp. 44–47) raised the question "How do you manage people whom you do not see?" His answer is that you do it by trusting them, but he acknowledges that the absence of face-to-face contact makes it difficult for traditional managers and leaders to deal with the "rules" of trust in an e-environment. Handy offers seven rules of trust:

- Trust is not blind.
- Trust needs boundaries.
- Trust demands learning.
- Trust is tough.
- Trust needs bonding.
- Trust needs touch.
- Trust requires leaders.

Really "knowing" someone in just the virtual world presents challenges; it is difficult enough in a face-to-face environment where you have nonverbal clues. One positive element for e-staff is that they went through some thorough assessment during the hiring process. As mentioned earlier, spending some time at the very start of the e-relationship in social exchanges before getting down to task messages helps gain some perspective about a person. One of this book's authors engaged in a project with a person he had never met; the first e-mail message from the coauthor-to-be contained only comments about what not to do, what was wrong with this or that aspect of the project, and what the person would not do. The negative tone of this initial message set the tone for the entire project. Although the work was successfully completed, the work relationship could be termed prickly at best—very unlike the relationship (open and trusting) between this book's authors. This is probably due, in part, as a result of having met one another at several professional meetings some years prior to engaging in our virtual collaboration, which has produced three books. We have met only twice during our six-year collaboration and have spoken on the telephone a few times. What has transpired is a wealth of e-mails, some of which have nothing to do with the work itself (personal activities as well as comments about world events) but which are the key to maintaining a trusting work relationship. Based on our experience, reinforced by the professional literature, we suggest that anyone with direct responsibility for e-staff have some face-to-face contact with them as soon as possible in the relationship. Although that is not always feasible, it is highly desirable and probably not a problem in most information service environments, except for some professional e-activities. Further, the initial e-messages should include some social exchanges, if not be completely dedicated to such exchanges, and other communication modes should be employed as well to help create and maintain a sense of sharing and of being people as well as workers.

Setting clear and measurable goals, including timelines, for e-staff establishes the boundaries of trust between leaders and remote personnel. As Handy states, in the e-environment, control comes into play after an activity rather than during—was the goal achieved and within the required time frame? We have mentioned several times the need for continuous learning for everyone in the organization. Remote staff must take on greater responsibility for self-learning in order to do their work effectively, which in turn builds trust. However, the e-leader must also be ready to provide coaching and mentoring and make it clear that she is willing to do this. Again, the absence of physical presence makes it harder to determine if assistance is needed.

If trust is misplaced, whether in the physical or e-environment, a leader must take immediate and firm action to correct the situation. There is a tendency not to take quick action in the case of remote workers because of uncertainty about what occurred. Letting the matter "slide" can cause additional problems with other staff when they become aware of the situation—and they will. Building commitment, as we have noted numerous times, is a major activity for the leader regardless of the environment; doing so in the virtual world calls for careful and thoughtfully written communication. When done well, the bonding will be as strong as in the physical workplace. Handy's "touch rule" reinforces the need for some face-to-face interaction with remote workers—"the more virtual an organization becomes, the more its people need to meet in person" (p. 46). His last rule also reinforces what others say about the need for multiple leaders, especially in the e-work world.

Check These Out

Susan Annunzio's book *eLeadership: Proven Techniques for Creating an Environment of Speed and Flexibility in the Digital Economy* (New York: Free Press, 2001) provides some useful guidance for leaders of not-for-profit organizations, although its main thrust is e-business. She has a particularly good section on generational differences and their implications for e-leadership. Gary Kissler's 2001 article ''E-Leadership'' (*Organizational Dynamics* 30, no. 2: 121–133) also focuses on e-business but contains ideas for any e-leader.

Becoming the Virtual Information Service

As we stated earlier, many information services are not yet truly virtual organizations, and they may not become so for some time to come. Providing remote access to electronic and other services is a small, but important, step toward becoming an e-organization. Yes, it is essential for providing the community served with what they expect and want, but it does not necessarily change the organizational structure or how staff goes about doing their work. To a large extent, people still come into a physical facility looking for in-person assistance and service. (The press notices about "deserted libraries" do not accurately reflect the reality, at least in the United States, where turnstile counts are stable and in many cases increasing. What *is* decreasing is book circulation as more and more full-text e-publications become available, and this is what the popular press refers to as deserted.) Moving slowly and thoughtfully, before it becomes imperative, toward greater and greater virtuality gives everyone time to learn what will and will not work in a given set of circumstances. Deciding where and when to make the move(s) calls for leadership that is thoroughly grounded in both traditional management issues and technology.

There is a continuum of virtual organizational structure. At one end is the most totally virtual organization. Examples include Amazon.com and Google, where customer interaction is all virtual in character and where the organization outsources noncore activities. Even these examples have a physical presence somewhere, with staff working at those locations. Information services are closer to the other end of the spectrum, making some use of technology to create an e-presence, outsourcing some activities, and using a limited e-staff.

Google's Way

Google Inc., like every organization, has a corporate culture. In Google's case that culture is recognized, valued, and maintained because it is viewed as a major factor in the growth and creativity of the organization. As the company expanded beyond the home office, thought and money has gone into maintaining the culture across time and space. Senior management decided on a strategy of employing a mix of technology (computers and videoconferencing) and "old-fashioned travel" as the way to address the challenge. "Set up some kind of video link and have them always running. Put them in common areas, get people out of their little workspaces. Expect people to travel some and don't skimp on interpersonal relationships" (Larson, 2006, p. D3).

Most organizations begin their movement along the continuum through office work and work teams. Before starting the process, leaders must be clear about the reasons for making the move. Helms and Raiszadeh (2002, p. 242) identify six common and valid reasons for increasing organizational virtuality—to reduce real estate costs, to increase productivity, as a means of reengineering, as an HR strategy, out of necessity, and to increase flexibility. Most, if not all, of those reasons can apply to information services. We would add another reason to the list, or a variation on the flexibility theme: to provide a new or better customer service. What is *not* a good reason is to make the move just because others are doing so.

Once the decision is made to change and clear goals and parameters are set, it is better to start the process on a small scale. Letting a few people try teleworking or establishing some teams operating with technology are ways to "test the water" before diving in. This second suggestion may sound counterintuitive to e-leadership, but successful leadership of face-to-face teams is essential for having success with e-teams. Additionally, both the organization and staff must have a clear picture of what "working out of the office" entails before committing to the concept.

Helms and Raiszadeh point out some essential but often overlooked issues when thinking about teleworking. Some of the most important issues are very individual in nature—the presence of potential distractions, the lack of an appropriate work space, the need for higher-level technology at home, and the need for socialization are some examples. Another crucial issue is the individual's self-motivation and ability to stay on task. Even such simple questions as whether the organization will pay for remodeling to create a suitable home office, including appropriate work furniture, not to mention the necessary technology, become serious issues. Another issue is providing the requisite high-level technical support 24/7 for the home worker, since one alluring aspect of working at home is that many times it can be done whenever it suits the person, as long as the goals are met. We need to emphasize the importance of monitoring task achievement of teleworkers. Frequent reviews of job descriptions and performance goals in light of changing needs and technological capabilities are also essential.

Questions to Ponder

Think about the following questions in terms of your present circumstances:

- What are the implications of technology for your leadership style?
- How can you integrate your leadership style with your available technology?
- Is your style an enabler of, or a constraint on, technology?
- Can your style coevolve with technology?
- Are there sound reasons to actively migrate to a more virtual organization?
- What organizational constraints to such a migration exist?
- Are there resource issues for such a move, and if so, how can they be overcome?

Two other important areas to think about are (1) what, if any, differences exist between the work of remote staff and those working on site and (2) what, if any, adjustments may be called for in vendor, control, assessment, and rewards systems because of the those differences. A third consideration, and probably the most important, is that of trust between the leader, the manager or supervisor, and the teleworker. Some managers and supervisors believe that teleworkers don't work as hard as the "people in the office" and may overlook remote employees when there are opportunities for promotion or staff development. The feeling that they can't watch all staff members all the time gets in the way of what can benefit the workers and the organization. Talking with teleworkers indicates that their output may in fact be higher than that of office-based employees. They have fewer office distractions and are aware that their output is monitored. Issues need to be addressed openly by both the employer and the employee—checks and balances must be put in place, with both sides having a clear idea of the quality and quantity of output required. Contracts need to be negotiated to protect both parties. It also becomes a matter of creating a new or significantly modified organizational culture.

E-Team Issues

There are two broad categories of e-teams—internal and external (multiorganizational)—that information services should think about. Keep in mind that the basics of team creation and maintenance outlined in chapter 4 apply equally to the virtual and face-to-face environments. A major difference is a leader seldom has as much control over the basic issues, especially in the case of external teams. The primary reason for using virtual teams is to overcome time or space (geography) issues.

Cascio and Shurygailo (2003) suggest a four-cell matrix for thinking about variation issues in virtual teams. One axis is for either a single or multiple leader situation, and the other axis represents either single or multiple locations. The least complex situation is the single leader, single location variation. We suggest that this is the place to start any migration to virtual teams or teleworkers because it gives everyone a chance to work out problems that arise. More complex arrangements can follow.

Internal information service teams, especially those created for a special project, usually consist of people from several departments who often engage in the team activities along with some or all of their normal duties. This creates a situation of multiple leaders or supervisors and, most commonly, a single location; where there are branch operations, multiple locations are possible. Some of the problems can arise from cross-departmental teams where normal duties exist alongside team responsibilities. Although the use of technology makes it easier to shift work activities to "off hours," it cannot reduce the pressure of performance expectations for team members with additional duties. We suggest that when first moving into team activities—traditional or virtual—team members should have some or all of their regular duties reduced or removed whenever possible. There is a significant learning curve for both leaders and staff when first making such a shift in operations, and burdening team members with maintaining their old responsibilities just compounds the complexity.

Once established, many face-to-face teams begin to use technology for facilitating their work without having the leader suggest the possibility. In time, there may be little to differentiate between virtual and face-to-face teams. Thus, leaders making the move to team-based work in what they believe will be a face-to-face environment would do well to think at least a little about the potential role technology may play in team activities and how to handle it when it does arise. Arnison and Miller (2002) suggest that traditional teams can realize some of the same technological benefits as virtual teams. The most obvious benefit is that technology can increase communication outside scheduled meeting times. Thanks to such tools as blogs, shared folders for documentation, or even group mail distribution lists or "reflectors," there is the potential for network building as well as increased flexibility in work and meeting times. Another major plus is that technology can increase the potential for cross-boundary collaboration. Faster response time for carrying out tasks is a possibility, as long as people are aware of the need to be thoughtful as well as quick. There may also be a carry-over in the area of measuring outcomes and contributions. All these potential benefits do, of course, require support by the leader and careful thought.

Check This Out

Chris Collison and Geoff Parcell's *Learning to Fly: Practical Lessons from One of the World's Leading Knowledge Companies* (Milford, CT: Capstone, 2001) is about knowledge management and expands on some of the points we make about working in teams and sharing information.

When leading a virtual team assigned to handle a project, whether an internal or external team, there are several significant areas to address if the team is to succeed. In the case of a multiorganizational team, such as one working on a nationwide 24/7 reference service, the challenges are more complex than for the internal team. Based on our experience, the first key activity is to ensure that senior leaders are committed to the project and are willing to devote the necessary resources to see it through. Senior leaders must work out several important details such as selecting one person to be the liaison between the team and the senior leaders. Establishing reporting and communication responsibilities is also a detail the group should work through before creating the team. A significant amount of time should go into discussing team milestones, timelines, assessment, and the skills team members need to bring to the table. The last item is very important, so that the leaders will, or should, select a staff person capable of making a contribution to team activities and not let local politics or feelings color the selection. Without such discussions it is almost inevitable that the team will have performance problems, the project could be delayed, and a growing sense of frustration will occur among the libraries.

Once the team is in place, the liaison leader should start the e-team process with some social e-mails. Early on, the team should select one of its members to serve as "chair" in the sense of initiating meetings and serving as the contact person for the liaison leader. These steps will smooth out communication and ensure that information is shared appropriately and in a timely manner. The leader must start these processes and make certain there is progress in building the trust between members that is so essential for positive outcomes.

In our experience, cross-organizational teams often encounter problems that are beyond their ability or responsibility to resolve. For example, when a vendor is involved, the team would rarely have the authority to make changes in an agreement or to commit to cost increases, as such issues normally remain with the senior leadership. On the other hand, there probably would be a significant amount of interaction between the team and vendor. Again, the liaison leader should be involved in creating a structure for that interaction. No vendor will be happy responding to multiple voices about an issue on one project. Another example of where senior leadership may be called on is when there is to be a workload distribution across organizational lines. In some cases, the team can make an effort and sometimes make solid recommendations on such issues; in other cases the problem will be beyond their "pay grade." One such issue might be, in our example of nationwide 24/7 reference service, the problem of fairly balancing the workload if there are not enough libraries participating in one or two time zones. Resolving such issues is the responsibility of senior leaders, but the liaison leader must be alert to such developing concerns and take proactive steps so that the team's activities can effectively continue. Clearly, that means the liaison should be monitoring team activities.

Regardless of whether the team is project oriented or not, or is internal or external in nature, it must establish some communication protocols. A small example is how to communicate an idea or opinion. Should an e-mail be sent to everyone? Or just to the leader, who then shares it? Should the idea be posted on a team website? Some of the options may call for additional software or other resources that may require funding or time to master. The leader will play a major role in this process. Some other options to consider using are blogs and wikis, each of which has certain advantages but requires some investment of time and energy.

Check This Out

Although most employees have experience with e-mail, few have any idea how to use it effectively. The performance of e-teams and e-workers depends, in part, on their using e-mail to its full potential. A good reference to share with e-staff is David Angell and Brent Heslop's *The Elements of E-Mail Style: Communicate Effectively via Electronic Mail* (Reading, MA: Addison-Wesley, 1994).

Teleworking teams are a little different from project teams. First and foremost, they are usually thought of as being long-standing. Second, they are composed entirely of institutional employees, so the leader usually has more knowledge of the staff involved and control over the team and its activities. It is easier to establish such things as the core hours team members will be available to one another and to leadership. An important point for leaders responsible for tele-workers, individual or team, is that "control" must be in terms of task outcomes and objectives rather than hours worked. This is something that may take time to get used to, both for leadership and staff. Although hours should not be an issue, the time frame allocated to complete a task or project becomes very impor-tant to establish at the outset, not after the fact.

Some practical communication concerns arise in teleworking beyond those mentioned earlier, such as establishing set times for contacting home workers, considering whether the service should pay for a separate work telephone line, and determining if there should be regularly scheduled "in the service" time (e.g., face-to-face meetings). Sometimes unexpected concerns come up, such as the need to help home workers establish reasonable boundaries between home and work; this can be a challenge for home workers with small children to do on their own.

By establishing realistic tasks and timelines, the e-leader also provides the context or structure of the agendas for e-workers, especially e-teams. According to Zigurs (2003, p. 345), research shows that having a "process structure" (agenda) for e-teams is a significant factor in their success or failure. Providing groupware tools helps develop such a structure. Such software will provide one or more of the following, to a greater or lesser degree: communication support, information processing, and process structuring. Communication support goes beyond e-mail and chat rooms, as some packages offer electronic brainstorming, group display screens, and discussion threading. Information processing mod-ules usually contain some modeling or SWOT analysis capability. Process structuring capabilities often include agenda setting, meetingware, and even par-ticipation "enforcement."

Some Things to Think About

- What can be done to build contextual cues into e-messages to reduce the chances of misunderstanding?
- How can you, as leader, provide team process structure while maintaining team flexibility?
- How can you, as leader, project a sense of ''presence'' in an e-environment?
- What can you do, as leader, to assist in building virtual team trust?

A challenge, as noted earlier, for the e-leader is building team member relation-ships that are at least similar to what can exist in face-to-face teams. There is a tendency for virtual teams to focus almost exclusively on tasks, with little effort to get to know one another. This does not always lead to failure but will almost always make the effort more difficult and often unpleasant for some or all of the team members. That in turn may make them less willing to engage in future e-team efforts.

Team trust, whether face to face or virtual, generally goes through a three-stage process. In stage one, performance is based on hope, expectation, and even fear rather than on true trust. That is, members have little or no knowledge of individual capabilities and just hope for the best. When that "best" materializes, the group moves on to the next stage. Fear can play a factor when the initial exchanges contain some doubts or negative thoughts on the part of one or more team members. This usually leads to significant problems and failure to move to a trusting work group. In stage two, members have a good knowledge of the abilities and work motivations of one another. They usually are able to predict performance outcomes. In stage three, team members identify with one another, share values, and are fully confident they can and will perform well. Some research (Coutu, 1998) suggests that although the three-stage process does occur in successful teams that exist only virtually, virtual team trust does or does not get established at the outset. That is, the initial exchange is *the* crucial point, just as we found in our experiences with virtual collaboration. Negativity in the first few exchanges underlies all future exchanges, and trust is unlikely to ever develop. There is an old saying that "a person never gets a second chance to make a first impression." In face-to-face situations that are long term, that is not an ironclad rule—early mistakes can be overcome. It would seem that for virtual teams, however, it is indeed irrefutable.

Check These Out

Judith Holton's 2001 article "Building Trust and Collaboration in a Virtual Team" (*Team Performance Management* 7, no. 3/4: 36–47) provides both a report on virtual team research projects and some excellent advice on building team trust. Stephan Zaccaro and Paige Bader published a fine essay that summarizes the key issues for e-leaders and virtual teams: "E-Leadership and the Challenge of Leading E-Teams: Minimizing the Bad and Maximizing the Good," *Organizational Dynamics* 31, no. 4 (2003): 377–387. For an overview of some of the technological tools one can draw on for e-work, read Darlene Fichter's "The Many Forms of E-Collaboration: Blogs, Wikis, Portals, Groupware, Discussion Boards, and Instant Messaging," *Online* 29, no. 4 (2005): 48–50.

An e-leader can attempt to address the first-impression issue by having an initial face-to-face meeting whenever possible. Lacking such an opportunity, then the leader should be the initiator of the first and perhaps second round of exchanges between team members. After providing a sense of what the team "charge" is, the leader can use the rest of the exchange for a storytelling session. One way to structure such an exercise is to ask each team member to respond to a question such as "What was the most exciting project you ever worked on, and what was it that made it exciting?" A wise leader will monitor later team exchanges for signs of distrust.

As a reminder, other principles of team management—such as performance assessment and rewards, as discussed in chapter 4—do apply to e-teams and must be considered by the leader when creating and maintaining virtual teams.

E-Mentoring

Just because there is little or no face-to-face contact in some virtual environments does not mean mentoring is not needed or effective. Mentoring has a very positive impact on career development and on work performance. E-workers should not have to go without the benefits of mentoring.

A review of the literature on mentoring suggests that while it has benefits, it is not as broadly available as might be desirable for all classes of employees. Two areas that appear to be weak are cross-gender and cross-ethnic mentoring. It may be that e-mentoring can help change these shortcomings because visual clues seldom, if ever, play a role. For e-mentoring to be effective, both the mentor and mentee must understand the pros and cons of technology when it comes to mentoring.

Check These Out

Hunt, Kevin, ``E-Mentoring: Solving the Issue of Mentoring across Distances,'' *Development and Learning* 19, no. 5 (2005): 7–10.

Mentors By Net, at www.MentorsByNet.co.uk (accessed May 1, 2006). A small-business mentoring site designed for European businesses.

Clearly, socialization exchanges are even more significant in e-mentoring than they are in face-to-face situations. The fact that electronic messaging tends to be more concise is both a plus and a minus for e-mentoring. It can be more fact laden and thus action oriented. On the other hand, so much of traditional mentoring deals with emotions and values, which do not lend themselves well to concise statements. For the process to be truly successful, both the mentor and mentee must resist the tendency to keep electronic messages short and the sense of needing to respond quickly. Time flexibility that comes with technology has the potential for sustaining mentoring relationships that might suffer or fail due to work time constraints.

In organizations that do not value or support mentoring activity, employees can gain access to professional mentoring from outside the organization. Certainly, finding a suitable mentor in such instances can be a challenge. A good place to start the search is with the professional associations and other groups that offer continuing education. Although they themselves may not have a mentoring program, there is a good chance they will be able to provide some direction.

Giving feedback on career options, providing guidance in ways to handle a situation, and suggesting how to prepare an effective résumé all work well in the e-environment. Two areas where e-mentoring has serious shortcomings are behavior modeling and providing mentees with challenging projects. Although it is possible to create challenging e-projects, they often resemble school assignments that are almost always abstract in character and usually lack the consequences of actual work. It is also true that few mentors have the time to develop sound projects. E-modeling, in what is today's (2006) typical workplace technology, can only be indirect at best. Giving some advice on behavior might be thought of as a substitute form of modeling, but a very weak one.

Successful Elements of E-Mentoring

For e-mentoring projects to be successful, both the mentor and mentee should be prepared for the following:

- Placing a heavy emphasis on social messages, especially at the outset of the mentor-mentee relationship
- Engaging in activities and practices that build trust—which becomes crucial for an ongoing relationship
- Realizing that long, detailed e-mail messages or other forms of correspondence should be the norm
- Exhibiting strong enthusiasm
- Being open and honest
- Having access to technology both at home and work in order to facilitate "staying in touch"
- Keeping response times as short as possible

Summary

Although virtual teams and e-work are relatively new concepts to some organizations, e-leadership is becoming ever more important for information service leaders. The subject of e-leadership itself will likewise become better understood as research into it progresses. Changes in technology, especially in terms of visual capabilities, may in time do away with the difference between face-to-face and virtual leadership. For the present, the e-leader must devote more time to honing communication skills in order to be effective. Creating an inspiring vision is only as effective as one is able to communicate it, and in the e-world of today, the written word plays a very significant role along with the range of other communication skills. A second essential skill is to ensure that trust is present and maintained. As stated at the outset of this chapter, e-leadership is not so much a matter of doing something different or new as it is about where one places the emphasis.

References

Arnison, Linda, and Peter Miller, "Virtual Teams: A Virtue for the Conventional Team," *Journal of Workplace Learning* 14, no. 4 (2002): 166–173.

Avolio, Bruce, and Surinder Kahai, "Adding 'E' to E-Leadership: How It May Impact Your Leadership," *Organizational Dynamics* 31, no. 4 (2003): 325–338.

Cascio, Wayne, and Stan Shurygailo, "E-Leadership and Virtual Teams," *Organizational Dynamics* 31, no. 4 (2003): 362–376.

Coutu, Diane, "Trust in Virtual Teams," *Harvard Business Review* 76, no. 3 (1998): 20–21.

Handy, Charles, "Trust and the Virtual Organization," *Harvard Business Review* 73, no. 3 (1995): 40–50.

Helms, Marilyn, and Farhad Raiszadeh, "Virtual Offices: Understanding and Managing What You Cannot See," *Work Study* 51, no. 5 (2002): 240–247.

Kanter, Rosabeth, *Evolve: Succeeding in the Digital Culture of Tomorrow* (Boston: Harvard Business School Press, 2001).

Larson, Jane, "Maintaining a Culture of Innovation," *Arizona Republic*, 13 April 2006, D1, D3.

Pulley, Mary Lynn, John McCarthy, and Sylvester Taylor, "E-Leadership in the Networked Economy," *Leadership in Action* 20, no. 3 (2000): 1–7.

Pulley, Mary Lynn, and Valerie Sessa, "E-Leadership: Tackling Complex Challenges," *Industrial and Commercial Training* 33, no. 6 (2001): 225–230.

Zigurs, Ilze, "Leadership in Virtual Teams: Oxymoron or Opportunity?" *Organizational Dynamics* 31, no. 4 (2003): 339–351.

Part 3

THE EXPERIENCE OF LEADERSHIP

CHAPTER 8

It Isn't Always Easy

This chapter focuses on the following:

• Preparing for the unexpected
• Handling tricky situations
• Being proactive

The final two chapters draw on real-world experiences taken from responses to our survey, conversations with colleagues, and our own careers. This chapter focuses on some of the tricky and unexpected situations that leaders may well encounter—the times when things don't quite work out as they might have intended. The next chapter takes a look at the other side of the coin, focusing on factors crucial for success.

However much we read about the theory of leadership, hear the experts, and enjoy some of the books written by and about the gurus, moving into a leadership role means the unexpected will always happen. This chapter alerts proactive leaders to what we call "banana skins"—factors that can be easily overlooked but that can result in a slipup.

Leaders vs. Managers

Hoadley (1994, p. 12) made a telling point by writing that "most of the research that has been done on the role of the director shows that directors continue to be primarily managers." Substitute the label *leaders* for *directors* and there is a suspicion that this may still, sometimes, be the case today. Leaders emerge from the ranks of managers and supervisors, and it isn't easy to make a change overnight from the old to the new role. There is often only a short period of time between job moves to think deeply about a new position. Time is spent leaving work in good order, with loose ends to be tied up. Moving from managing to leading presents increasing challenges. The leadership role is more politicized, more technological, and probably more fundamental. Accepting a new challenge isn't always easy, and the person moving into the new role may feel more comfortable continuing with familiar tasks.

So, to recap the differences between managing and leading—drawing on Caroselli's (2000) description of the different perspectives—you are a manager if you do the following:

- Direct the work rather than perform it
- Have responsibilities for hiring, firing, training, and disciplining employees
- Exercise authority over the quality of work and the conditions under which it is performed
- Serve as a liaison between employees and upper management
- Motivate employees and contribute to a culture of accomplishment

If you do the following, you are a leader:

- Believe that, working in concert with others, you can make a difference
- Create something of value that did not exist before
- Exhibit positive energy
- Actualize—going beyond vision to create a new reality
- Welcome change

> **BANANA SKIN NO. 1**
>
> Believing that leadership is just managing at a higher level: *Understand the fundamental differences between managing or supervising and leading.*

Balancing Delegation: Not Too Little, Not Too Much

The first challenge is understanding the parent organization and the information service, which involves a lot of listening, asking questions, and looking at internal documentation. It is vital to gather information, but it takes time. Effective leaders delegate and make sure an effective feedback system is in place. But they must avoid the danger of reaching the point where contact with the team, the users, and the governing body is lost. Sometimes the leader becomes overwhelmed with the importance of his new role. Porter (2004) illustrates the question of "how much delegation?" when identifying seven surprises for new CEOs and their warning signs. We have adapted them for the information sector because they have resonance for leaders in any setting.

Surprise 1: You can't run the information service. The warning signs follow:

- You are in too many meetings and involved in too many tactical discussions.
- There are too many days when you feel you have lost control over your time.

Surprise 2: Giving orders is very costly. The warning signs follow:

- You have become a bottleneck.
- Employees are overly inclined to consult you before they act.
- People start using your name to endorse things, as in, "Sally says . . ."

Surprise 3: It is hard to know what is really going on. The warning signs follow:

- You keep hearing things that surprise you.
- You learn about events after the fact.
- You hear concerns and dissenting views through the grapevine rather than directly.

Surprise 4: You are always sending a message. The warning signs follow:

- Employees circulate stories about your behavior that magnify or distort reality.
- People around you act in ways that indicate they're trying to anticipate your likes and dislikes.

Surprise 5: You are not the boss. The warning signs follow:

- You don't know where you stand with board members and your management team.
- Roles and responsibilities of the management team are not clear.
- The discussions in meetings of the management team are limited mostly to reporting on results and management's decisions.

Surprise 6: Pleasing stakeholders is not the goal. The warning signs follow:

- Board members and the management team judge actions by their effect on statistical evidence only.

- People who don't understand the information sector push for decisions that risk the health of the service.

Surprise 7: You are still only human. The warning signs follow:

- You give interviews about you rather than the service.
- Your lifestyle is more lavish or privileged than that of other senior people in the organization.
- You have few, if any, activities not connected with the organization.

> **BANANA SKIN NO. 2**
>
> Delegating but failing to get the balance right: *Not too little, not too much.*

Team Expectations

The hardest expectations to meet are likely to be your own. You've made it. You've done your homework. Of course you will make a success of it. The preparation is done, you've got the position, so others think you have the capability, so why shouldn't you succeed? But circumstances can conspire against you, and we'll examine this along the way. But staying on a high for too long means your expectations are probably a little unrealistic. . . . Staff will expect the following:

- Their leader will demonstrate trust in them.
- When a critical decision is being made, everyone will be involved in the same room, at the same time, to give their input and listen to the leader.
- They will be asked how long it will take to complete a task delegated to them. If it is needed sooner, account will need to be taken of the risks involved.
- Before change is introduced, they will be consulted and a pilot will be run.
- When measuring output, everyone remembers that what gets measured gets manipulated.
- Their leader will concentrate on the big picture, leaving the managers and supervisors to do their work.

The leader will show that he has respect for his predecessor and successor. The team members were there before the leader and will still be there when the leader moves on.

Failing to meet the expectations of the staff can create a dangerous situation. Kets de Vries has written extensively on organizational psychology and comments on "top executives' vulnerabilities which are often intensified by the way followers try to manipulate their leaders" (Coutu, 2004, p. 66).

BANANA SKIN NO. 3

Believing you are the only person who has expectations: *The boss, users, and staff also have expectations and ways to use their power. Don't forget Porter's list of surprises.*

Gender Issues

Women who move into a position previously held by men may encounter challenges. This is well documented, but we suspect that gender issues may challenge both men and women. Staff will be a little wary of a new boss, and strong bosses of the same, or opposite, gender may publicly demonstrate that they have power and can rock the boat. Just listen and observe.

Research on this point indicates that there may be differences in the leadership styles exhibited by women and men, and this needs to be understood by the leader and the team.

Check This Out

One paper on gender issues that is worth reading is Steven Appelbaum, Lynda Audet, and Joanne C. Miller, "Gender and Leadership? Leadership and Gender? A Journey through the Landscape of Theories," *Leadership and Organizational Journal* 24, no. 1 (2003): 43–51.

BANANA SKIN NO. 4

Being a woman leading a team used to having men in this role, or vice versa: *Be sensitive to feelings, and be prepared.*

Being in the Public Eye

Being in the public eye doesn't come easy for everyone, but a new leader can't avoid being in the limelight. Everyone is watching and waiting. If you feel uncomfortable, you'll look unhappy and disturb everyone around you. Without an understanding of emotional intelligence, the situation is exacerbated and a downward spiral is created.

It's one of the reasons some people are reluctant to move into a leadership position. The higher up the organization you move, the more you are exposed. Making decisions that may be controversial and that introduce change can be unpopular. There is a feeling that everyone is looking at you, and in a very critical way. People listen to what you say and how you say it, looking for idiosyncrasies if they feel uncomfortable with what you are saying. It's a natural feeling to want to be liked and to have the respect of colleagues. But respect may not come easily, particularly if your style differs from what they are used to. Don't try to follow your predecessor's ways, but learn enough about him to understand where colleagues are coming from. Have courage and hang on to the knowledge that you were selected for the position. Remember that someone is likely to disagree with any decision you make. Know why there might be resistance. One way to bolster self-confidence is to present an image that makes you feel comfortable and that fits the role.

BANANA SKIN NO. 5

Not knowing yourself well enough to have and demonstrate self-confidence: *Think about the image you need to present.*

Watching the Horizon

Monitoring changes in the operational environment is vital. Getting buried in learning about the immediate role can mean that scanning the horizon takes a lower priority.

Tip

Sometimes the potential for new inventions can be overlooked. The British Museum Library used an early form of fax at the end of the 19th century, but it took rather a long time to gain general application in the wider world.

Organizations exist in a state of constant flux. Observing what is happening in the organization at large informs strategy. Board members come and go, policies are reframed, and opportunities emerge. The makeup of the community served changes. Perhaps a TV program generates an upsurge of interest in family history, bringing new users to a genealogical collection. The provision of Internet access to public libraries draws new users who need training and support. Anticipating change and planning ahead is vital. Potential demands and change must be factored into planning. Technological developments have a radical impact, but selecting the winner is a challenge.

To add to the challenges is the question of competition as users increasingly have access to alternative sources of information. They don't need to visit a service point in person and may prefer to pay for convenience and immediacy. Commercial services have moved into the market.

Leaders must exercise judgment, understand risk management, and be well informed about what is happening in the operating environment.

BANANA SKIN NO. 6

Being unaware of what is happening outside the service: *Be an informed leader, and reflect on the intelligence gathered.*

Interdependency of Services

After performing the environmental scan and factoring issues into planning comes the awareness of the nature of collaboration that will be needed to achieve goals. Getting to know the service and its staff is vital to ensure collaboration. However, the pressure to make a mark *within* the service can result in a degree of isolation from what is happening *outside* in the wider world.

But no service is an island. Failing to work collaboratively with the peer group within the organization, to everyone's benefit, is a shortsighted policy. It can limit information flows from within the organization and does not encourage allies who may be needed at some point. Governing boards welcome cooperation between the different parts of their organization. This also means collaborating with external bodies and agencies. The information sector has long relied on cooperative work to maximize the resources available to their users. Collaborating on staff training programs, publicity campaigns, and disaster plans can cut costs and bring people together from other services so that informal networking develops. People feel valued if they get out and about as part of their work. Good ideas emerge, and staff feel refreshed.

BANANA SKIN NO. 7

Allowing isolation of the leader, staff, and service: *The leader and the team must be visible to the user and professional communities.*

Managing Change

Staff anticipate that a new leader will bring changes, and the governing board expects the service to move forward. People anticipate change with varying degrees of enthusiasm, and a new leader wants to make an impact. One of the most challenging responsibilities is having the skills and experience to introduce change successfully.

Kotter (1996) suggests eight reasons why organizations fail in managing change, which can be applied equally to the private and public sectors:

- Not establishing a sense of urgency and allowing too much complacency
- Failing to create a sufficiently powerful guiding coalition
- Underestimating the power of vision
- Undercommunicating the vision by a factor of 10 (or 100 or even 1,000)
- Permitting obstacles to block the new vision
- Failing to create short-term wins
- Declaring victory too soon
- Neglecting to anchor changes firmly in the corporate culture

Kotter spells out some of the consequences: New strategies are not well implemented; reengineering takes too long and costs too much; and quality programs don't get the hoped-for results. Sometimes it's reassuring to know that some challenges haven't changed over time—reflect on Machiavelli's words of wisdom written in the 16th century:

> There is nothing more difficult to arrange, more doubtful of success, and more dangerous to carry through than initiating changes. . . . The innovator makes enemies of all those who prospered under the old order, and only lukewarm support is forthcoming from those who would prosper under the new. Their support is lukewarm partly from fear of their adversaries, who have existing laws on their side, and partly because men are generally incredulous, never really trusting new things unless they have tested them by experience. In consequence, whenever those who oppose the changes can do so, they attack vigorously, and the defense made by others is lukewarm. So both the innovator and his friends are endangered together. . . ." (Machiavelli, 1961, p. 51)

Change needs reflection—a consideration of "what would happen if," an understanding of the implications of introducing change, an estimate of the costs, an assessment of likely support and opposition, and a strategy and plan to manage the process.

BANANA SKIN NO. 8

Introducing change without adequate planning: *The well-informed leader anticipates and plans for change by working with the team.*

Perfectionism

We all want to do a good job; it's what drives job satisfaction, but there is danger in trying to become a perfectionist. For some people, being a perfectionist is deeply embedded in a lack of self-esteem. Perfectionists want to do a flawless job and to succeed better than anyone else has. They seek high levels of achievement—but at a cost. Engrossed in their work to the exclusion of others, they become diffident. It takes longer for them to meet a deadline. They procrastinate and have a "reason" (which is really an excuse) for not meeting deadlines. Time management skills are absent, and often the problem hasn't been picked up during an appraisal.

Lack of preparation can go unrecognized by the team, but it may be diagnosed by peers (e.g., who note that papers have not been adequately prepared for meetings). The problem should be picked up by the leader's boss and handled sensitively, by coaching or counseling. If an intervention isn't made early enough, the perfectionist starts to freeze, moving into a state of mind of becoming afraid to take any action. That is a potential disaster for the leader, the team, and the service.

> **BANANA SKIN NO. 9**
> Believing that every task undertaken can and should be done perfectly: *Working effectively and efficiently should be the aim. Learn to work smarter and to delegate.*

Risk Taking and Risk Aversion

Taking risks and flying by the seat of the pants are seen by some as being an attribute of a successful leader. Risk aversion is a personality trait that should be overcome. It can be tempting to be overly cautious and not make a "brave decision," but to avoid making a decision is as dangerous as taking too much risk. Recognizing a path between the two develops with experience and from understanding the organizational culture and how risk management is viewed. If the governing board operates in a blame culture, then taking too high a risk should clearly be avoided. On the other hand, part of the learning process comes from taking a risk. Healthy organizational cultures recognize that some risks must be taken and encourage employees to learn from their mistakes. We agree with this approach.

> **BANANA SKIN NO. 10**
> Taking risks without understanding how the organizational culture views risks: *Balance risk taking and risk aversion. Without risks the service will never move forward and may well slide backward.*

Learning from Your Failures

Everyone has disappointments from time to time. Perhaps the budget request doesn't get board approval, a paper submitted to a professional journal is not accepted for publication, or a member of the team is not performing as well as she should. Failures will, and do, happen. They are a fact of life, but they shouldn't happen too often. Learn from the experience. Take a quiet moment to review the situation and perhaps make notes. Talking with a mentor can be helpful. Work out how it might have been avoided—and learn the lesson.

The Japanese use the following saying: "You should repeat a problem nine times—by the ninth you'll have the solution."

BANANA SKIN NO. 11

Failing to recognize that not everything will always go as expected: *Recognize a failure, learn from mistakes, and demonstrate humility. We are all human.*

Values and Ethics

Moving to the top can go to a person's head. There are examples in business and the public sector, such as the leader who builds a power base that works to his advantage, rather than that of the team, or perhaps negotiates a salary and benefits beyond the norm for the position.

Power can be abused. The manner in which dissent is handled can be unethical. Dissenters may be denied privileges (e.g., conference attendance, merit increases, preferred leave dates).

Checks and balances need to be in place, including a 360-degree appraisal system for all staff, a regular survey of staff morale, and a transparent arbitration or adjudication system.

Beware of "using" people when networking and of seeking unreasonable favors. Work with the network, but give as well as take, and share information unless it is confidential (or gossip).

Organizational politics may uncover unethical behavior. Von Zugbach (1995, pp. 1–2) provides an example in the attitude that "power in the organization is about deciding what you want and making sure that you get it." You might like to use his thirteen "winner's commandments" to identify people who could be stepping over the ethical line:

- Me first. Nobody else will put your interests before theirs.
- There are no absolute rules. Other people's ideas of right and wrong do not apply to you.

- The organization is there to serve your interests, not the other way round.
- You are on your own. Nobody is going to help you become a winner.
- Be paranoiac. Watch out, the bastards *are* out to get you.
- Suck up to those who matter and suck up well. Identify the key people in the system who will help you.
- Say one thing and do another. You need to pay lip service to the organization's cherished notions of how things should be done.
- Be a team player, but make sure you beat your fellow team members.
- Remember the truth is not always to your advantage. Those who control your future do not necessarily want to hear the bad news.
- Manipulate the facts to suit your interests. Even when things are bad you should come up smelling of roses.
- Get your retaliation in first. When there is blood on the organization's carpet, make sure it's not yours.
- Blow your own trumpet—better still, get someone else to do it for you.
- Dominate your environment or it will dominate you.

This raises interesting questions. You might stop at this point and consider how you would approach the problem if you felt that someone was behaving unethically and following the "winner's commandments." Would you talk with him over a coffee, seek a second opinion in confidence, or be a whistle-blower? Or is there another tactic you would use? The way that politics is played in some organizations can be a real dilemma.

The values of honesty, goodwill, loyalty, quality, fairness, responsibility, cooperation, and, in the leader, humility, sometimes get lost in the pressure to reduce overheads and speed up the process of change. At one time this happened only in the private sector, but with the push to reduce spending, leaders in the public sector become vulnerable. Pressure can mount to overlook fundamental values and ethics when leaders find that their governing boards place pressure on them. Making decisions in this situation is not as clear-cut as it may appear, and the leader may be isolated. Loyalty to the service, and to the organization, can produce isolation and inner conflict. Playing politics may produce paranoia. And that is fatal.

BANANA SKIN NO. 12
Failing to recognize when the organization's values and ethics are being challenged: *When values are challenged, take appropriate action.*

Not Being Arrogant

Leaders who have been in a post for a time, who have built up a power base, who are perceived as successful by their followers, and who are pushing through a radical change program can become arrogant. They can become smooth talkers, persuaders, or arm twisters. The symptoms of arrogance include the gradual reduction of consultation and listening to other viewpoints. The leader pushes through his decisions, limits his networking, surrounds himself with sycophants, fails to recognize his personal limitations, and refuses to be accountable. The arrogant leader doesn't compromise with anyone about anything—he thinks he is always right. Eventually the arrogant leader fails. The sad point is that he may not recognize why it has happened. Hopefully he wakes up to his growing isolation or a peer or his boss takes action.

BANANA SKIN NO. 13

Being right all the time and failing to recognize growing arrogance and isolation: *Listen to users, the boss, and colleagues—and be sensitive to their body language as well as their words.*

Work and Life Management

There is a great deal to pick up and learn when taking up a new senior appointment. And it is a steep learning curve. In common with other life experiences, the more you learn, the more you realize how much there is to learn. It's a fact of life that there are only twenty-four hours in the day in which to plan, execute, consult, network, attend meetings (both formal and informal), and socialize in the work role. It is very easy to lose focus and become a workaholic. That is not good for anyone, especially the people with whom the leader works and lives. Workaholics become bores, have limited small talk that is essential for socializing, and are stressed, which limits their energy and creativity. . . . We can go on with the negatives. Everyone understands the need to avoid becoming a workaholic—but, hey, there is so much ground to cover. . . . Somehow the balance needs to be achieved.

Having a close family relationship that is valued, not staying in the office or at the bar too late in the evening, taking the entire vacation entitlement, ensuring that reading for relaxation extends beyond the *Harvard Business Review* and the professional journals—all will help. Another way to "turn off from the office" is to have an absorbing hobby that is an antidote; some go sailing, others run marathons, and many volunteer in the community.

The most difficult circumstances in which to achieve a balance is having a young family or caring for an elderly relative. Then both work and family life are especially demanding, but getting the balance right is very rewarding. Benson (2005) has written an article that offers good advice: "Are You Working Too Hard?"

The way not to have a balance lies in poor time management skills. To keep work under better control, plan each day and week effectively; indicate times when the office door will be open or firmly shut; check e-mail, voicemail, and text messages at specific times of the day; keep your desk clear; delegate tasks; and avoid micromanaging and procrastination.

Although too much stress is not good for anyone, some stress can help people give their best. This is where understanding emotional intelligence pays dividends.

BANANA SKIN NO. 14

Not ensuring that there is a balance between work and personal life: *Achieving balance is important for every individual and those around her. Remember, stress can be both bad and good for you.*

Staying Connected to Users

As a junior assistant in a public library, one of the authors of this book learned the importance of keeping in touch with users. The chief's office overlooked the lending library. He worked there unobtrusively, but if a problem arose his ears pricked up, he came downstairs, and without embarrassing his staff, he quietly observed what was happening. It was usually a discussion about why there was a long waiting list for a new popular novel. He kept closely in touch with what users wanted. (He also had a good way to keep in touch with junior staff, who went to his office for two hours each week while the seniors did the daily task of straightening the shelves. He talked about new books and users. Meanwhile, the seniors checked on how well routine tasks were being carried out, titles on the shelves, and wear and tear on the stock.) He had his finger on the pulse, and everyone had a great respect, and affection, for him.

In an industrial research library, the head librarian demonstrated the value of spending about a third of the working day showing the flag and seeing what was happening around the laboratories and offices. In both examples, the people at the top kept in very close touch with users. Their teams provided feedback in other ways and they had statistics to refer to, but seeing the users and talking with them indicated how needs might be changing and how improvements could be made. And this feedback was discussed with their staff so that quality was built into the service and the staff felt valued.

As society becomes more pressured, there is also increasing diversity among users, with technology playing a greater role in delivering information. Information professionals have become more aware of the anxiety that users can experience in using services. There has been only a limited amount of research carried out on the topic, but it has been studied in the academic library sector (Onwuegbuzie, Jiao, and Bostick, 2004).

Yet with the time pressures on leaders, it is all too easy to overlook the individuals in the community served. Many of the national and state archives and libraries have excellent coffee bars, and the chiefs can be found there taking their breaks—or just gently taking in the atmosphere and reactions of users. . . .

BANANA SKIN NO. 15

Failing to recognize the value of informal feedback from users: *The views of users don't have to be gathered through a survey. And get concerned if colleagues don't provide informal feedback.*

Remaining Accessible

Sometimes the job can seem to be overwhelming, and one way out is to close the door and "catch up." But closing the door on reality can have serious consequences for the service and the leader. Losing visibility means the information that comes by osmosis stops flowing and the team hesitates to "bother you." The gossip and rumor mills get busy—and the situation may well reach the ears of the board. It can be the start of a downward spiral. It is important to recognize the symptoms and go to the watercooler, get out in the wider community, find a mentor, and face reality. Don't get stale. Maintain the momentum.

BANANA SKIN NO. 16

Undervaluing visibility: *Getting out of the office is refreshing—and it may produce a solution to a problem.*

Expecting the Unexpected

Leaders must be prepared for all eventualities. Many crises can affect an information service, including mergers and takeovers, budget cuts, staff redundancies, layoffs and systems failures, or perhaps a company handling an outsourcing contract goes bust. Natural disasters such as fires, earthquakes, hurricanes, and floods occur; a gunman runs loose in the library; or a member of the team is raped. A staff member may have a serious illness and perhaps die. . . . These are all happenings reported in the professional press. You can't be prepared for all of them, but you can have a procedure in place to handle the most likely (e.g., a disaster plan and a computer backup system located at another site). It is also essential to have a communications tree within the service, where the leader notifies a senior staff member who notifies two others and they notify another two, or whatever is an appropriate communication chain to quickly get accurate information out to the staff.

BANANA SKIN NO. 17

Failing to anticipate that disasters can happen: *Identify the most likely crises. Create a communication tree. Poor communication works like the children's game where one whispers into another's ear; the message that passes around the room becomes very garbled.*

Dealing with an Administrative Change

Some leaders report to a more senior colleague and others to the chair of the governing board. The working relationship with the boss develops over time as each gets to understand the other's vision, ways of working, preferences for communicating, and likes and dislikes. A stable relationship helps the service and organization develop. But bosses also change jobs, introducing a new person to report to, and it doesn't always happen at the best of times. In the worst circumstance the person the leader reports to leaves involuntarily. She may have committed a misdemeanor, or perhaps the board felt she was not holding the confidence and trust of the staff. Concern on the part of her team, or people who reported to her, will be related to the degree of attachment they had to the person who has left. If the wider organization feels they were closely aligned, then the standing of the group may be affected. Reading the runes accurately in these circumstances is vital, and such an event usually occurs without warning. The replacement may start very cautiously in making relationships within the organization that could affect the leader's influence, within both the organization at large and the information service.

If the boss has left of his own choosing the situation is easier, but it still needs to be handled carefully. The leader and the person he reported to will have shared much information, both formally and informally. The former boss will have known the service well. The replacement may well be unknown to the leader, and while being friendly, it may be wise to keep the powder dry for a short time until he has talked of his vision and intent. Be cautious, but don't withdraw.

BANANA SKIN NO. 18

Breaking in a new boss: *Be very slightly cautious until understanding and trust are established, then ensure he or she is well informed.*

Team Difficulties

From time to time the staff of the service may exhibit signs of being "difficult," with a sharp questioning of decisions or viewpoints. People may be reluctant to make changes to their schedules or be more demanding of resources. Cooperation may be withdrawn. Gossip and rumors emerge. The leader needs to have the staff on her side but perhaps not entirely on her terms. A team that assumes power can finish a leader. Offerman (2004) has described what can happen "when followers become toxic."

Clearly the reason for any change in attitude must be identified at a very early stage, before matters escalate to a state of noncooperation. Reasons may become clear if the leader steps back from the situation. Perhaps annual pay awards are smaller than expected. Changes in working conditions, increases in workloads, new technology, and radical change may be taking place. Talking with managers and supervisors informally in the first instance should reveal the problem and the resulting strength of feeling.

Being honest, listening, motivating the staff, and staying relaxed but concerned should stop the situation from escalating. But if it doesn't, then a mediator should be able to assist with resolution. Leaders should work hard so that it doesn't reach this stage—but if it does they shouldn't hesitate to take this direction. It requires fast and effective resolution. But don't confuse strong argument with creativity. All teams need to be creative, and this can produce passionate feelings.

BANANA SKIN NO. 19

Ignoring staff members who are exhibiting signs of stress: *A leader needs to understand why and take effective action.*

Generational Differences

Many information services have paid and volunteer staff born in different generations. Members of each generation have their own viewpoints shaped by their life experiences. Gen-Xers may find it challenging working alongside volunteers drawn from the same age group as their grandparents.

Older volunteers may well draw on their experience in the workplace to offer comment and advice. Many attracted to information services are likely to have been professionals in another sector. Members of generation X and generation Y can help the veterans and the baby boomers learn new skills—and a new vocabulary. All generations have much to offer in the workplace.

BANANA SKIN NO. 20

Not dealing with tension arising from intergenerational attitudes and experiences: *Ensure that everyone values the input of others, drawing on the skills and experience acquired during their careers.*

Not Being a Toxic Leader

Earlier we wrote of toxic followers, but leaders can be toxic too. Toxic leaders have great designs, for themselves rather than the team. A toxic leader exhibits destructive behavior patterns and dysfunctional characteristics. When he takes up the position he may appear, to the organization and the team, to offer the certainty and security that he is the right person for the job. Toxic leaders create expectations they cannot fulfill and have a destructive effect on the team and the service.

BANANA SKIN NO. 21

Showing self-interest: *The prospect of a senior position may be tempting, but check out how your experience, personality, and skill base suit the position. A mentor could prevent a big mistake.*

Personality Traits

Dotlich and Cairo (2003) prepared a list of personality traits that can result in leaders failing:

- Arrogance
- Melodrama
- Volatility
- Excessive caution
- Habitual distrust
- Aloofness
- Mischievousness
- Eccentricity
- Passive resistance
- Perfectionism
- Eagerness to please

Some have been discussed earlier, but the list draws attention to factors that do not necessarily come to mind—perhaps eccentricity and eagerness to please. . . .

BANANA SKIN NO. 22

Not understanding oneself: *Understand your emotional intelligence—another point to check out with a mentor.*

Final Thoughts on Banana Skins

We noted earlier that Kets de Vries explores the psychological issues of organizational behavior and leadership in his research, and his papers are always worth reading because they focus on the people factors. In *The Leadership Mystique* (2001), he explores the factors that contribute to leadership failure:

- Conflict avoidance
- Oppression of subordinates
- Micromanagement
- Inaccessibility
- Manic behavior
- Game playing.

Drawing on experience, we add to the list:

- Change must be seen as a journey and not an end in itself—it needs to be continuous.
- Over time a risk-averse culture can emerge, which stifles innovation.
- The leader may see the vision but fail to put energy into planning, preparation, implementation, and monitoring progress.
- Goals are set too far into the future to be visible and realistic to the staff.
- The views and input of nonusers and ex-users are as essential as those of the users
- Following the direction of similar services may be reassuring, but you must take at least one step forward to stay ahead.
- A service that sees itself as being successful may not realize that the world outside is changing.

Our experience indicates that everyone is likely to slip on one of the banana skins at some point—we are all human. But this experience also tells us that leaders quickly learn to spot them. So don't get paranoid. Just ensure that you listen to honest feedback from those around you, and develop a good team spirit.

References

Benson, Herbert, "Are You Working Too Hard? A Conversation with Mind/Body Researcher Herbert Benson," *Harvard Business Review* 83, no. 11 (November 2005): 53–58.

Caroselli, Marlene, *Leadership Skills for Managers* (New York: McGraw-Hill, 2000).

Coutu, Diane L., "Putting Leaders on the Couch: A Conversation with Manfred F.R. Kets de Vries," *Harvard Business Review* 82, no. 1 (January 2004): 66.

Dotlich, David L., and Peter C. Cairo, *Why CEOs Fail: The 11 Behaviors That Can Derail Your Climb to the Top* (San Francisco: Jossey-Bass, 2003).

Hoadley, Irene B., "Introduction," *Library Trends* 43, no. 1 (Summer 1994): 12.

Kets de Vries, Manfred, *The Leadership Mystique: A User's Manual for the Human Enterprise* (London: Financial Times Prentice-Hall, 2001).

Kotter, John P., *Leading Change* (Boston: Harvard Business School Press, 1996).

Machiavelli, Niccolò, *The Prince*, translated by George Bull (London: Penguin, 1961).

Offerman, Lynn R., "When Followers Become Toxic," *Harvard Business Review* 82, no. 1 (January 2004): 54–60.

Onwuegbuzie, Anthony, Qun G. Jiao, and Sharon Bostick, *Library Anxiety, Research, and Applications* (Lanham, MD: Scarecrow Press, 2004).

Porter, Michael, "Seven Surprises for New CEOs," *Harvard Business Review* 82, no. 10 (October 2004): 62–84.

von Zugbach, Reggie, *The Winning Manager: Coming Out on Top in the Organization* (London: Souvenir Press, 1995).

CHAPTER 9

Crucial Success Factors

This chapter focuses on the following:

• Personal factors crucial for success
• Job factors crucial for success
• Important concepts for successful leaders

Several points stand out from our reading, our observation, our own experiences, and our survey of directors of information services. Taken together, these form a set of crucial factors that contribute to success.

They can be grouped into three categories. The first relates to the innate talents of a leader. The second covers the position and the delivering of a high-performing information service. The third deals with understanding. Together they form a checklist that might not produce a perfect row of ticks, but it will indicate areas needing development.

Personal Factors

SHOWING PASSION, ENTHUSIASM, AND COURAGE

Passion contributes to successful leadership. Leaders we have enjoyed working with have shown a strong commitment to their roles and a passionate interest in their work and that of people around them. Everyone is motivated to feel enthusiastic, which brings out a strong motivation to make things happen. Ciampa and Watkins (2005, p. 169) put it well: "An effective vision . . . generates passion in the new leader—a passion that in turn motivates others."

Passion is communicated through the spoken word and body language, enthusiasm, and emotion. New ideas emerge from the way enthusiastic leaders communicate with the people around them. Passion contributes to building a confident, happy team that knows exactly where it is heading. Feeling passionate about their work means that leaders are less likely to accept the status quo.

Knowing when to operate on instinct and respond to a gut reaction requires courage and comes with experience in the role. Arigho, quoted in Lucas (2000, p. 10), says it well:

> I would describe my style as being very open, honest and enthusiastic. I am also quite decisive and very instinctive—I have learnt over time to trust my gut feelings. I think consistency is also important. I don't like a culture of fear and unpredictability. And you have to have that little bit of fun as well—because humor reaches out to people.

Although information aids decision making, human reaction also plays a part. Sometimes it pays to follow a hunch and bring intuition into play. Hayashi (2001, p. 61) notes, "Our emotions and feelings might not only be important in our intuitive ability to make good decisions but may actually be essential."

Courage is vital when faced with unpleasant decisions. If you feel you must please all the people all the time, think twice before accepting a leadership role.

Crucial success factor no. 1: Demonstrate passion, enthusiasm, and courage to stakeholders. *Don't be afraid to show positive emotions. It shows you are human and committed to your work.*

BEING ADAPTABLE

Taking a flexible approach doesn't always come easy to a new leader. Organizations change and are rarely stable for any length of time, and staff come and go. Sometimes things don't work out, and tactics and strategy have to be rethought. Successful leaders develop the skill to "reframe" and reshape a problem so that it has a good outcome. And a sense of humor and a quick wit help.

Crucial success factor no. 2: Adapt to new situations and take the team with you. *Learn how to take the team with you, and communicate convincingly with a little humor.*

SHOWING IMAGINATION AND CREATIVITY

Imagination and creativity contribute to creating the vision for the service. Theme parks demonstrate these factors, and the Disney team of "imagineers" describe how to create a working environment that fosters creativity (The Imagineers, 2003). Another term linked to creativity is *innovation*. Creative ideas are transferred to the workplace when they move to the stage of innovation.

Definitions

Creativity is the reorganization of ideas in a way that throws a different light on a situation. *Innovation* is the generation of a new service or a new way to provide an existing service. Creativity generates new ideas; innovation implements the ideas for the benefit of the organization.

Breaking away from received wisdom and being creative requires courage, but it is vital for visualizing goals for the service and the means of achieving them. Creativity needs to be cultivated in the thinking of the staff and embedded into the culture of the service. It is generated through brainstorming and focus groups. Explore ideas with stakeholders, and select the most appropriate for piloting. Consultation generates an open culture that drives the service forward.

Experienced leaders ensure that creative employees who submit suggestions that are adopted receive due recognition through appraisals, annual salary reviews, or employee-of-the-month awards.

Crucial success factor no. 3: Use imagination and be creative. *Think outside the box.*

HANDLING CRITICISM

New leaders feel vulnerable when they hear criticisms of the service or themselves. People want to give a new leader the benefit of their wisdom if they believe there is a better way to do things. Sometimes the criticism can be more personal. Staff may find it difficult to adjust to a new leadership approach or style; they may want to speed up change or slow it down. The service may hit challenges. It becomes trickier if the criticism comes from a member of the governing board. There can be a sense of vulnerability and isolation.

Leaders must know how to handle criticism before it escalates. Set designated times for an open-door policy, and if there are rumors, seek informal feedback. Use listening skills to help the feedback process, and reflect before responding. Keeping calm helps resolve the problem, and resolution should avoid escalation.

Crucial success factor no. 4: Know how to handle criticism. *Accept that not everyone will love you all the time—listen and reflect before responding.*

STAYING INFORMED

Keeping informed comes naturally to information professionals, and there are many sources about international as well as national and local developments, along with management and leadership. It is easy to become myopic. Encourage staff to read widely, and build up a staff collection for their use.

Internal documents are essential reading—papers for meetings, briefing documents, the intranet and website, annual reports, and so on. They are important for what they say, how they say it, and what they don't say. Take notes at committee meetings of who speaks and what they say, and compare them with official minutes. See if there is any discrepancy between the two. And don't forget to network around the organization, the local community, and those vital e-groups.

Crucial success factor no. 5: Keep well informed. *Refresh speed-reading skills, and read widely.*

FOLLOWING THROUGH

Leaders have many tasks and need the temperament to be able to juggle, keep the eye on the ball, and follow through. Don't overlook a task that gets pushed back as organizational priorities change. Set up a system, either electronically or on paper, and check it regularly to ensure that deadlines are met and tasks are completed.

Crucial success factor no. 6: Set up a system to ensure that all tasks are followed through—and use it. *Prioritize and allow adequate time for completing tasks—don't forget the management skills.*

Job Factors

ACCEPTING THE RIGHT POSITION

Making the right move is important. If a job appeals, examine the advertisement and decide whether your experience and qualifications match the basic requirements and the move is feasible. Family considerations or the cost of housing may rule out some moves. Research and assess the organizational culture and climate.

Crucial success factor no. 7: Ensure that you suit the position and the

position suits you. *Reflect before applying for a job. Gather relevant information to ensure a good decision is made.*

ADAPTING LEADERSHIP STYLE

We noted earlier that personality factors influence leadership style. This point came through in responses to our survey.

"She is a leader with high expectations, high energy, and tons of vision, and she is a lot of fun. I think I learned from her the trick of planning out all possible scenarios that might result from events—and we had plenty of opportunities to practice this."

"I think one's personality contributes greatly to management style, and I've always been comfortable with collaborative decision making and less than comfortable making decisions in a vacuum."

But leadership style must be in harmony with the organizational culture. Some are informal; others are more formal. Certain cultures require frequent and rapid change, and staff anticipate this. Other cultures are reluctant to introduce change, and staff may not anticipate that change will come about or the ways it may affect them.

Crucial success factor no. 8: Ensure that your approach to leadership is in harmony with the organizational culture. *Leadership style is a function of personality, and personality isn't easy to change.*

KNOWING HONESTY IS THE BEST POLICY

Leaders are human, too. Mistakes happen or something is overlooked. You can be sure this will be spotted. Acknowledge it quickly and put it right. Thank the person who has drawn attention to it. A little humility goes a long way.

A trickier situation occurs when major changes emerge, from circumstances beyond your control, that will affect team members. You then have divided loyalty—to the organization and to the team—but your loyalty must remain with the organization. It is not a comfortable situation, but stay calm on the outside and develop an action plan to minimize the surprise factor. Be prepared for anger, and avoid false pretenses. Negotiate with the board and those affected. This sensitive situation requires courage and the skills to motivate the team to ensure the service continues to operate.

Crucial success factor no. 9: Remember that leaders may be faced with divided loyalties. *Understand where your loyalty lies.*

UNDERSTANDING GENDER AND LEADERSHIP

Mann (1995) suggests that power in organizations is biased in favor of men, and women's views of organizational politics indicate that they fail to recognize the importance of political competence and the need to acquire and exercise power. Women need political competence. Arroba and James (1987) define two dimensions of political competence. The first dimension is an awareness, or understanding, of the organization (e.g., the ability to "read" the organizational world). The second dimension is the awareness of one's predisposition to behave in certain ways (e.g., understanding what one brings to a situation).

Research based on 360-degree feedback suggests that women are rated as being significantly more transformational as leaders than are men. The transformational behavior is derived from women's respect and concern for the needs of others, the empowerment of their staff, staff development, and being open to receiving feedback. The findings also indicate that women underrate themselves in terms of effectiveness. By contrast, men rate themselves as being much more effective in terms of leadership than others do (Powell, 2004). In the post-Enron era, it is now suggested that transformational leadership and looking after the needs of all stakeholders become vital (Pollitt and Owen, 2005).

Crucial success factor no. 10: Women shouldn't underrate their effectiveness in a leadership role. *Hone political and communication skills.*

FOCUSING ON THE COMMUNITY SERVED

The community served must be at the center of the service. Many texts focusing on leadership and management put staff first, and it is easy to see why they take this approach. Without having the right staff, doing the right things in the right way at the right time, user services will be less effective. But team building and staff development follow on from assessing and planning how needs can best be met. It is only when needs have been identified and changes to these needs tracked that the most effective way to deliver the service can be assessed. Staffing requirements follow.

Information seeking and user needs are topics that have slipped in the information curriculum in recent years and in some programs have been replaced by marketing. However, marketing doesn't always focus on the individual user, either actual or potential. Satisfying information needs results in user satisfaction and effective champions of the service.

Crucial success factor no. 11: Ensure that the community served is at the forefront of planning. *Maintain a dialogue with users, ex-users, and nonusers. Users can be valued champions of the service.*

STRIVING FOR QUALITY

Use of the service must be measured both in quantitative and qualitative terms. Data can be manipulated, but the soft information about how people feel about the service is a vital input to planning. Examine data and information collected with the staff, and identify what can be done to increase both user satisfaction and employee job satisfaction. Coaching users adds to the value they derive from the service, helping them work seamlessly with new sources, technology, and procedures.

   Crucial success factor no. 12: Ensure that quality remains at the core of the service. *Work with stakeholders and examine ways to increase all aspects of service quality.*

ANTICIPATING THE EXPECTED AND WATCHING FOR THE UNEXPECTED

Scanning the operating environment yields essential feedback to inform planning and strategy. Balancing the immediacy of today with what will be expected tomorrow becomes more challenging as the rate of change increases.

   Planning produces models to test against "what would happen if" scenarios and indicates where information and evidence are thin and where gaps should be filled. As an exercise, it builds confidence and draws people into anticipating change.

   One of the most enjoyable and rewarding ways to gather information is to attend national conferences and network. Building up strong relationships with a range of vendors pays dividends. And watch the political scene and decode what the politicians are saying.

   Crucial success factor no. 13: Be well informed. *Gather information, reflect on tomorrow, and ask yourself, "What would happen if?"*

COMMUNICATING

Leaders spend their time communicating, with the team, their boss, the community served, politicians within and outside the organization, and their professional colleagues. It is a key task in supplying and gathering information. And good news, and sometimes bad news, must be given to the boss and governing body if trust is to be maintained.

   Messages must be delivered convincingly and consistently. It's a skill to develop, especially when working with the media, which can carry messages to a wide community.

Crucial success factor no. 14: Keep the service in the public eye. *Communicate effectively to get the message across.*

PREPARING AND REHEARSING

First impressions are important. Acting on clues determines style and image, but tweak the image from time to time. When briefing the team or board or when making public presentations, keep the following in mind:

- Prepare and rehearse—get the timing right.
- Have a strong opening to catch listeners' attention.
- Use short sentences.
- Be specific.
- Select words carefully, and avoid long ones.
- Pause after key points.
- Repeat key words to reinforce a point.
- Alliteration strengthens a point—"It needs to be done efficiently, effectively, and economically."
- Paint a picture; rather than "We are expecting 200 boxes of records," try "The boxes will overflow two bays of shelving."
- Use humor, and wait for the laughter to end before starting again—but if you are bad at telling jokes, don't try!
- Remember the power of storytelling to make a point.
- Tell the audience what you are going to say, say it, and recap at the end.
- When using technology, know how it operates, know what can go wrong, and try it out beforehand in the place you will be using it.
- Confidence and comfort in public speaking come with experience.

Crucial success factor no. 15: Prepare for briefings and public speaking. *Rehearse frequently, and remember that experience brings confidence.*

WORKING WITH THE TEAM

Make sure you understand the job of everyone you are leading—you don't have to be able to do it, but know enough to make intelligent decisions. According to Drucker (2005, p. 107), "The first secret of effectiveness is to understand the people you work with so that you can make use of their strengths."

Good leaders are good judges of people. It is a key requirement, given the proportion of an information service budget that is spent on staff and staff development. ALA president Carla Hayden offers the following words of wisdom: "Leadership is more than a position or place you find yourself in. It is a mind-set that recognizes the potential of actively working with others to achieve significant goals" (Anderson and Lapsley, 2004, p. 121).

Bring together the right mix of skills and personalities and the team will achieve its goals. Understanding the basics of diversity management is essential. Leaders need to win the respect of their staff; it doesn't come with the position. The followers, or staff, bestow respect upon the leader. Goffee and Jones (2001, p. 148) suggest that people seek, admire, respect, and follow leaders who produce three emotional responses:

- A feeling of significance
- A feeling of community—a unity of purpose around work and a willingness to relate to one another as human beings
- A buzzing feeling of excitement and challenge

Provide opportunities for staff development, and encourage staff to identify a mentor. A respondent to our survey underlined the value of a mentor: "Mentors have been very important in each of the positions I have held. I learned how to be a better librarian and a good leader by working with and emulating the mentors at each location. I still have a mentor in the larger metropolitan library community. I hope that I am serving as a mentor, an example, to people on my staff and other librarians in our consortia."

Crucial success factor no. 16: Quickly understand the strengths and weaknesses of the team. *Ensure that staff development programs are in place and working effectively.*

RECOGNIZING THAT YOU CAN'T BE THERE ALL THE TIME

Since most information services operate beyond normal office hours, every staff member needs someone to act as a deputy. Clearly the leader won't be present all the time, and having a rotation of nominated deputies provides the opportunity for them to experience what it's like to act at a higher level. It also demonstrates confidence. A debriefing indicates how much has been gained and what still needs to be learned. It is a way to spot high flyers.

Ensure that a deputy has access to the information she will need, the office diary, and relevant nonpersonal e-mail, and provide a briefing on current and hot issues. Notify the stakeholders of who is in charge.

Guidelines for accessing e-mail need to be in place so that service can continue seamlessly when a member of the team is off duty. It is a sensitive but vital issue to address.

Crucial success factor no. 17: Have coverage for absences. *A system of informed deputies should be in place to provide coverage for the absence of everyone working in the service.*

FITTING EVERYTHING INTO THE WORKDAY

Trying to get the proverbial quart into a pint-sized pot is a challenge for the team and its leader. There are only so many hours in a day. Use the KISS approach to administration—keep it simple, stupid! Take a regular health check of the service, and work with the team to identify unnecessary tasks and routines—yes, they can be found. Although change occurs in working practices, sometimes the whole process continues even though a part is now redundant. Get managers and supervisors to work with their teams to see what can be streamlined, then convene a meeting of the managers and supervisors to assess the impact if a process is changed. It's a good learning curve for staff.

Crucial success factor no. 18: Cut out redundant processes and tasks. *Get everyone to recognize the benefits of KISS.*

Important Concepts

THEORY SHOULD UNDERPIN PRACTICE

It is easy to be preoccupied by professional practice and overlook the theory that lies behind it (e.g., leadership and communication). Remember the theoretical content studied during your first professional course, and keep up with emerging theories.

Crucial success factor no. 19: Understand that sound theory underpins excellent practice. *Keep up to date with theory- and evidence-based practice.*

LEADERS NEED TO MAKE DECISIONS

Leaders need to know when a decision has to be made and be prepared to act decisively. This involves being well prepared, reflecting on relevant information, knowing when and how to convey the decision, and anticipating the consequences. This is a crucial success factor for leaders, and a major reason for success is having the understanding this process requires.

Crucial success factor no. 20: Leaders must make decisions. *Be prepared both technically and psychologically to act decisively.*

VALUE YOUR EXPERIENCE—BOTH THE GOOD AND THE LESS GOOD

A number of survey respondents indicated that the experience gained in earlier positions had shaped their leadership style. It wasn't always a good experience:

"I learned 'what not to do'—in my pre-MLS professional position. The way I was treated by a superintendent of schools after I had resigned my position taught me, as an administrator, to treat people the way I would want to be treated given the circumstances. This helped me develop my humanistic style of leadership."

Communication with the boss is also important:

"I learned this about management: Don't run ahead of your support structure. Your immediate boss needs to know what you intend, and why you intend it, and if he says "no," don't do it or resign. I learned one other thing: Listen carefully to those around you, and use a combination of caution and abandon in carrying our your responsibilities, all the while communicating as though communicating were going out of style."

Leaders have the responsibility to ensure all members of their staff know how their tasks relate to the overall operations of the information service. Team members must also realize the benefits of collaborative working, which raises the level of job satisfaction, which, in turn, is a lever for raising the performance of the service:

"When I was younger and employed as a library assistant and had a few individuals reporting to me, most assignments were task oriented. At the time I was perhaps too stringent on making sure tasks were completed for the sake of just being completed. Later my communication style changed, and that allowed me to see tasks as they related to much bigger operations. I began to notice how things could change in part due to process analysis of certain operations. This brings in more stakeholders, and you begin to realize that the way you interact with others can affect tasks or projects. Having a good mentor in my early library clerk days allowed me to change before I went down a 'hard-nosed' path. I also changed by believing or trying to see great qualities within individuals and using their strengths, or at least instilling the belief that together we can do great things."

Following is an insight into personal values and how they influence daily work and overcome the danger of developing an ego problem. The passage also draws attention to the need to make sure you have all the facts before making assumptions:

"One key experience was my studies at a Jesuit Seminary . . . in which I came to understand and affirm the basic value of the personal over the corporate and that the interests of the corporate tend to be served best when the individual 'good' is understood and affirmed. This leads to the overriding question in my management style: What is the good, and how can it best be achieved? Moreover, this helps tremendously in transcending 'ego' problems.

"Another formative experience was an occasion when I felt I, as a new librarian, was treated unfairly and without adequate understanding of the situation achieved by my supervisor. Assumptions were made and poor judgments resulted. While this situation was not of career-making or breaking magnitude, it did convince me of the value of fully understanding the relevant circumstances, giving persons involved a fair and adequate opportunity to express their interpretation of events, and seeking a just and equitable judgment and solution. It showed me how unfair jumping to conclusions is and the true value of due process.

"An early developed (and continuing) intentional experience of personal reflection on what I do or might feel about a decision or situation causes me to always ask the question of how others might also feel about a decision or situation. Being considerate of others in this way is an important aspect of my leadership style; it stems from my studies in philosophy and theology."

Another aspect of personal values centers on trusting people. Without trust a team will not operate effectively, and the leader will be overwhelmed with decisions. Micromanaging is to be avoided, as one respondent recalls:

"The first event that I think influenced me was at my first job. I had a supervisor who stood over me and watched everything I did—and I hated it. I vowed right then to never do such a thing. I decided that I would place a lot of trust in people I work with and never make them feel the way that manager made me feel.

"My first boss . . . stressed the importance of trusting people to do their jobs well without close supervision. He wanted to be kept informed about the big issues and projects, but then he got out of the way and let you do your job. My second boss was a micromanager, and I decided I never wanted to be that sort of supervisor."

How experience indicates that information may not necessarily provide a clear solution to an issue, and that there may be more than one possible outcome, is seen in the next quotation. It also makes the point that fear can affect thinking; we echo this point. Fear raises stress levels, which is not conducive to good decision making, and all organizations go through periods of stress:

"For a long time I believed that, if adequate and reliable information was available on an issue, the best solution would be clear to those involved or it would be clear that more than one option was viable. I remember a management team meeting in my first directorship when it became very clear that my belief was not always supported by my experience. In particular, I learned that when people are fearful, they often do not think clearly or rationally."

Crucial success factor no. 21: Recognize that all experience contributes to the development of a leadership style. *Sometimes the less good may be more easily recognized than the good.*

IT'S ESSENTIAL TO CONTINUE LEARNING

No one ever stops learning, and all professions place an emphasis on continuing professional development. Getting away from the service, working in a peer group, and identifying and filling gaps in understanding and knowledge are vital ways to stay fresh. Ideas and approaches change over time, and it is good to be tested and refreshed.

Aside from keeping in touch with professional skills and knowledge so that you can talk with new recruits with professional degrees and understand what they are talking about, it is vital to keep ahead of developments in the fields of management and leadership. Smart leaders are members of the national management organization.

Communication skills need to be updated because language changes over time. It happens in management-speak and in daily life, as anyone who has a teenager in the family knows. Using the right words in the right situation demonstrates sensitivity to the person you are talking with. Language becomes both more fascinating and more important as we get older. Think of the metaphors that have been used to convey organizational cultures.

Try this

List three terms you might use to describe the culture of your organization. Then add three terms you might use to describe the culture of your team. Is there a difference? If so, why?

Make sure you can use the latest terms to convey ideas effectively. And ensure that you can operate the latest technology. Some gurus making conference presentations are a bit lost when they don't have their technicians nearby to operate the laptops, PowerPoint presentations, and so on.

A valuable contribution to informal learning comes from having a mentor you trust, in a relationship you value. The relationship can be a rewarding experience for both parties. Respondents to our survey described their experience of having a good mentor, and their comments shed light on the nature of the relationship. The first quotation brings out the different learning experiences that can be gained from different mentors at stages in a career. The interaction between the younger person and the older mentor demonstrates that the relationship can be warm and, at times, amusing:

"I had three mentors. One was the earnest young director, and another was the acquisitions librarian with whom I worked at that same library for about six months. The third was a woman who was about the age I am now, who was seasoned and had much to impart.

"The first had something to do with my being offered the job I have now. He and I had maintained contact after he went to the . . . library. He frequently invited me to interact with what he was doing, and through that, my horizons were raised.

"The second mentor helped me develop a point of view. He was the acquisitions librarian at the same . . . library. He didn't really see eye to eye with the director, but he was not insubordinate. Through his approach to things, I learned how a staff could learn to work together, in spite of differences of opinion, and develop respect for one another.

"The third mentor helped me see the job from inside out. She was seasoned in the kind of library we were working in. Some of its common features were that it was resource poor; it was staffed by dedicated but not necessarily trained people; and it was not esteemed highly by the faculty, students, or administration. She knew we would always struggle with that, so she made a virtue of the struggle. She had a fund of aphorisms that I find myself using. "It's time to put feet on our prayers." Being interpreted, it means "Let's get to work." She was very kind, and we went to all kinds of library events together. I must tell you that her favorite thing to watch on TV was professional ice hockey. (This is an aside. One day she and I set out for a meeting of . . . librarians that was to be held somewhere in the southwestern suburbs. . . . We always met at 1:00 p.m., so we had to leave early enough to get there, get a meal, and then go to the meeting. We stopped at a place that seemed busy but capacious. Picture this: a sixty-plus lady and a young thirty-ish man in a restaurant together where the feature of the afternoon was an intimate apparel style show. When we realized what we had walked into, we both bubbled with mirth. She was a great lady!)"

The second quotation indicates that the relationship with a mentor doesn't necessarily focus on management or supervisory skills. We have noticed that the literature doesn't always cover the intellectual side of the professional's work. It's often found that managerial and supervisory skills are valued more highly than knowledge of the subject matter of the collection. Encouraging your professionals to develop this side of their work adds to their personal development and benefits the community served:

"Mentors can help teach you to strategize and to see the big picture. Often, one's mentors are one's supervisors. You can learn the good and the bad of supervising from them. Some of the best mentors I've had are true intellectuals who read widely and worry about the intellectual depth of a collection. This skill is not highly valued [but it] should be."

The third quotation draws attention to the way an experienced leader can help a younger person understand risk taking and how to sharpen analytical skills. It requires courage on the part of the mentor, and probably some difficult experiences along the way in his career, to be able to let the staff fail in order to learn "how to do it better next time":

"The greatest influence has probably been in how I have developed my areas of strength. Letting me fail but not destroying me for it; encouraging me to take risks even though the outcomes were very uncertain; and listening closely and asking me the right questions improved my abilities to analyze problems or issues."

Some mentoring relationships last a long time, as the fourth example illustrates. It also highlights the value of humor in friendship and the need to work in a collaborative way with colleagues to achieve goals—you can't do this alone:

"As far as mentors go, I have had only one really great mentor, though I also have had great colleagues and friends whom I could occasionally seek advice from. My mentor later became a very good friend in life, and to this day we still bounce around ideas on emerging trends—after enjoying a great laugh, of course. When it came to leadership, he was very well respected and liked by many, and I remember his words when he once said, 'I am not here to supervise or manage you. . . . You are smart enough to make wise decisions, otherwise we would not have hired you. I am here to accomplish, with your help, big projects and goals that benefit the library as a whole.' So if this could be tied into any managing or leadership style, I quickly learned to gather up your allies and instill in them the ability to accomplish great projects together rather than going it on your own."

Many professionals take an additional master's after they have completed their qualifying courses, perhaps in the subject field of their bachelor's degree and MBA. But in responses to the survey of directors, we were struck by the number who had taken a PhD and commented on the value of the higher degree, though at the time some didn't foresee what it might lead to:

"Pursuing my doctorate. For a while after I received it, I didn't think that was a good decision. However, today, I know it was because when dealing with other deans, having the doctorate levels the playing field in terms of respect—you become one of them because you have successfully jumped all the same hurdles they jumped."

"Getting a PhD in Library Science. It was a good idea, but at the time I did it, I wasn't sure."

Some respondents indicated that it was a conscious decision that helped them pursue their personal goals. Possessing a doctorate assists a move into a leadership role and puts the director of an information service into a peer group that respects the higher degree:

"The decision to earn a PhD was the crucial point in my career. It was the key to pursuing my dream of improving the provision of information services in indigenous communities. The degree, in turn, led me to opportunities for administrative positions in such communities, as well as the opportunity to teach and conduct research in those communities. I believe, especially now, that the choices for both administrative and teaching positions have been good ones. I am content with my choices and have no unresolved regrets."

Study for a higher degree doesn't have to come at an early stage in a career. In some cases family responsibilities can intervene. We think the key factors are knowing what you want to research and that you want to do it:

"Going back for my PhD at the ripe age of forty-one. My career has advanced rapidly since graduating at forty-five. I think in higher education, this remains a principal entry ticket.

"Given my desire to be in control, I guess a major decision point in my life came about fifteen years ago when I realized that I probably needed a doctorate to move ahead in library management. (I had been on a search committee for a director, and some of the faculty, with whom I had worked very closely, made the comment that they couldn't envision a library director without a doctorate.) Well, I had always wanted to move into a directorship, so it seemed the next thing for me to do. Some individuals can do that on the strength of just an MLS or an MLS and another master's degree. I probably could have also depending on where I could go. However, with a family, one's choices are more limited. My husband, knowing me better than I know myself, told me in the late 1980s that I should go for my doctorate. Once he indicated that he supported that decision (we had teenage boys at the time), I was ready. I took the GRE and was accepted into graduate school. Afterwards, I was able to move forward in my career with no further obstacles. I might have done the same thing without the doctorate, but never as easily. It was the best decision for an academic librarian."

"From a professional viewpoint, I wish I had gone for my doctorate sooner. But, on the other hand, the demands of my family would have made it more difficult, so it is just as well that I waited until I did. Probably the timing was perfect for me."

But one respondent did have regrets: "I am sorry I did not finish my PhD. . . ."

Crucial success factor no. 22: Value continuing professional development, for yourself and the team. *We all need to learn new skills and approaches to the job we do—learning never stops.*

THE DAY WILL COME

At some point in your career, you'll decide it's time to take a break or move on. Everyone gets stale on the job from time to time, that feeling of "having enough" and the need to recharge batteries. Before taking the drastic step of considering a job change, consider a career break. Some organizations recognize the value of sabbaticals and build them into their human resource policy to ensure that staff do not become so stressed that their health, and hence the quality of their work, is affected.

But more professionals are choosing to take a gap year. It's now common for teenagers, so why not the higher flyers who may have a bank balance to match their aspirations?

Another way to take a shorter break and get some good ideas is to apply for a professional travel award. A number of organizations offer scholarships that provide an opportunity to travel overseas and see how the job is done in other parts of the globe. Both of the authors of this book have been fortunate to receive travel awards, which have contributed to their career development. Sometimes, too, governments request an expert to advise on professional matters as part of an overseas aid program. Learning fast in such circumstances quickly brushes up ideas and brings new insights into situations that can be taken for granted.

From time to time, opportunities come up unexpectedly and you get head-hunted for a vacancy. It's flattering and should be followed up just to see what your market value is and whether the post is attractive. Proceed positively but with a little caution. Tease out the arguments for and against. Find out what the job entails and how it matches your track record; consider the organization and its direction. Does the position involve a radical change? Where is it located? What will it mean for your family? What benefits are offered? What is your standing in the current job? Realistically, what would be the future prospects with the current employer? Prepare carefully before entering the selection process.

But you might just feel you need to move on and want to sound out the labor market. Know the reason, whether you want to stay in the same field or assume a leadership role in a different sector or at a higher level (e.g., to provost or vice-chancellor level in a university). Here is one word of warning—the grapevine is very active in professional fields. How will the board or your boss react if she hears? Remember, you'll need references. . . .

Another decision that is less easy to make today than it was in the past is retirement. The fixed age for retirement no longer exists, and so the individual sets a leaving date. It may be determined by financial issues, by a wish to pursue other interests—one of us has a passion for narrow-gauge steam railways—or perhaps by the need to care for an elderly relative.

There is also a tricky side to retirement, because our faculties decline as we get older, and making an assessment about one's state of health may not be easy. An annual health check may be an insurance policy taken out by the employer. Sometimes employers have a policy whereby employees are able to step down from a senior role and take a part-time or reduced-hours contract, recognizing the value of the benefits and experience these individuals can continue to contribute.

In chapter 1 we drew attention to the seven ages of the leader identified by Bennis (2004). The penultimate age was that of the Statesman, with Spectacles on Nose, and it underlines our view that perhaps leaders shouldn't stay in their jobs for a long period of time. It was interesting to read a comment by one of the survey respondents:

"I've often wondered if moving into management in 1980 (head of Reference and Circulation) was the right choice in terms of personal happiness. While being able to apply my philosophies of service and management in different situations over the past twenty-four years has had its rewards, there have also been frustrations and disappointments.

"At this stage of my career I sometimes feel I might be happier, career-wise, with less responsibility and fewer obligations, although I still enjoy being able to encourage and support my staff in the work they are doing."

When the decision to leave is voluntary, giving adequate notice is essential for a smooth handover to the incumbent. Then there is the involuntary layoff or termination that can arise. The higher up the ladder you move, the more likely you will receive notice of termination. Leaders do fail to meet expectations, both their own and those of the organization, and there may be a mutual understanding that it is time to go. Look at what has happened in the business world in recent years.

When you, as leader, leave a job—for whatever reasons—leave behind the legacy of a strong team, documentation for decisions made, an outline of possible development for the service, and a list of useful contacts. Then step aside and let the new leader assume his role.

CRUCIAL SUCCESS FACTORS 237

Crucial success factor no. 23: Know when it's the right time to go, and leave a good legacy. *Ensure that the next person in the position has all the information he will need, and leave a contact address.*

Summing Up

One of the survey respondents puts it well: "I received some great advice from one of my earliest supervisors—Always remember you don't know all the answers, and more important, you don't even know all the questions. The more power you share, the greater power you have. Never blindside your boss, and always tell the truth." To this, we add the following guidelines:

- Deliver more than you promise—to users, to the team, and to the organization.
- Don't look back to what might have been—focus on what's to come.
- Be decisive.
- Buy a copy of Bennis and Goldsmith's *Learning to Lead: A Workbook on Becoming a Leader* (2003)—it's full of useful exercises that make you think about the role of a leader.
- Enjoy being a leader!

References

Anderson, Paul, and Andrea Lapsley, "Leadership: An Interview with ALA President Carla D. Hayden," *Library Administration & Management* 18, no. 3 (Summer 2004): 121.

Arroba, Tanya, and Kim James, "Are Politics Palatable to Women Managers?" *Women in Management Review* 3, no. 3 (1987): 123–130.

Bennis, Warren G., "The Seven Ages of the Leader," *Harvard Business Review* 82, no. 1 (January 2004): 46–53.

Bennis, Warren G., and Joan Goldsmith, *Learning to Lead: A Workbook on Becoming a Leader*, 3rd ed. (New York: Basic, 2003).

Ciampa, Dan, and Michael Watkins, *Right from the Start: Taking Charge in a New Leadership Role* (Boston: Harvard Business School Press, 2005).

Drucker, Peter F., "Managing Oneself," *Harvard Business Review* 83, no. 1 (January 2005): 107.

Goffee, Robert, and Gareth Jones, "Followership—It's Personal Too," *Harvard Business Review* 79, no. 11 (December 2001): 148.

Hayashi, Alden M., "When to Trust Your Gut," *Harvard Business Review* 79, no. 2 (February 2001): 59–65.

The Imagineers, *The Imagineering Way: Ideas to Ignite Your Creativity* (New York: Hyperion, 2003).

Lucas, Erika, "Tooling Up for Leadership," *Professional Manager* (September 2000): 10.

Mann, Sandi, "Politics and Power in Organizations: Why Women Lose Out," *Leadership & Organization Development Journal* 16, no. 2 (1995): 9–15.

Pollitt, David, and Hilarie Owen, "What Women Can Bring to the Boardroom in the Post-Enron Era," *Human Resource Management International Digest* 13, no. 2 (2005): 36–38.

Powell, Sarah, "Interview with Beverly Alimo-Metcalfe," *Journal of Health Organization and Management* 18, no. 6 (2004): 393–398.

Index

About the Authors

Dr. G. Edward Evans is librarian of the Harold S. Colton Memorial Library and Archives at the Museum of Northern Arizona. His career has included both practice and teaching, often during the same period of time. He recently retired as university librarian at Loyola Marymount University, Los Angeles. During his tenure there, he taught part time at UCLA's Graduate School of Education and Information Studies and also taught courses in anthropology and archaeology for Loyola Marymount's Sociology Department. As a Fulbright scholar, he taught at the University of Iceland and has offered courses in management at library schools in Norway, Denmark, Sweden, and Finland. He has served as an external examiner in management for the Department of Library Studies at the University of the West Indies. He holds two degrees in anthropology, an MLS, and a PhD.

Professor Patricia Layzell Ward is honorary archivist to the Festiniog Railway Company in Wales, has worked in public and special libraries, and enjoyed a longtime involvement in teaching and research. She was director of the Centre for Library and Information Management at Loughborough University, England, and chair in library and information studies at Curtin University in Perth, Western Australia, and the University of Wales, Aberystwyth. She is emeritus editor of *Library Management*, author of conference papers and journal articles, examiner to a number of universities, and an overseas consultant. She holds a master's and PhD from University College, London; is a fellow of the Chartered Institute of Library and Information Professionals and the Chartered Management Institute; an associate of the Australian Library and Information Association; and a member of the American Library Association.